Macworld® Photoshop® 4
Instant Expert

Macworld® Photoshop® 4 Instant Expert

by David D. Busch and David Field

IDG Books Worldwide, Inc.

An International Data Group Company

Foster City, CA ⊡ Chicago, IL ⊡ Indianapolis, IN ⊡ Southlake, TX

Macworld® Photoshop® 4 Instant Expert

Published by
IDG Books Worldwide, Inc.
An International Data Group Company
919 E. Hillsdale Blvd., Suite 400
Foster City, CA 94404
http://www.idgbooks.com (IDG Books World Wide Web Site)

Library of Congress Catalog Card No.: 96-075398

ISBN: 1-56884-884-6

Printed in the United States of America

10 9 8 7 6 5 4 3 2 1

1B/QU/RS/ZW/FC

Distributed in the United States by IDG Books Worldwide, Inc.

Distributed by Macmillan Canada for Canada; by Contemporanea de Ediciones for Venezuela; by Distribuidora Cuspide for Argentina; by CITEC for Brazil; by Ediciones ZETA S.C.R. Ltda. for Peru; by Editorial Limusa SA for Mexico; by Transworld Publishers Limited in the United Kingdom and Europe; by Academic Bookshop for Egypt; by Levant Distributors S.A.R.L. for Lebanon; by Al Jassim for Saudi Arabia; by Simron Pty. Ltd. for South Africa; by Pustak Mahal for India; by The Computer Bookshop for India; by Toppan Company Ltd. for Japan; by Addison Wesley Publishing Company for Korea; by Longman Singapore Publishers Ltd. for Singapore, Malaysia, Thailand, and Indonesia; by Unalis Corporation for Taiwan; by WS Computer Publishing Company, Inc. for the Philippines; by WoodsLane Pty. Ltd. for Australia; by WoodsLane Enterprises Ltd. for New Zealand. Authorized Sales Agent: Anthony Rudkin Associates for the Middle East and North Africa.

For general information on IDG Books Worldwide's books in the U.S., please call our Consumer Customer Service department at 800-762-2974. For reseller information, including discounts and premium sales, please call our Reseller Customer Service department at 800-434-3422.

For information on where to purchase IDG Books Worldwide's books outside the U.S., please contact our International Sales department at 415-655-3172 or fax 415-655-3295.

For information on foreign language translations, please contact our Foreign & Subsidiary Rights department at 415-655-3021 or fax 415-655-3281.

For sales inquiries and special prices for bulk quantities, please contact our Sales department at 415-655-3200 or write to the address above.

For information on using IDG Books Worldwide's books in the classroom or for ordering examination copies, please contact our Educational Sales department at 800-434-2086 or fax 817-251-8174.

For press review copies, author interviews, or other publicity information, please contact our Public Relations department at 415-655-3000 or fax 415-655-3299.

For authorization to photocopy items for corporate, personal, or educational use, please contact Copyright Clearance Center, 222 Rosewood Drive, Danvers, MA 01923, or fax 508-750-4470.

is a trademark under exclusive license to IDG Books Worldwide, Inc., from International Data Group, Inc.

ABOUT IDG BOOKS WORLDWIDE

Welcome to the world of IDG Books Worldwide.

IDG Books Worldwide, Inc., is a subsidiary of International Data Group, the world's largest publisher of computer-related information and the leading global provider of information services on information technology. IDG was founded more than 25 years ago and now employs more than 8,500 people worldwide. IDG publishes more than 275 computer publications in over 75 countries (see listing below). More than 60 million people read one or more IDG publications each month.

Launched in 1990, IDG Books Worldwide is today the #1 publisher of best-selling computer books in the United States. We are proud to have received eight awards from the Computer Press Association in recognition of editorial excellence and three from *Computer Currents'* First Annual Readers' Choice Awards. Our best-selling ...*For Dummies*® series has more than 30 million copies in print with translations in 30 languages. IDG Books Worldwide, through a joint venture with IDG's Hi-Tech Beijing, became the first U.S. publisher to publish a computer book in the People's Republic of China. In record time, IDG Books Worldwide has become the first choice for millions of readers around the world who want to learn how to better manage their businesses.

Our mission is simple: Every one of our books is designed to bring extra value and skill-building instructions to the reader. Our books are written by experts who understand and care about our readers. The knowledge base of our editorial staff comes from years of experience in publishing, education, and journalism — experience we use to produce books for the '90s. In short, we care about books, so we attract the best people. We devote special attention to details such as audience, interior design, use of icons, and illustrations. And because we use an efficient process of authoring, editing, and desktop publishing our books electronically, we can spend more time ensuring superior content and spend less time on the technicalities of making books.

You can count on our commitment to deliver high-quality books at competitive prices on topics you want to read about. At IDG Books Worldwide, we continue in the IDG tradition of delivering quality for more than 25 years. You'll find no better book on a subject than one from IDG Books Worldwide.

John Kilcullen
President and CEO
IDG Books Worldwide, Inc.

Eighth Annual Computer Press Awards ≥1992

Ninth Annual Computer Press Awards ≥1993

Tenth Annual Computer Press Awards ≥1994

Eleventh Annual Computer Press Awards ≥1995

As always, for Cathy, mother of four great kids, and who, in another world, could be Amy Hollerith's twin.

Preface

Has this ever happened to you?

"Pat, you know Photoshop, don't you?"

"Uh, I *have* Photoshop. I haven't really mastered all, er, *any* of its features yet."

"That's good enough. The boss isn't happy with the way his head-and-shoulders picture looks in the presentation we're giving at noon. Can you remove that glare from the top of his head, erase a few of those frown lines, and maybe change that double-breasted suit into a more fashionable Italian number?"

"What?"

"Here's a disk with the photo. Give me a nice PICT file in about 30 minutes so I can drop it into the presentation."

"Okay, sure," you reply, while trying to recall if your brother-in-law's company has any openings in the mail room. You figure that in 30 minutes, you just may be able to figure out what a PICT file is....

Despite what you might think, Photoshop isn't more complicated than auto mechanics, gourmet cooking, and brain surgery combined. When a task is broken down into easy steps, nearly anyone can learn to replace a radiator, sauté some onions, tie a suture—or combine two photos seamlessly into one. All you need are some engaging projects and a few hints on how to complete them. *Macworld Photoshop 4 Instant Expert* gives you 18 real-world projects, each designed to furnish essential expertise *not* by the miracle of osmosis, but by hands-on work with useful techniques and typical work scenarios. Each project builds on what you learned in the previous one, and is laced with enough good humor to keep things interesting. Even if "Photoshop Guru" isn't in your job description, you can easily tack that accolade onto your résumé by working your way through this book.

THE CHALLENGE

Imagine you're the art director for Schotzie & Schotzie, an up-and-coming advertising/PR agency. Your firm has just been retained by Kitchen Table International, the world's leading manufacturer of trailing-edge computer hardware, software, and limpware. In just four short years, KTI has risen from oblivion to obscurity, and is looking forward to having your agency furnish the company with a complete image makeover. Because KTI has virtually no image at all right now, this should prove to be a challenge.

As art director, you've been asked to create everything from a logo to an annual report cover—but on the condition that you abandon your airbrush and X-Acto knife in favor of Photoshop and a Macintosh, tools more suitable for a high-tech client. Learning Mac basics took you three days, and now you're set to tackle Photoshop. Are you ready to become an Instant Expert?

In the next 18 chapters, we're going to ask you to create good-looking art, combine images, and do sophisticated photo-retouching quickly and efficiently. We also come right out and admit it: We're no artists, and having to work with the less than awe-inspiring visuals KTI has dumped into our laps does little to hide this sad truth.

Our forte is to get creative people like you up to speed on Photoshop quickly. We'll give you all the tools you need, even some basic images on the CD-ROM packaged with this book, while intentionally keeping the techniques simple so you become comfortable with each tool one at a time. Once the gloves fly off, we'll show you some more advanced ways of putting individual tools and features to work. By the time you're through with this book, you'll be well on your way to giving your creative vision more form, shape, and color through the use of the most powerful and popular image editing program available for the Macintosh.

We don't plan to teach you how to use your computer, nor do we offer instruction on using the rudimentary features of your operating system. If you don't know the essentials of using your Macintosh, you shouldn't be reading this book—just yet. Nor will we spend time explaining how to install Photoshop. If you weren't willing to crack the shrink-wrap around the manuals, why would we think you'd be eager to have us rehash the same material here?

Nor will you have to wade through tons of background information to get to the good parts. Lots of computer books pack 300 pages of solid information between their covers. Unfortunately, they are often 800-page books! Photoshop Instant Expert contains *only* the good parts.

WHAT YOU WILL NEED

To become a Photoshop Instant Expert, all you need are this book, the accompanying CD-ROM, a CD-ROM-equipped Macintosh with Photoshop installed on it (and *please, please* have from 16 to 32MB of RAM, or more), and at least 50–60MB of free hard disk space so you can work with the projects comfortably. While none of the files you'll be working with makes unreasonable demands on the average Photoshop user's Macintosh, you won't be having as much fun as the rest of us if you have to wait while Photoshop unloads part of an image from your meager RAM and puts it on your hard disk to make room for another portion of the image.

You'll find the CD-ROM to be a bit different from those bundled with most books. We haven't loaded it up with demos, shareware, and advertisements for vendors. Instead, you'll find tons of files that enable you to work alongside us on the projects. These files include:

- The actual beginning, intermediate, and final files for most exercises, so you can load them into Photoshop and try out the functions for yourself, using the exact files we used. The files are located in folders on the CD-ROM labeled with the chapter numbers.

- Full-color versions of each of the figures printed in this book. You can load any of the screen shots into Photoshop and see exactly what we saw on our screens. In a way, that's even better than printing this book in full color all the way through, because you can examine any of the images in detail, and still not have to pay $75 for fancy four-color printing.

- A gallery of additional color and black-and-white artwork you can use to practice your F/X skills. These are low resolution (if you consider 300 dpi low resolution) images, many with slight imperfections, similar to what you might produce yourself. You'll find portraits, scenery, still lifes, and other subjects. Because many readers might not have access to a color scanner, we've incorporated these pictures as fodder for F/X enhancements.

HOW TO USE THIS BOOK

Computer books invariably begin with incredible insights, such as a suggestion to read the book from front to back, skim over boring parts, and then review any portions you don't understand until the information finally sinks in. We don't think *Macworld Photoshop 4 Instant Expert* requires an instruction manual, and we relegated all the boring parts to the bit-bin long before the book hit the printing press. So, we'll start you off with one piece of advice: just go do it!

Acknowledgments

Our names are on the cover, but many other creative people worked long and hard to contribute to the final version of this book. We would like to thank our untiring editors, Michael Koch and Michael Welch, for their help in making this book real. Thanks, too, to Phyllis Beaty and the production staff for doing such a good job on a tight schedule. We would also like to thank Michael Roney for giving us the chance to write this book. Finally, we would like to tip our hats to our imaginary friends Scott Nolan Hollerith and his mother Amy, for their aid in making the 18 projects unreal.

Contents at a Glance

Table of Contents

Designing a Simple Logo

Basic Tools and Functions

Kitchen Table International (KTI) needs a simple, abstract logo for its introduction of VRMLcelli, the company's new "virtual reality" software product. This is an excellent time for you to fire up Photoshop and learn how to use its basic tools. You've got 20 minutes to work on this project, so how hard can it be?

THE TOOLS

- ☐ Photoshop's File menu
- ☐ Status box
- ☐ Rectangular/elliptical marquee and magic wand tools
- ☐ Copy and paste commands
- ☐ Move, gradient, and zoom tools
- ☐ Palettes

GETTING STARTED

Before we start creating a logo, it's worthwhile to first get you oriented and make sure your computer's up to the task. Photoshop demands rigorous work from your computer, requiring it to manage swarms of individual picture elements—called *pixels*—if not calculate values for millions of these image components in a few seconds. You can't move on to your next design step until your Mac applies the various effects and color changes you select, so if your machine is too slow or too hungry for RAM (random access memory), an inadequate system sharply limits your experimentation.

Although we've actually run Photoshop on a Macintosh II with a 68020 processor, System 7, 8MB of RAM, and a pair of slow 80MB SCSII hard drives—a setup that approximates Adobe's "minimum" requirement—the machine invariably kept us waiting for agonizing minutes just to load or work with any image larger than a postage stamp. Unless you have something to keep you occupied while Photoshop processes files on a slow system, we suggest you settle for Adobe's "recommended" system configuration: a 68040 Macintosh or Power Macintosh with System 7.1.2 or greater and at least 16MB of RAM (24MB for a Power Mac).

Should you be working with a 68020 or 68030 machine, consider some form of accelerator to bring your computer up to at least 68040 or Power Mac speed. Accelerator cards are available from a variety of manufacturers, and you can often install them yourself. (For high-end systems, PCI-based ultra-wide SCSI drives and video accelerators can also improve performance.)

Extra RAM can be even more important in boosting your Mac's speed, because it enables Photoshop to keep multiple copies of the image (or images) you're working on in memory. The more memory, the better—always. Photoshop tries to load the entire original image in RAM, plus a copy it uses to undo the most recent operation, if necessary. If you divide an image into several levels or *layers*, Photoshop needs even more RAM. Whenever Photoshop doesn't have enough memory to juggle all the necessary image information, some data has to be temporarily placed on your hard disk—a process that reduces most operations to a crawl. The process is slow (painfully so) because even the fastest hard disk is thousands of times slower than memory.

The standard rule of thumb is to have RAM equal to three to five times the size of the largest image you'll be working with. If you plan to manipulate 2MB images, you'll need at least 6MB of RAM, just to work comfortably with a single image. Such images aren't particularly large, however. A full-color 1024 × 786-pixel image only amounts to about 2.4MB if there isn't any squeezing, or *compression*, schemes built into the software to reduce the image size. The Photoshop program itself likes to have another 5MB, and when you add 3 to 5MB for the Mac operating system (OS), you can see why 16MB is a more realistic bare minimum for serious work.

What's more, Photoshop users need real RAM, not the simulated kind created by utilities such as RAM Doubler, which works great for other applications but has been known to interfere with Photoshop's built-in memory preservation routines, called *virtual memory*.

utility (u-til'-i-ty), *n*. **1:** A small Macintosh program that optimizes your system's resources until they are all gone. **2:** An essential software component that is not included and must therefore be purchased at extra cost. **3:** Any useful feature that the developers of an application or operating system forgot to include, didn't foresee a need for, or simply elected to skip because the beta testers couldn't figure out how to use it.

Luckily, memory is even easier than accelerator cards for you to install yourself. You can purchase additional RAM from Macintosh dealers or mail-order catalogs in the form of Single In-line Memory Modules (SIMMs) or Dual In-line Memory Modules (DIMMs), which usually come with complete installation instructions. With most older Macs, RAM replacement is fairly easy. With later Macs, however, placing RAM in the appropriate bank can be a bit tricky for the neophyte, and is best left to a qualified Mac technician.

With a fast enough processor and enough RAM, most other hardware considerations become secondary. You'll want a hard disk that's large enough to hold all the files you want to work with, of course, with some space left over for Photoshop to use to simulate RAM when you finally do run short. Even gigabyte drives are cheap these days, and removable drives such as Iomega's Jaz give you open-ended storage of large image files. You'll also need a decent monitor and enough VRAM (Video Random Access Memory) to display millions of colors. Recent Power Macs have at least 2MB of VRAM, enough for millions of colors at 832×624 resolution, and can be upgraded to 4MB, sufficient to display millions of hues at 1024×768. If your computer meets the specs we've outlined in this section, you're ready to roll.

THE PHOTOSHOP DESKTOP

When you launch Photoshop and open a new document, you'll see a working screen like the one shown in Figure 1-1. Depending on how Photoshop has been set up, you'll see a toolbox and a number of palettes—small dialog box-sized windows that have tools and options you need to work with images. Don't worry if your first view of Photoshop looks a little different. You can hide or reveal the palettes shown in Figure 1-1 all at once by pressing the Shift-Tab keys. We'll describe these components only very briefly and save the longer explanations for when you actually start to work with them.

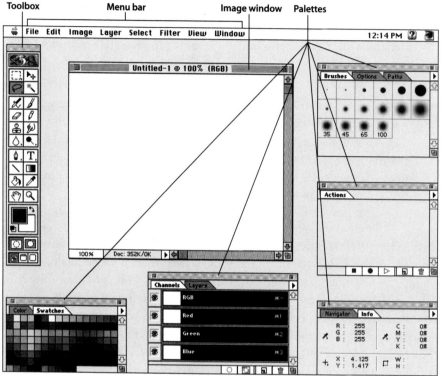

FIGURE 1-1
Photoshop's opening screen, with toolbox and palettes

THE TOOLBOX

The toolbox contains 20 *tools* that enable the user to select, draw, paint, fill, crop, and erase images or add text. To select a tool, click on its icon, then use it inside the image window.

Below the tool icons are three sets of controls. The *color controls* enable you to change foreground and background colors; the *mask controls* provide a choice of Standard or Quick Mask mode (in case you would like to create your masks with paint tools); and the *screen display controls* enable you to switch from the standard display to one with fewer windows and menus on the screen.

You can hide and restore the toolbox (as well as the other palettes) by pressing the Tab key. This is a quick way to clean up your screen to provide an unobstructed view of your image. Figure 1-2 shows the toolbox in detail.

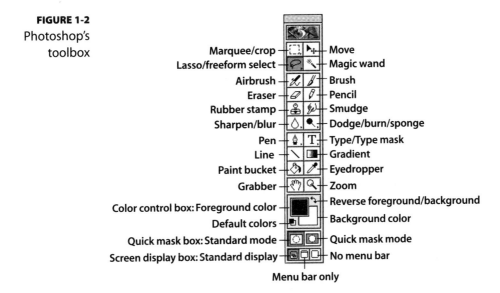

FIGURE 1-2
Photoshop's toolbox

Marquee/crop — Move
Lasso/freeform select — Magic wand
Airbrush — Brush
Eraser — Pencil
Rubber stamp — Smudge
Sharpen/blur — Dodge/burn/sponge
Pen — Type/Type mask
Line — Gradient
Paint bucket — Eyedropper
Grabber — Zoom
Color control box: Foreground color — Reverse foreground/background
Default colors — Background color
Quick mask box: Standard mode — Quick mask mode
Screen display box: Standard display — No menu bar
Menu bar only

THE PALETTES

Photoshop also offers ten palettes, each of which enhances your ability to work with an image. As mentioned before, you can hide or reveal all the palettes at once by pressing the Shift-Tab keys. Figure 1-3 shows Photoshop's palettes. We'll describe them in alphabetical order, although they don't appear that way in Figure 1-3.

ACTIONS PALETTE Choose this palette to record macros representing whole series of commands that can be carried out on multiple images and accessed at the click of the mouse.

BRUSHES PALETTE This palette enables you to select various brush sizes and store brushes you create yourself. Press F5 to show or hide this palette.

CHANNELS PALETTE You can work with individual color channels, or create new ones called Alpha channels, using this palette.

COLOR PALETTE This palette makes it easy to dial in an exact color by typing values for red, green, and blue combinations in the boxes provided, or by using the sliders to produce a color you like. Press F6 to show or hide this palette.

INFO PALETTE This underused palette provides information about the color value and position of the pixels under the cursor. You can use this information to determine the colors or image coordinates of a particular pixel. Summon this palette or hide it by pressing F8.

LAYERS PALETTE You'll use the Layers palette to slice your image into separate overlays that you can work on individually and then combine in creative ways. Pressing F7 shows or hides this palette.

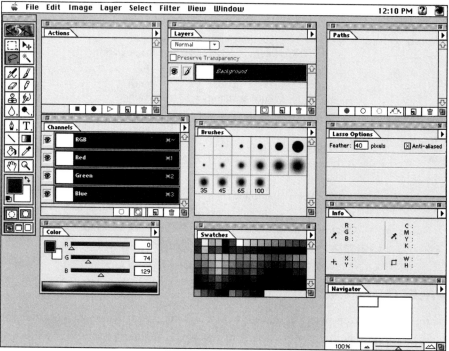

FIGURE 1-3
Photoshop's palettes

NAVIGATOR PALETTE This palette presents a miniature view of your image, which you can use to move the cursor from one spot to another quickly.

OPTIONS PALETTE This palette provides options for the currently selected tool, and the choices you have will vary depending on the tool (for example, Lasso options appear in Figure 1-3). Drawing tools may have controls that affect each tool's opacity or how the tool is applied to the image. The blur tool has controls that determine how much blurring is used. The text tool has no options at all.

PATHS PALETTE This palette enables you to add line-oriented shapes, or *paths*, to a Photoshop image with the pen tool. The paths can be used to select precise areas of your image. The pen tools are also available from the toolbox.

SWATCHES PALETTE This palette is a simple collection of user-modifiable color swatches that enables you to add or delete colors to create a custom palette or choose a foreground or background color.

TIP You can also access (or show or hide) any of the palettes by selecting Window ⇨ Palettes from the menu bar.

KEEPING YOUR PALETTES ORGANIZED

You may find that the palettes either show up in the same places each time you start Photoshop, or they reflect however you left them in your last session. To change your current setup, select File ➪ Preferences ➪ More from the menu bar. Look at the very last check box, Restore Palette and Dialog Positions. If this box is not checked, the palettes appear in the default positions each time you start Photoshop; if it is checked, the palettes remain in the same positions as you left them during your last session. Select this option to keep Photoshop's palette display customized the way you want it.

You'll also notice that some palettes come in groups. The Options and Paths palettes appear with the Brushes palette, for example. Click on any tab (the areas of each palette that look like ordinary file tabs) and you'll bring that palette to the front. If you click on the zoom box in the top right corner of any of the palettes, you'll see them shrink so that only the tabs are showing. This is handy if you want to get a palette out of your way, without clearing it from your screen. Click on the zoom box again to return the palette to its full size.

Also, you can easily customize the arrangement of your palettes. To set up a palette as a stand-alone element, grab its tab and drag the palette out of the set in which it is included. Release the mouse button, and the palette will remain on your desktop all by its lonesome. To rearrange palettes in new groups, you can drag each palette to another set of palettes and drop it inside. We've customized our setup so that the three palettes we use the least—Paths, Color, and Info—are collected together in one palette, while the five we use the most—Layers, Channels, Swatches, Brushes, and Options—all reside in a single group. To avoid cluttering up the screen, we hide the trio we use least, leaving plenty of room for the set we use most.

STEP 1: LOADING A NEW DOCUMENT

Now that you've familiarized yourself with Photoshop's basic tools and functions, we can focus our attention on the task at hand: creating a stunning, colorful logo for KTI's latest software package, VRMLcelli. We begin by loading and sizing a "canvas" or surface to work on. To load a blank Photoshop document and set its dimensions, follow these directions:

1 Select File ➪ New from the menu bar. The New dialog box appears (see Figure 1-4).

2 Replace the default file name, Untitled-1, by typing in a more useful name, such as VRMLcelli Logo.

3 In the Image Size box, select *pixels* (instead of inches) as the unit of measurement (it's convenient to use pixels as a reference when we don't need a project in a particular size), and type 800 into both the Width and Height fields. (While this is more space than we need, it allows some extra room to manipulate components of the image. We'll crop the image to finished size in Step 5.)

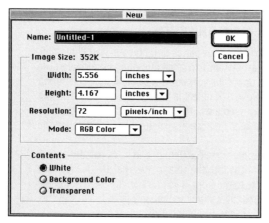

FIGURE 1-4
File ➩ New dialog box

4 Change the value in the Resolution field to 300 pixels per inch. The default value, 72 pixels per inch, corresponds to the resolution of your monitor display, which is rather coarse. A value of 300 provides an image with a higher resolution that is more suitable for reproduction on a laser printer or other output device.

5 Select RGB Color from the Mode drop-down list box. As you open the box, you'll notice that Photoshop gives you the option of creating an image in Bitmap (black/white only with no intermediate shades), Grayscale (a full range of black and white tones), RGB Color (a full-color image made up of the red, green, and blue pixels that your monitor can display), or CMYK Color and LAB Color (two alternative ways of displaying full color).

6 Make sure the White radio button in the Contents box is checked. Photoshop will create an empty file that is filled in with a white tone we can use as a background. You can also choose Background Color, or specify that the frame be left Transparent. Usually a plain white background is the best choice.

7 Click on OK to create an empty, white window.

The window looks like any Macintosh window, with a title bar, scroll bars, and size and close boxes. A status box at the bottom left corner displays one of four sets of information that you can change by clicking on the arrow to the right of the box. You can see the status box in Figure 1-5. The most important information for an Instant Expert is the default, Document Sizes, indicated by two figures divided by a slash. The figure on the left shows the basic size of the file, which tells you how much space is required to save it to your hard disk as an uncompressed bitmapped image. The figure on the right indicates how much space is required to store the image, including any extra layers or channels we might have created. We'll tell you more about layers and channels later.

FIGURE 1-5

The status box in the lower left corner of the file's window displays information about a particular file.

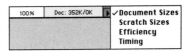

While working with your image you should always keep an eye on your status box, because it enables you to roughly gauge the size of your file. For example, if you had a 40–50MB file, you would know you might have problems getting that image printed or even transported to another computer. By the time you finish this book, you'll know some tricks for making file sizes smaller.

TIP When you hold down the Option key and click on the status box, you can see information about the file, including size and color depth.

STEP 2: CREATING A 3D ELEMENT

Now that we have a "canvas" to work on, we can actually start working on our logo. You'll be surprised how easy it is to create shapes of varying sizes with Photoshop's selection tools and a few menu commands. Just follow these directions:

1 Press Command-R to display Photoshop's rulers, if you haven't done so already. Two rulers appear along the top and the left side of your VRMLcelli Logo window.

2 Click on the marquee icon (located at the top of the left column in the toolbox—refer back to Figure 1-2 if you need help finding it), move the cursor to the right, and select the rectangular marquee tool. Alternatively, you can hold down the Option key while clicking the icon to cycle through all five choices: the rectangular and elliptical marquees, vertical and horizontal line marquees, and the crop tool.

3 Move the cursor to the upper left corner of the VRMLcelli Logo window, about ¼ inch from the top and the left side. The exact distance doesn't matter. Hold down the mouse button and drag down and to the right to enclose a portion of the window in a tall, narrow dotted marquee, about ⅜ths of an inch wide and 1½ inches tall, as shown in Figure 1-6.

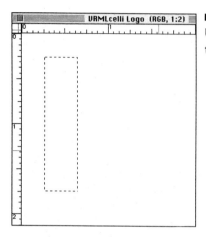

FIGURE 1-6
Use the rectangular marquee tool
to select areas with rectangular sides.

4 Return to the toolbox, and Option-click the marquee tool icon until you've selected the elliptical marquee tool.

5 Go back to your dotted marquee and position the cursor at the top edge of the selection about one quarter of the distance in from its right edge. Press the Option key, then the mouse button, and then drag down. This action removes a rounded section from the rectangular selection, as shown in Figure 1-7.

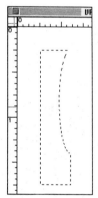

FIGURE 1-7
Holding down the Command key while
dragging a selection tool removes the
selected portion from the original selection.

NOTE From now on, you'll want to remember that holding down the Command key while using a selection tool enables you to remove anything you "select" from an active selection. You can use this capability to fine-tune rough selections.

6 Use the Option key and elliptical marquee tool to remove a section from the lower left side of the rectangular selection, as shown in Figure 1-8. What we've done here is create half of a stylized "V." We'll make the other half appear in a moment.

FIGURE 1-8

Another section carved from the original selection, using the elliptical marquee tool

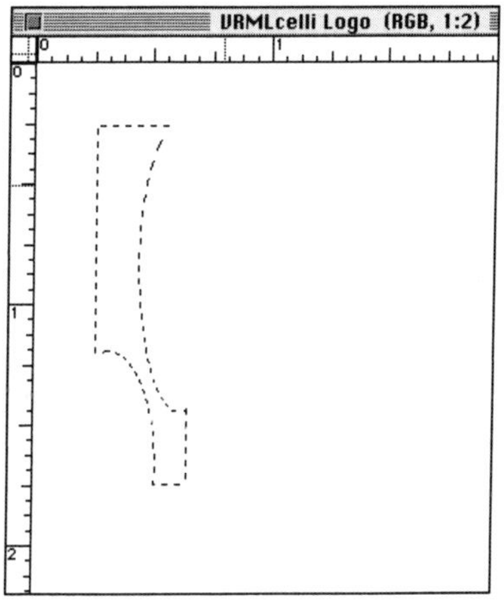

7 Next, we want to make the selection solid black. Because our goal is to make you an Instant Expert, rather than an Instant Novice, here are two ways to accomplish the task:

⊡ Make sure the color control box in the toolbox shows a black square in the upper left corner, overlapping a white square underneath it. If not, click on the miniature black/white squares in the lower left corner of the color control box to return to Photoshop's default black/white scheme. Select Edit ⇨ Fill. The Fill dialog box appears (see Figure 1-9). Make sure the options are as shown—Use: Foreground Color, Opacity: 100%, and Mode: Normal—and click on OK. The selection will be filled completely with a black foreground color.

FIGURE 1-9

Filling the selection with solid black

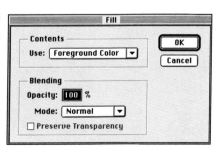

⊡ A quicker way to fill a selection with a solid color is to click on the double-headed arrow placed between the two color control boxes. Clicking this arrow tells Photoshop to swap the two colors, turning the black foreground into the background color, and vice versa. If you press Delete, or Option-X (Cut), Photoshop deletes the selected area and replaces them with the background color. Although this second method is the quickest way to fill a selection with a solid color, you'd want to use the first procedure, if you chose to use a special option, such as an opacity level less than 100 percent (in this case adding some gray value instead of solid black) or one of the mode options we'll explore later in the book.

8   To complete the "V" we need a mirror image of the black object we've created so far. Select Edit ⇨ Copy (or press Command-C) to copy the object to the Clipboard. Then select Edit ⇨ Paste (or press Command-V) to immediately place a copy on top of the original as a new layer. You won't see any difference, as yet, because both images are superimposed.

9   Select Layer ⇨ Transform ⇨ Flip Horizontal to turn the new copy into a mirror image. The duplicate will flip sideways, as shown in Figure 1-10.

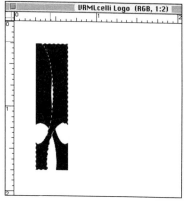

FIGURE 1-10
The original selection has been copied, pasted, and flipped horizontally to provide a mirror image of itself.

10 Next, we need to align both halves. Select the move tool (the top tool in the right column in the toolbox), then click on the flipped object, and drag it to the right to create a V-shape.

NOTE You can fine-tune the position of the object by using the keyboard's arrow keys. Using these keys enables you to nudge a selected object up, down, right, or left one pixel at a time.

STEP 3: ADDING A 3D EFFECT

What we have created so far is actually the drop shadow of our stylized "V." To create the accompanying body of the character and fill it with an interesting color effect, we need to use another selection tool, the magic wand, and the gradient tool, respectively. Just follow these directions:

1   Select the magic wand tool from the toolbox (the second tool from the top in the right column), then click on the left portion of the "V." The magic wand automatically selects all the continuous pixels that are within a brightness range (called a *tolerance level*). Because the pixels inside this section of the "V" are all a uniform black, the magic wand grabs all of them. (We'll show you later how to change the tolerance level to select pixels that fall into a particular range of tones or colors.)

2   Hold down the Shift key, and click in the right portion of the "V." The pixels there are added to the current selection.

 NOTE From now on, you'll want to remember that holding down the Shift key while you select items adds the new selection to an existing one, just as holding down the Option key subtracts the new selection from an existing one.

3   With both halves selected, use Command-C (or Edit ⇨ Copy) to copy the "V" to the Clipboard, then paste it right back down on top of the original using Command-V (or Edit ⇨ Paste).

4   Next, we want to add an interesting color effect to the duplicate. Click on the Swatches palette tab (if it isn't already visible on your screen) and select a light and a dark shade of red to represent one of KTI's corporate colors. (In the real world, a corporation probably has strict rules defining the exact hue of its "trade dress," and we'll show you how to create a color "by the numbers" later on. For now, you only need to know how to extract colors from the Swatches palette.)

5   Move the cursor to the bright red square in the upper left corner of the Swatches palette. Notice how the cursor changes to an *eyedropper* as it passes over the swatches (see Figure 1-11). Click the mouse button, and the color under the eyedropper is copied to the *foreground* box in the color controls section of the toolbox.

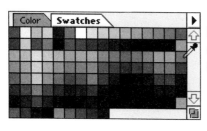

FIGURE 1-11

Foreground and background colors can be copied using the eyedropper and the Swatches palette.

6 Move the cursor to the lighter red (pinkish) square, and Option-click. The color is copied to the *background* box in the color controls section of the toolbox.

 NOTE From now on, you'll want to remember that clicking on a color in the Swatches palette (or the Color palette) or anywhere in an image when the eyedropper tool is active, makes that color the foreground color. Option-clicking under the same circumstances generates a new background color.

7 Select the gradient tool from the toolbox (the eighth tool from the top in the right column), then click on the Options palette tab. Make sure the settings for the gradient tool correspond to those shown in Figure 1-12 (Normal; Opacity 100%; Gradient: Foreground to Background; and Type: Linear).

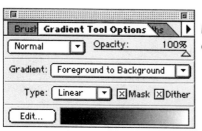

FIGURE 1-12

Make sure that the gradient options are set to their defaults.

8 Move the cursor down to the lower right-hand corner of the "V," hold down the mouse button, and drag to the upper left corner. You'll get a cool gradient effect, as shown in Figure 1-13. Dragging diagonally makes the gradation a tiny bit lighter on the left side than on the right, giving the impression that a light source lies in that direction.

9 Next, use the arrow keys to move the colored selection a few pixels to the right and a little down, so that the black original version shows behind it. Adjust the position until you get a 3D effect that pleases you. Figure 1-14 shows the results.

FIGURE 1-13
The finished gradient adds
a cool effect to the logo.

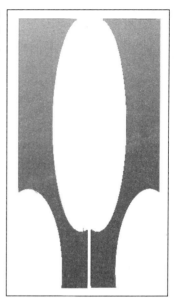

FIGURE 1-14
The underlying black shape provides
a 3D effect in the finished "V."

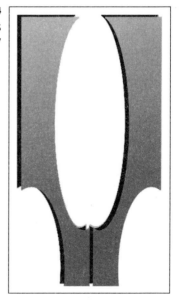

TIP Hold down the Command key, and press H to hide the selection marquee. Doing so makes it easier to view the colored shape and the original version underneath. You can use this trick any time you want to hide the selection's outline or "marching ants." Pressing Command-H again restores the selection marquee.

STEP 4: ADDING A STYLIZED LETTER

We've got a "V" for VRML, but no "c" for celli, yet. We'll add this component while introducing another option of the gradient tool. Follow these directions:

1 Click (or Option-Click) on the marquee tool icon in the toolbox to activate the elliptical marquee tool.

2 Move the cursor about halfway down to a point on the right edge of the "V." Hold down the Option and Shift keys, then press the mouse button and drag to the right. The selection will appear as a perfect circle, centered on the point where you first clicked. Make the circle a little less high than the upper arm of the "V," as shown in Figure 1-15.

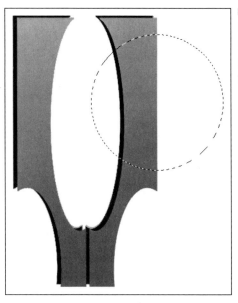

FIGURE 1-15
Holding down the Option and Shift keys while dragging with the elliptical marquee produces a perfect circle centered around the original cursor position.

3 Use the Swatches palette to select a light blue as the foreground color, and a dark blue as the background color. These choices will represent KTI's other corporate color.

4 Select the gradient tool, and then click on the Options palette. Change the Type option to Radial. Then click the Edit button, and in the dialog box that pops up, use the midpoint slider to move from the

default value, 50 percent (which makes the gradient change smoothly from one color to the other about halfway across the object) to 38 percent, which causes Photoshop to "favor" the background color over the foreground color in a 62:38 ratio. We want most of the circle to be dark blue, with the light blue as a highlight. Click on OK when you've edited the gradient's midpoint.

5 Place the cursor at the upper left edge of the selected circle, and drag to the lower right edge. The result is the 3D sphere shown in Figure 1-16.

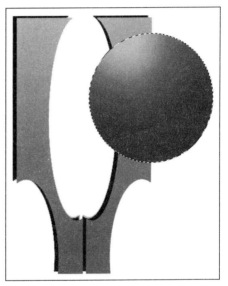

FIGURE 1-16
A radial gradient applies
a shaded 3D effect.

6 Click on the miniature black/white boxes in the color control area of the toolbox to return to the default colors, then activate the elliptical marquee tool. Click on the Options palette and make sure that the Anti-Aliased box is *not* checked. *Anti-aliasing* is a technique that helps blend shapes together by "fading out" rough edges. In our example, however, we want the drawing tool to carve out a "clean," sharp section rather than a fuzzy one, hence anti-aliasing should not be activated.

7 Choose a section of the sphere you've just created to carve out a "C" shape with the elliptical marquee tool, and then press Delete. Your logo should now resemble the image shown in Figure 1-17.

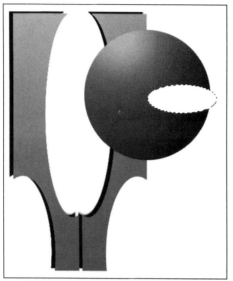

FIGURE 1-17
The finished VRMLcelli logo,
created from scratch in Photoshop

STEP 5: CROPPING AN IMAGE

The image area we have been working with is actually larger than needed. Because it's often a good idea to give yourself plenty of space to work, Photoshop makes it very easy for you to crop an image to any particular size when you're done. Just follow these directions.

1   Activate the rectangular marquee tool and select an area around the finished logo, leaving a little room on all four sides.

2   Select Image ⇨ Crop from the menu bar. Photoshop reduces the size of the working canvas to encompass only the rectangular area you selected. Using this technique, you can work with a larger image area, then crop to the final size you want.

STEP 6: SAVING YOUR FILE

Although Photoshop stores files on your disk in much the same way as other Macintosh applications, it provides some options you won't find outside of image editing programs. The following directions demonstrate how to save a new copy of the current file, using Photoshop's format options:

1   Select File ⇨ Save As from the menu bar.

2   In the Save This Document As dialog box, you can type in a file name of your choice.

3 Select a file format from the Format drop-down list box. The most common formats are PICT (a file type that can be opened by many Macintosh applications, but not too many in the PC world); TIFF (a bitmapped format common on both Mac and PC platforms); and Photoshop's native format (which allows saving all the layers and channels you've created). The extensions that most commonly represent these formats are .pct, .tif, and .psd. Although the Macintosh doesn't need PC-like extensions, many users like to add them when naming files as a hint to what file format has been used.

4 Click on the Save button, and your file will be stored on the disk.

GETTING CLOSER TO THE PIXELS

Appendix A explains how a Photoshop image is made up of pixels. You can see a representation of what these pixels look like using Photoshop's zoom tool. When Photoshop zooms in, it shows each pixel at a larger magnification. When you zoom in to 2:1, Photoshop makes four pixels show what one pixel showed before. The actual pixel size doesn't change, but the representation of the image does. If you zoom in to 16:1, you'll see 256 actual pixels representing one pixel of the original image; instead of 72 pixels to the inch, the image is now represented by four and a half to the inch. Naturally, you only see a small part of the original image. Although we haven't reached a point where we need to zoom in and out on an image, you might enjoy playing with this capability. Take a break, and try it out, as follows:

1 Select the zoom tool in the toolbox (tenth icon from the top in the right column) and click on the upper edge of the "V" in our logo (zooming in looks like the image shown in Figure 1-18). The image becomes twice as large as before. You can also use the slider in the Navigator palette to adjust magnification, or click on the small triangle/large triangle pairs at either end of the slider to zoom in and out.

FIGURE 1-18
The VRMLcelli logo at twice its original size

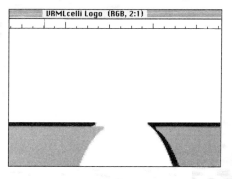

(continued)

GETTING CLOSER TO THE PIXELS *(continued)*

2 Keep clicking on the image until you reach the limit of 16:1. At this point the pixels are clearly visible (see Figure 1-19). What appeared to be smooth curves and transitions of color at 1:1 you can now see as just blocks of pixels, including the lighter colored pixels that create the smooth, anti-aliased effect.

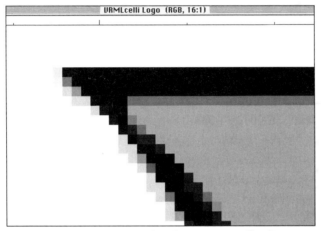

FIGURE 1-19
The same image at 16 times magnification

3 Hold down the Option key and click on the image. The zoom ratio goes down to 8:1.
4 Keep clicking, and hold down the Option key until you reach 1:1.
5 Now return to 16:1 by clicking without holding down the Option key.
6 Double-click on the zoom tool—the image returns to 1:1.

You can also zoom in and out on your whole image by pressing Command-spacebar (zoom in) or Option-spacebar (zoom out) as you click with the mouse. This method is usually quicker. The zoom in or out centers around the current cursor position.

WHAT YOU'VE LEARNED

Even though this is the very first chapter of the book, you've learned quite a few basic elements, tools, and techniques that you can apply to your own projects. You know that:

- A fast processor and 16MB of memory are recommended to make your system work acceptably fast.

- Pressing the Tab key can hide or show the toolbox and palettes.

- The F5, F6, F7, and F8 keys hide or display the Brushes, Color, Layers, Info, and Commands palettes, respectively.

- Palettes can be dragged out of their default locations to create new sets, or can stand alone.

- Pressing Command-R turns the rulers on and off.

- Holding down the Shift key while making a selection *adds* to a selection, while pressing the Command key *subtracts* from a selection.

- Pressing Command-H shows or hides the selection marquee.

- Anti-aliasing can smooth out rough edges by providing lighter or darker pixels to blur them.

- Objects can be copied, cut, or pasted using the standard Macintosh menu commands and key shortcuts.

- Choosing Layer ⇨ Transform ⇨ Flip Horizontal/Flip Vertical is a fast way to flip a selection horizontally or vertically.

- Images can be repositioned with both the move tool and the arrow keys.

- Clicking and Option-clicking in the Swatches palette or anywhere in the image when the eyedropper is visible selects foreground and background colors, respectively. The two colors can be swapped by clicking on the swap colors arrow, or restored to the default black/white values by clicking on the miniature color control boxes.

- Pressing Command-spacebar or Option-spacebar as you click the mouse button enables you to zoom in or out, respectively.

In Chapter 2 we're going to use our VRMLcelli logo to create images for KTI's upcoming World Wide Web page. This will give you an opportunity to discover more Photoshop tools, including the wonderful world of brushes—which are flexible in more ways than one.

Creating a Web Page Graphic

Using the Brush Tools

The client liked your logo well enough to ask you to adapt it for Kitchen Table International's new World Wide Web page devoted to VRMLcelli. Can you incorporate the logo design into some graphics, navigational buttons, and rules (lines) for the company's Webmaster? Even though you've had only one Photoshop session, you'll be pleased to know you can perform some very cool tricks using simple-to-learn brush tools, a few new techniques, and the tricks you've already learned.

THE TOOLS

☐ Photoshop's Select and Preferences menus

☐ Brushes and Layers palettes

☐ Magic wand and toning tools

☐ Image Size and Scale commands

☐ GIF98a Export filter

Many Web pages can be improved by a distinctive graphic—a good-looking logo or other image that gives visitors an idea of where they are. Photoshop's brush tool provides a slick way to build such an image. And, because we are not limited to the brush set Photoshop provides, the brush tool enables us to reuse the VRMLcelli logo we designed in the first chapter—as a custom brush. In this exercise we'll first create a frame around our image, and then paint in a custom background, using the VRMLcelli logo as a brush. As before, the project is divided into several easy steps.

graphic \graf′ic\ *n* **1:** In desktop publishing, image-oriented material used to interrupt the flow of less essential components in a publication, such as text. **2:** In Internet parlance, anything that delays loading a Web page, thereby reducing the number of visitors to a site. *adj* Vividly realistic and involving large, audience-pleasing explosions, as in *graphic violence*.

STEP 1: CREATING A FRAME WITH BRUSHES

The first step is to open an empty Photoshop document, and begin drawing a frame. Follow these directions:

1 Select File ➪ New and replace the default name with a more useful name, such as VRMLcelli Web Graphic. Make it 400 pixels wide by 400 pixels high, leave the Resolution setting at 72 pixels per inch (this image is for a Web page, remember), and select RGB Color from the Mode drop-down list box. Leave the contents of the new document white, as in the previous exercise.

TIP Always choose a resolution and size suitable for your intended application. We chose the resolution of 72 pixels per inch because the final image will be viewed on a display screen with a resolution on roughly the same scale. The 400 × 400 pixel size we've chosen is actually a little large for a Web graphic, but we wanted to give you enough room to work. You can always reduce the graphic's size later on to fit better on a Web page. Because visitors to a Web site may be viewing your page through a window that's 640 × 480 or smaller, you need to keep graphics within that size, too. Also, larger images take too long to download, and tend to discourage visitors from hanging around.

2 Click the rectangular marquee tool, and select a square that's about a quarter inch smaller than the document itself. You should leave only a small border around the outside edge.

3 Next, round off the corners of your rectangular selection by choosing Select ⇨ Feather. A dialog box pop ups asking for the "Feather Radius." This is the number of pixels Photoshop uses to blur the edges of your selection, including the corners. Enter a value of 5 and click on OK. Your selection will look like Figure 2-1.

FIGURE 2-1
Your "rounded" selection

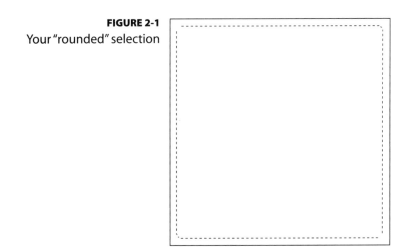

4 Click the brush tool in the toolbox (the third icon from the top in the right column—if you need to, refer back to Figure 1-2 in Chapter 1 to find the right tool), then click on the Brushes palette. You'll see various brush types, including hard-edged ones in the top row and softer, blurry brushes underneath. The icons show the approximate screen sizes of the brushes, until the final row where their size is indicated by a number representing the diameter of the brush in pixels. Choose the 35-pixel brush.

5 Next, choose a color for your frame. We selected a bright green from the Swatches palette.

SETTING YOUR PREFERENCES

Photoshop lets you specify certain parameters as preferences, including the way painting tools are represented on the screen. We'll look at many of these preferences in this book, but now is a good time to set the painting tools preference. To do this, choose File ⇨ Preferences ⇨ Display & Cursors. A Preferences dialog box appears (see Figure 2-2).

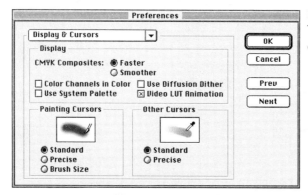

FIGURE 2-2

The Preferences dialog box

In the Painting Cursors box, you'll notice three choices. The Standard radio button sets the cursor to a simple icon representing the tool (for example, brush or pencil) with the tool's "hot spot"—the place where painting begins—at the point of the icon. You can also choose a Precise cursor, which is a cross-hair that locates the hot spot in the center of the cross-hair. We prefer the Brush Size selection, which shows you the actual coverage size of the brush or other painting tool on screen. You have less of an idea where the hot spot is, but more control over how much of your image is covered. Click the Brush Size radio button. In the Other Cursors box you'll probably want to click the Precise button for all the tools, such as eyedropper and lasso, as long as you're here.

6 Move the brush to the upper left corner of your selection and click once. Then move the brush to the upper right, hold down the Shift key and click again. You'll notice that the brush traces a path from the last place you "touched down" to the new place. Now, move to the lower right and Shift-click. Repeat, using the lower left and upper left corners again until you've drawn a fuzzy green frame around the selection, as shown in Figure 2-3.

NOTE   Shift-clicking enables you to draw continuous, straight figures without having to drag the cursor manually.

FIGURE 2-3

The border so far

USING THE SWATCHES PALETTE AND COLOR PICKER

The Swatches palette is a good source of repeatable colors, because the swatches remain the same until you add or delete one, or create special colors of your own. You can always save sets of swatches for reuse later using the fly-out menu. However, if you want a greater selection or particular color and don't need to reproduce the color later on, you can select your color(s) from the Color Picker. Just click on either the foreground or background color control boxes in the toolbox and the Color Picker appears, as shown in Figure 2-4. You can use the controls to type in values using one of the four color systems Photoshop supports (for example, actual values for red, green, and blue components), or select any color you wish with the round cursor. Click on the Custom button to select a Pantone color or another predefined color. If you do need to reuse a color you select in this way, you can add it to a swatch in the Swatches palette, or grab it from the image, using the eyedropper.

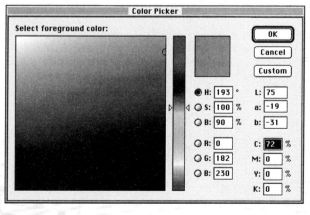

FIGURE 2-4

The Color Picker offers a whole spectrum of colors to choose from.

7 Select the magic wand tool, then click on the Options palette. In this palette, make sure that Tolerance is set to 32, and the Anti-Aliased box is checked. The Tolerance level is the range of tones from 0–255 that Photoshop uses to include pixels in a selection. With the Tolerance level set to 255, all pixels in an image will be selected; at 0, none will be selected. With our setting of 32, all pixels with a brightness range that is plus or minus 16 of the pixel you click will be included.

8 Click twice anywhere in the middle of your green frame. The magic wand tool automatically selects all the green pixels that match the one you click in, plus any others that have brightness values plus or minus 16. In effect, you've selected the center of the frame, and ignored the fuzzy outer edges, which are lighter than the tolerance level you've chosen.

9 Select a darker green from the Swatches palette, and then choose Edit ⇨ Fill to fill the selection. Make sure the Opacity setting in the Fill dialog box is set to 100 percent.

10 Choose Select ⇨ None, or click anywhere outside the selection to deselect the area you just filled.

11 Click on Brushes to select the smaller fuzzy brush in the middle row, immediately above the one labeled "65."

12 Repeat your Shift-click trip around the frame, painting with white in the middle of the frame/border. You'll end up with the interesting 3D border shown in Figure 2-5. Note that you achieved this great effect using nothing but the selection tools and a few brushes!

FIGURE 2-5
The 3D border is finished.

STEP 2: CREATING A CUSTOM BRUSH

This next effect is even more impressive. You're going to convert the VRMLcelli logo we created in Chapter 1 into an artistic brush. Creating your own brushes gives you more flexibility than if you used Photoshop's built-in round brushes. Here's how to do it:

1 Load the VRMLcelli Logo file into Photoshop.

2 Create a copy of the logo with the Image ⇨ Duplicate command. It's always a good idea to work with a copy of your original. If you modified and saved the original, you'd have no way to retrieve it later on. Don't let that happen to you!

3 Close the original version to keep it safe.

4 Select Image ⇨ Image Size. In the resulting Image Size dialog box you can adjust the dimension of the image or change its resolution. The measurements used can be in percentages, inches, pixels, or centimeters, as well as points, picas, or columns (see Figure 2-6).

FIGURE 2-6

The Image Size dialog box enables you to adjust the dimensions and resolution of an image.

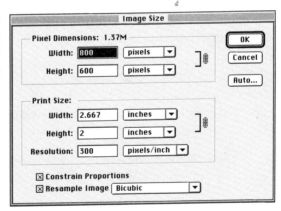

TIP If you type in a new width, Photoshop adjusts the height of your image proportionately. If you type in a new height, Photoshop changes the width accordingly. The key is that the Constrain Proportions box must be checked (at the bottom of the dialog box), which displays the chain link icon that joins the height/width in the dialog box, "locking" them together proportionally. Uncheck the Constrain Proportions box, and you can specify a new height or width and leave the other measurement unchanged. Although doing this destroys the image's original proportions, it may not make a difference with abstract visuals, particularly textures.

5 Make sure the measurements are set to percentages, that the Constrain Proportions box is checked, and that the Resample Image box unchecked. Then change the width to 25 percent. Click on OK, and Photoshop will shrink the VRMLcelli logo to one-fourth its original size.

6 Next, we want to sharpen up the reduced logo, while increasing the contrast a little. Select Sharpen from the Filters ⇨ Sharpen menu.

7 Select the magic wand tool, and then click anywhere in the white area outside the logo. Photoshop selects everything but the logo itself.

8 Choose Select ⇨ Inverse to reverse the current selection, so that only the logo is selected. You've just learned a quick trick for selecting an object that is not of a uniform color itself, but rests on a plain background. Select the plain background itself, then inverse your selection. This is much easier than trying to select the object piecemeal.

9 With the logo highlighted, click the Brushes palette, and find the fly-out menu at the right side. Select Define Brush.

Congratulations—you've just created a new brush that's a grayscale version of the VRMLcelli logo. It appears at the end of the Brushes palette. You can use this brush to paint creatively, and add backgrounds, as we'll do next.

STEP 3: ADDING A BACKGROUND

Now we're going to use our new custom brush to add an interesting background to the frame, as follows:

1 Activate the magic wand tool, and then click inside the frame you created earlier. This enables you to paint only in the selection, while leaving the border itself alone.

2 Click the Brushes palette, and then select your new custom brush.

3 Click the Swatches palette and select a color. Notice that the cursor for the brush tool changes into an eyedropper as it passes over the swatches. Click on a color to make it the foreground hue.

4 Move over to the selection inside the border, and click with the brush. Notice that the shape painted with a single click is an exact image of the VRMLcelli logo. If you kept the mouse button pressed and dragged, you could paint with little logos. For now, however, just stamp a couple of copies in the selected area by single-clicking.

5 Change colors in the Swatches palette, and stamp a few more copies of the logo. Repeat, changing colors a few more times, until you have some overlapping background images, as shown in Figure 2-7.

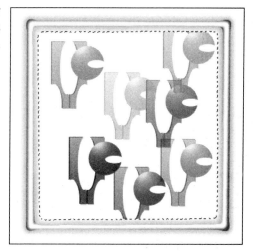

FIGURE 2-7
Overlapped background images produce an interesting effect.

STEP 4: SAVING IN A WEB-FRIENDLY FORMAT

The final step involves saving our graphic in a format that enables it to be placed on a Web page and viewed inline with the text, links, and other components that KTI's Webmaster will place there. Here's how to create your first interlaced, transparent GIF file—and learn what *that* is at the same time.

1 Save your work now, if you have not done so already, or create a duplicate of this file using the Image ⇨ Duplicate command. We're about to make some changes to our Web graphic and then save it in a new file.

2 Because we want only the graphic, and nothing else, to show through on the Web page, we'll need to crop the image. But because the outer edges are fuzzy, we'll do it in a different way than in the previous chapter. Select the magic wand tool, and click on the white area outside the graphic. Then use Select ⇨ Inverse to reverse the selection, so only the graphic itself is chosen. By now, you should be fairly comfortable with selecting portions of images in this way.

3 Copy the selected graphic using Command-C.

4 We're not going to do a standard Paste, as we've done so far. We're going to use a special Paste option, available only from the Edit menu. Choose Edit ⇨ Paste Layer. The New Layer dialog box pops up, as shown in Figure 2-8. Name your new layer Transparent GIF, then click on OK. This pastes a copy of the selected graphic in a new, transparent layer of its own. The surrounding area is fully see-through, as if we'd glued the graphic onto a clear piece of plastic.

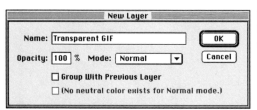

FIGURE 2-8
Create a new layer with the New Layer dialog box.

TIP   Photoshop can work with multiple layers, which you might think of as overlays. You can turn individual layers on and off, and change the way they are "stacked" so that certain features show through, or are obscured by objects layered on top of them. Layers are also a great way to work with individual objects separately, without changing any of the other elements in an image. We can combine the layers later on in many different ways.

5 We want to save a "transparent" version of the image, so click the Layers palette tab, shown in Figure 2-9. Your original image is labeled Background, while the new layer is called Transparent GIF. Both layers have an eyeball icon in the left-most column, which means they are currently visible. In addition, the Transparent GIF layer will be highlighted, indicating that it is the active layer. Several layers can be visible at one time, but you can work only on the active layer.

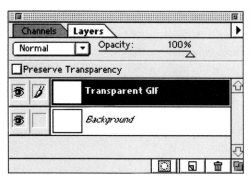

FIGURE 2-9
The Layers palette shows all the available layers in an image.

6 Turn off the background layer by clicking on the eyeball icon. It will vanish, leaving only the new layer, as shown in Figure 2-10. The background layer still exists of course—you just can't see it at the moment. Notice that the white area surrounding the image has vanished, leaving only a gray checkerboard pattern. The gray checkerboard is Photoshop's default way of indicating a transparent area. You may change the grid size and color of this pattern any time by selecting File ⇨ Preferences ⇨ Transparency, although that's not a good idea, because it keeps any of the information in the other layers from showing through.

FIGURE 2-10
The gray checkerboard pattern shows the transparent areas of the image.

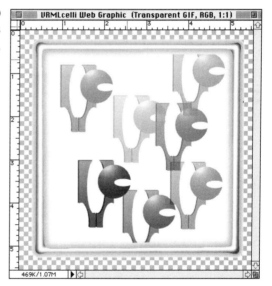

7 Next, we use Photoshop's special GIF export facility to create a Web-style GIF file. Choose File ⇨ Export ⇨ GIF89a Export to display the dialog box shown in Figure 2-11. While you can set various options in this dialog box, the way we've created this image has already taken care of most of the choices for us. What Photoshop is about to do is convert the image from millions of colors down to 255 of the 256 that are allowed in a GIF-format file. The final color is set aside to represent transparency when the GIF is loaded by a Web browser. In addition, the image will be *interlaced*, so that the Web browser can display alternating lines as the image is shown a little at a time. You can click on OK, then type in a file name for the graphic in the resulting dialog box.

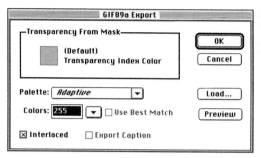

FIGURE 2-11

The GIF89a Export facility enables you to create Web-friendly files.

NOTE   The Graphics Interchange Format (GIF) was created by CompuServe Information Service as a common file format for 256-color images that could be viewed on Macintosh, PC, or other platforms. All you need is a viewer capable of displaying GIF files. Because GIF is so widely used, viewing capabilities were built into the first graphical Web browsers. When they encounter a GIF file while downloading a page, the GIF can be displayed right on the page along with the text. Although GIF files have been squeezed, or compressed (unneeded or redundant information is discarded when the file is saved), they still take some time to download, so they are often interlaced. The browser can receive every other line of the image first, display a coarse version quickly so you'll have some idea of what the image looks like, and then fill in the missing lines as they are received.

STEP 5: CREATING A CUSTOM BUTTON

Given what you've learned so far, it will take you only a few extra minutes to create a custom button for the KTI Web site. When clicked, this button will take visitors to various links within the company's Web site.

This task also gives you an opportunity to work with filters. Photoshop's filters are little stand-alone programs that plug into the imaging application and provide a way to process the pixels of a selection or the entire image. Filters can blur, sharpen, or move pixels from one place to another (all the Distort filters do this), change their color, or perform other magic. Follow these instructions, and you'll have a nice, vivid button in no time:

1   Select the elliptical marquee tool and move the cursor to the VRMLcelli Web Graphic image we created in this chapter. We're going to select a portion of the background to use as the texture for our button.

2   Hold down the Shift key to create a perfect circle, and drag until you've grabbed around one-quarter of the graphic.

3 Copy the contents of the circular selection by pressing Command-C.

4 Choose File ⇨ New, and the New File dialog box pops up. Notice that Photoshop has already filled in a width and height corresponding to the dimensions of the selection you've copied to the Clipboard. Photoshop makes it easy to create a new file that closely fits the area you've selected and copied.

5 Check Transparent in the Contents box and click on OK. Photoshop creates a new, empty file showing the gray checkerboard pattern that represents transparency.

6 Press Command-V to paste down the circular selection you copied. Your new image should look like the one shown in Figure 2-12.

FIGURE 2-12
The button pasted down in a new file

7 This isn't quite button-like enough, so we're going to use one of Photoshop's native filters again. Select Filter ⇨ Distort ⇨ Spherize. When you do this, the Spherize dialog box appears, as shown in Figure 2-13. Make sure you set the Mode to Normal, and that you move the slider to 100 percent (as shown). Then click on OK.

FIGURE 2-13
The Spherize dialog box

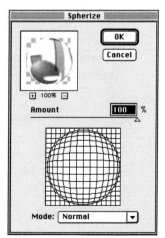

8 Choose Filter ➪ Sharpen ➪ Sharpen to make the image a little more vivid. The button should now resemble the one shown in Figure 2-14.

9 To make the button look a little more spherical, we're going to add a radial gradient. Make sure the layer containing the button is active, then click outside the button with the magic wand to select the surrounding area. Then use Select ➪ Inverse to reverse the selection so only the button is selected. We need to select the button to make sure the gradient we add in the next step is applied only to the button itself.

FIGURE 2-14
The circular Web button looks like this once it's been spherized.

10 Select the gradient tool, then choose a dark and light blue as your background and foreground colors respectively. Click on the Options palette, and then choose Radial as the Type of gradient. We don't want to fill in the button with color, so move the Opacity slider to the 15 percent point. This setting enables us to add a touch of transparent color to the image. Place the cursor at the upper right edge of the circle, and drag to the lower left to apply the gradient.

11 Because the button is way too big, use Image ➪ Image Size, then change the Width unit of measurement to Percent, and type in 25 percent as the new value. Make sure the Resample checkbox is unchecked. Click on OK.

12 Apply the Filter ➪ Sharpen ➪ Unsharp Mask. Unlike the Sharpen and Sharpen More filters, Unsharp Mask has three sliders that enable you to control how sharpening is applied. For now, just use the Amount slider and set it to 50 percent. (We want you to become accustomed to using this filter, as we'll get plenty of benefit from it in this book.)

13 Our button is already on a transparent background, so you can use the File ➪ Export ➪ GIF89a Export command to create a transparent, interlaced GIF (as you did before) that makes it easy to include the file in a Web page. Choose a name such as `button.gif` to make it easy to identify this file.

STEP 6: CREATING A HORIZONTAL RULE

Web browsers provide their own rules (or lines), but many Webmasters like to include custom rules that adhere more closely to the visual theme of the page. We can create a color-coordinated rule in a few minutes. Here's how:

1   Return to your duplicate of the VRMLcelli Web Graphic. Choose the rectangular marquee tool, and then select a long, narrow strip, as shown in Figure 2-15.

FIGURE 2-15
Select a long, narrow
strip from the graphic.

2   Choose Layer ⇨ Transform ⇨ Scale from the menu bar. Small boxes called selection handles will appear at the four corners of the horizontal selection.

3   Drag on the boxes to make the selection both longer and thinner. The pixels in the image stretch and compress to accommodate your modifications. You can cancel the changes you've made anytime by pressing the Escape key. Pressing Return tells Photoshop to go ahead and make the changes permanent. Press Return.

4   Use Command-C to copy the stretched selection to the Clipboard.

5   Select File ⇨ New to paste the new, elongated object into a file, and accept the default dimensions Photoshop has filled in for you, as they correspond to the selection on the Clipboard.

NOTE The toning tool enables you to use a brush-like tool to make sections of an image darker (*burn*) or lighter (*dodge*), without changing the other values, or to remove some of the color brightness, or saturation (*sponge*). The *dodge* and *burn* terms derive from photographic techniques in which a darkroom worker held a dodging object, including his or her hands, in the enlarger's light path as an image was exposed (burned) onto photographic paper. The object could be used to allow more or less light to fall on the paper for a particular area of the image, making it darker or lighter. The sponge version of the tool has no direct darkroom equivalent, but it can come in handy nevertheless.

6 The final step is to give the rule a tubular appearance. Select the dodge/burn/sponge tool, also known as the toning tool, from the toolbox (the sixth tool from the top in the right column).

7 Click on the Options palette. Make sure Exposure is set to 100 percent, and Highlights is showing in the drop-down list box. In the Tool list, choose Burn, if it isn't already showing.

8 Click on the Brushes palette to choose a toning "brush." Choose the one in the second row above the 45-pixel brush.

9 Drag the burn tool along the bottom edge of the rule. Then repeat and drag along the top edge. You'll produce a smooth, tube-like effect, as shown in Figure 2-16.

FIGURE 2-16

The rule has been transformed into a tube-like object.

10 We're not going to save this one as a GIF. Instead, use File ➪ Save A Copy, and select JPEG as the output format. Name the file `Vrule.jpg`. The JPEG Options dialog box appears (see Figure 2-17) when you click on OK, giving you several choices. Choose the Standard format, and select Medium image quality from the top drop-down box, and click on OK again. Note how the slider moves to indicate your choice: The higher the quality—that is, the sharper the resolution—the larger the file.

NOTE Web pages support both GIF and JPEG file formats for a good reason. Each has different strengths. GIF files have 256 colors and display well on any monitor, whether the user's machine supports 256 hues or millions of colors. GIFs also compress fairly well without actually losing any information, so they are small and retain all the sharp edges and detail of the original. JPEG files, on the other hand, use what is called a *lossy* compression scheme, that actually discards image detail to make the file smaller. That's why you had to choose from four different quality levels in step 10. When you save a JPEG file, you can decide for yourself what tradeoffs to make in terms of image quality and file size. The rule we created squeezes down to about 1.5K as a JPEG, but requires twice as much disk—and download—resources when stored as a GIF. The JPEG version, however, can include a full 16.7 million colors, producing a smoother-looking image. Use GIF when fine details are important or you need transparency, and JPEG when smooth colors are your primary concern.

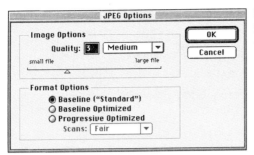

FIGURE 2-17
Select the JPEG image quality you desire from the JPEG Options dialog box.

WHAT YOU'VE LEARNED

In this chapter, you picked up some basic tricks you can apply to much of your work with Photoshop. You know that:

- The Select menu has options that enable you to modify a selection. The Feather command, for example, can blur or fade the edges of a selection by the number of pixels you specify.

- The Brushes palette provides a selection of hard- and soft-edged brushes with which you can paint.

- The way brushes and other tools are represented on the screen by the cursor can be modified in the File ➪ Preferences ➪ General dialog box. You can choose from a generic brush icon, a precision cross-hair, or a cursor that corresponds to the actual coverage of the brush.

- You can double-click on the color control boxes to select a hue from the Color Picker.

- Straight lines can be drawn with a brush by clicking at one end of the line, then Shift-clicking at the other end.

- The magic wand tool can select an area based on how close adjacent pixels are to the pixel you clicked first. The range Photoshop uses to select these pixels is called the tolerance level, and can be changed in the Options palette.

- Any selection can be converted into a custom brush, which is added to your Brushes palette.

- The Image Size option can be used to change the dimension of an image, either proportionately or in just one direction. You can also modify the resolution, as well as the size of an image, by typing in a percentage instead of a dimension or number of pixels.

- World Wide Web images most commonly use GIF or JPEG file formats.

- The GIF format is best for images that have fine detail and look good with 256 or fewer colors.

- The JPEG format is best for photographs and images that don't suffer when compressed.

- Photoshop can store image elements in separate overlays called layers. The active layer is highlighted, and an eyeball icon appears next to a layer that is currently visible. Click on an eyeball to hide or reveal a particular layer.

- Photoshop uses a special File ⇨ Export ⇨ Export GIF89a filter to create interlaced and transparent GIF files.

- Selections can be resized by using the Image ⇨ Effects ⇨ Scale command, and dragging on the selection's sizing handles until you achieve the desired proportions. Clicking inside the selection sets the new size; clicking outside cancels the operation.

- The toning tool lightens, darkens, or removes color from areas of an image.

So far you've worked with images created from scratch. Now it's time to get your feet wet with manipulating a photographic image. In Chapter 3, we'll show you how to use the brightness/contrast controls to spiff up a seriously deficient original.

Creating a Price Tag

Image Correction with Photoshop

THE PROJECT

Management reports that the big computer superstores just can't keep Kitchen Table International's products on the shelves—they keep sending them back for credit. KTI's marketing whizzes feel that some fancy price tags may help overcome the widely held belief that KTI's products are unencumbered by special features. Your job is to design an attractive tag that lists the price for KTI's slow-moving D-RAM chip line. You don't bother to tell your client that most computer users have switched to SIMMs or DIMMs, and instead decide to learn more about Photoshop's image correction tools.

THE TOOLS
- ▣ Brightness/Contrast controls
- ▣ Variations dialog box
- ▣ Levels Control
- ▣ Monitor Setup
- ▣ Text tool

Our price tag will include a full color, photographic image, because consumers tend to think packaging and marketing materials with photographs are more impressive than those containing simple line art and text. Unfortunately, KTI provided you only with a rather poor black-and-white photo. Don't worry, we'll show you how to dress it up, and add a splash of color.

OBTAINING IMAGES

In the first two chapters we used images created from scratch. Doing so gave you some experience with Photoshop's basic selection and drawing tools. While Photoshop can be used to paint images in an artistic way, it is predominantly an image editing program, with tools to improve and manipulate photographic images for printing, desktop presentations, or publishing.

To edit images, you must first get them into the computer. If you have a scanner or digital camera, or own a Mac equipped with camcorder video capture capabilities, you can roll your own images, so to speak. Many of these products come with a plug-in for the Filters menu or a TWAIN driver that plugs into Photoshop's Acquire menu, and enables you to grab images with a scanner directly into Photoshop, or to download them from a digital camera or other source. Instructions for installing TWAIN or plug-in support and acquiring images should come with your hardware, and won't be covered in this book.

Photofinishers can process your film and provide you with a Kodak Photo CD containing high-resolution scans of each picture on the roll (plus lower resolution versions to play with). Existing prints, slides, and negatives can also be converted to Photo CD. The cost can be as little as $1 an image. Kodak's Web site (`http://www.kodak.com`) contains a list of sources for Photo CD scanning.

If you have a CD-ROM drive suitable for Photo CD images, you can also get good photographs from commercial and shareware CD-ROMs. If you decide to add a desert background to an image, for example, you'll find several CDs with desert scenes. One company with a large number of reasonably priced image CDs is Corel Corporation. Their CD-ROMs are widely available at $20–$40 each, perhaps a little less if purchased in packages. In addition, shareware CDs sell for as little as $15. The CD-ROM bundled with this book has images, including the ones we use here, that you can use at no extra cost.

STEP 1: CORRECTING BRIGHTNESS AND CONTRAST

The first thing we need to do is load a picture—a TIFF file—into Photoshop, and doctor it up. TIFF is a kind of bitmap format, like GIF and JPEG. It shares with GIF a lossless compression scheme that can squeeze images down in file size without losing any picture information. Unlike GIF, however, the TIFF format can store up to 16.7 million colors. An additional difference is that various types of TIFF files abound, including different ways of ordering the bytes in an image for Macintosh computers and for PCs. Luckily, programs such as Photoshop can read and write all the common TIFF formats, and create files that can be used on both Macs and PCs.

 file \fil\ *n* **1:** The smallest quantity of information that can be accidentally erased by a computer user. **2:** A small tool with cutting ridges or teeth that can be used to make an expansion board fit better in a tight slot. *v* To store something you don't mean to find again. From the Old English *fylan*: befoul. See also *defile*.

USING THE BRIGHTNESS/CONTRAST CONTROL

Many pictures you'll work with have some brightness and/or contrast defect. The picture may be too dark, or too light, or it has plenty of dark and light tones, but not enough in between. By the time you're asked to work with an image, it's probably too late to have it reshot, so you'll have to make the best you can of it. We're going to show you three simple ways to fix these types of problems. Two are pretty easy, but don't offer the degree of control you really need. The third way only *looks* complicated. Here's how to get started:

1 Locate the Chapter 4 folder on the CD-ROM bundled with this book, and load the file ram.tif into Photoshop. At around 1.5MB, it's a fairly big file, but prepare to be disappointed as it loads—KTI did not send you a first-rate scan to work with. In fact, it's low in contrast, and looks something like Figure 3-1.

FIGURE 3-1
The original TIFF image
you have to work with.

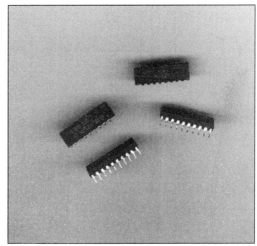

2 Zoom in (Command-spacebar) and you'll see the image has plenty of detail. It just looks faded.

3 Select Image ⇨ Adjust ⇨ Levels (or press Command-L). In the resulting Levels dialog box, the most important part is the histogram, shown in Figure 3.2 (see the sidebar for an explanation of histograms). As you can see, our ram.tif image is a mess. There's a little clump of pixels halfway between the black point and middle gray point, a small slope of medium gray pixels, and a huge Devil's Tower of pixels that extend right off the top of the chart. That's our problem: All that space at the left of the histogram, and the smaller amount at the right end, are wasted.

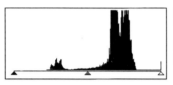

FIGURE 3-2
The histogram displays the amount of each gray value in an image, using vertical bars.

A HISTOGRAM IS NOT A COLD MEDICINE

You can see just what's wrong with many kinds of images by studying a kind of chart called a histogram, which you can view from the Image ⇨ Histogram menu, or manipulate from Image ⇨ Adjust ⇨ Levels.

Histograms are a kind of bar chart, with 256 lines extending from completely black (represented by the black triangle at the left in Figure 3-2) to completely white (represented by the white triangle). In the middle is a gray triangle used to represent a number called *gamma* that measures the contrast of the midtones of an image. For now, we'll just worry about the black and white points, and learn how to adjust gamma later on.

Grayscale images like ram.tif can have 256 different gray tones. The fewer of these gray tones that are used, the higher the contrast of the image. If the picture used only 10 different gray tones, we'd find it to be a very high-contrast image indeed. If it uses all 256 evenly, we see it as a low-contrast image.

The histogram's 256 line positions each show how many pixels are represented by that gray value. An average photograph will have a histogram that looks something like a mountain, with some pixels at the black end, some at the white end of the scale, and a peak in the middle, where lots of gray tones reside. Few images will neatly fit between the black and white end points, and the mountain frequently has a steeper slope at one side than the other.

4 The most tempting way to change the image is with Photoshop's Brightness and Contrast sliders. Try it: create a duplicate of ram.tif using the Image ➪ Duplicate command. You can also create a duplicate by pressing the Option-D keys. Select the duplicate.

5 Use the Image ➪ Adjust ➪ Brightness/Contrast menu command to display the dialog box shown in Figure 3-3.

FIGURE 3-3
The Brightness/Contrast dialog box has sliders that help you control the parameters separately.

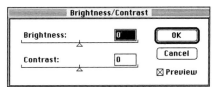

6 Make sure the Preview box is checked, so Photoshop will show you what's going on in your original image as you play with the sliders.

7 Move the Brightness slider until a value of +22 appears in the Brightness window—or place the cursor in the box and type in 22 directly. Click on OK to apply your setting to the duplicate image. The picture looks a little better, doesn't it? The chips are brighter and easier to read, and the gray background has been given a cleaner white tone. But, in truth, we haven't fixed the image as well as we might. The real situation is revealed in the histogram produced by these brightness/contrast settings, shown in Figure 3-4.

FIGURE 3-4
The modified histogram reveals what's going on.

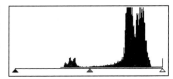

8 Compare the two histograms presented so far. You can see that all we've done is move the values up the scale towards the white end of the chart. Fewer pixels are wasted at the white end of the scale, but we're still not using all those black tones at the left side of the histogram. The picture is still low in contrast. Let's try to fix that.

9 Press Command-B again to display the Brightness/Contrast sliders, and move the Contrast slider until a value of +33 is shown, or type 33 in directly. Click on OK to apply the change.

10 Look at the histogram (shown in Figure 3-5) now. It shows that alternating lines have been removed, increasing the contrast of the image. You can often improve an image by fiddling with the brightness and contrast controls, but as you can see, it's often a trial and error process that doesn't produce optimum results.

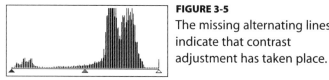

FIGURE 3-5
The missing alternating lines indicate that contrast adjustment has taken place.

USING VARIATIONS

1 Make another duplicate of ram.tif, and select it.

2 Select Image ➪ Adjust ➪ Variations. Photoshop displays an interesting arrangement of images in the Variations dialog box (see Figure 3-6) that show what your original image would look like with various degrees of lightening and darkening applied to the very lightest highlights, middle tones, and shadows.

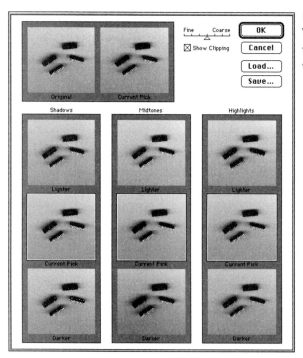

FIGURE 3-6
Variations provide you with several different views of an image.

3 Unfortunately, the Variations are small and sometimes difficult to gauge. We can fix that. Click Cancel to return to the original image.

4 Select one RAM chip with the rectangular marquee tool. Then, choose Image ⇨ Adjust ⇨ Variations again. This time, the variations are centered only around the selection, so we can see what's going on much more easily, as you can see in Figure 3-7.

FIGURE 3-7
You can work with a selection to enlarge the area displayed by the Variations dialog box.

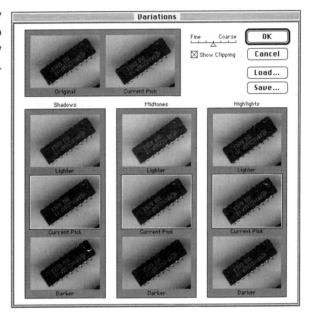

5 We already know that the background area should be lighter. The background is the closest thing we have in the picture to a highlight—not counting the legs of the RAM chips. We can lighten those highlights by clicking on the upper box in the Highlight column. Click it five times to give all those highlights a boost. If you look carefully, you'll see black spots appear on the legs of the RAM chips (if the Show Clipping box is checked, as it should be). That means that the settings you apply won't enable all the detail in that area to be shown—it will be "clipped" out. We'll ignore that warning for now.

6 Next, click on the Darker box in the Midtones column. That will darken only the tones in the middle area of the image, and make the RAM chips look a little spunkier.

7 Compare the Original and Current Pick images at the top of the dialog box. This seems to be the best we can do. But don't click on OK! If you do, the changes will be applied only to the selection. You can choose to remember what you just did (five times Highlight/Lighter, once Midtones/Darker) or click on Save, and store the current settings on your hard disk. Then click Cancel.

TIP When working with Variations, you can move the Fine . . . Coarse slider to increase or decrease the amount of change a given adjustment will produce. Set the slider toward Coarse if you want more dramatic changes or toward Fine if you'd like to work with subtle modifications. If you're working with several photos all shot under the same conditions, you can Save the settings you arrive at, and then Load them later on to apply them to a different image.

8 Choose Select ➪ None, or click anywhere outside the selection to unselect the chip.

9 Select Image ➪ Adjust ➪ Variations once more, and either load your settings from disk, or apply the settings you remember from Steps 5 and 6. Then click on OK to apply the change. The histogram of this latest image looks like the one shown in Figure 3-8. It's lower in contrast, but still wastes tones in the dark end. You can see from the image that it has no true black tones. What can we do? It's time to investigate the third and most flexible way of adjusting the tonal values of an image.

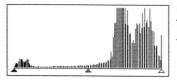

FIGURE 3-8
Tones are still wasted, as this histogram shows.

USING THE LEVELS CONTROLS

1 Duplicate ram.tif once more, and select the duplicate.

2 Choose Image ➪ Adjust ➪ Levels. The Levels dialog box appears (see Figure 3-9). The three fields to the right of Input Levels show the current setting for the black point (in this case 0, at left), the white point (255, at right), and the gray gamma indicator in the middle, which is set at a neutral value of 1.00. It's easiest to think of gamma as a kind of brightness indicator, that can be adjusted from the "normal" value of 1.00 to very dark (.10) or very light (9.99). However, the gamma control changes the brightness only of the middle tones, without affecting the lightest and darkest areas. That's why it receives a special name of its own. The Levels dialog box can be used to adjust the brightness and contrast in sophisticated ways. You'll even find an Auto button that can make some corrections for you.

FIGURE 3-9
The Levels dialog box includes the histogram we've been viewing all along.

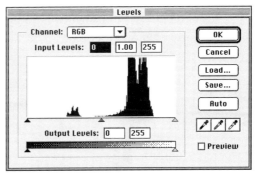

3 Click the Auto button. The histogram immediately changes to one like that shown in Figure 3-10. Notice that the black point has been moved in from the left to a point just to the right of the first black tones in the actual image, while the white point has been moved in to where the white tones actually end. The Auto setting actually ignores the 5 percent darkest and 5 percent lightest pixels, and allocates the 256 gray tones of the image in the area where detail exists. You probably won't use the Auto button much, because you can achieve greater control making these modifications manually.

FIGURE 3-10
Photoshop can provide automatic adjustments, as it has done here.

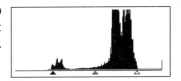

4 Evaluate the underlying image of the RAM chips. The picture looks better, although now it's a bit too contrasty. You can adjust that by moving the left Output Level slider at the bottom of the window to the right, until a value of about 50 shows in the left Output Level box. The Output Level slider adjusts the contrast of the final image.

5 Click Cancel to nullify the changes, and then select Image ⇨ Adjust ⇨ Levels once more to display the Levels dialog box again.

6 Manually adjust the black and white points so they are set at the beginning and the end of the dark and light details, respectively.

7 Next, move the gamma slider to the left. Notice how the gray middle tones become lighter, while the dark tones remain relatively unchanged? Stop moving the slider when the image looks really good to you. In our case, that was when the gamma reached 1.88. Your results may vary depending on how you've set Photoshop's own gamma control to match your monitor (see Appendix C for more information on calibration). The dialog box should look like the own shown in Figure 3-11.

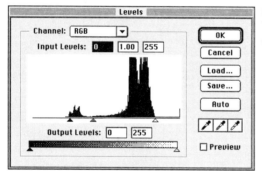

FIGURE 3-11
The gamma control adjusts the contrast of midtones.

USING EYEDROPPERS

While the image we have on the screen is good enough to use, we want to show you one more way of adjusting brightness and contrast, as follows:

1 Click Cancel again to nullify your changes, and choose Image ⇨ Adjust ⇨ Levels to display the Levels dialog box again.

2 Click on the black point eyedropper (the one at the left of the set of three in the lower right of the dialog box). You can use this eyedropper to select the actual darkest point of your image.

3 Move the dropper to the dark strip on one of the lower two RAM chips, and click. The black point on the histogram moves to the right, roughly to the point where it was set with the Auto control.

4   Select the white point eyedropper, and click on the lightest area of the
    image that has detail. That's not the legs of the chips but the upper
    right corner of the image, in the lightest portion of the background.
    The white point will move left on the histogram.

5   Next, adjust the gamma slider manually to produce the best image.
    Click on OK to save and finish.

NOTE What you've learned here applies equally well to color as well as grayscale
images. The only reason we tackled a black-and-white picture first was to let you
tackle some potentially confusing concepts without dragging in hues. Use these
techniques to spiff up your color images, either as a whole, or by working with
individual color layers. You'll learn how the red, green, and blue elements of an
image can be handled separately later in this book. Also, you should know that
you have yet another way to adjust gray values—with the Image ⇨ Adjust ⇨
Curves dialog box. We don't need this advanced tool to do our work here, though.

STEP 2: CONVERTING A GRAYSCALE IMAGE TO COLOR

KTI's price tag will be printed in dramatic full color, but the photo you received is
black-and-white. Fortunately, Photoshop makes it easy to convert a grayscale picture to
color. Here's how:

1   From the Mode menu, select RGB Color. Photoshop instantly
    converts the picture to a color image. Unfortunately, it still contains
    only grayscale information. We can fix that.

2   Choose Image ⇨ Adjust ⇨ Hue/Saturation. The Hue/Saturation
    dialog box appears (see Figure 3-12).

FIGURE 3-12
The Hue/Saturation dialog box can
be used to colorize an image.

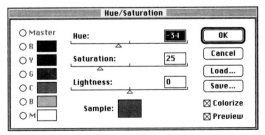

3 Check the Colorize box. This tells Photoshop to add color to the image, based on the settings of the sliders.

4 Move the Saturation slider to the 25 percent level. This sets the amount, or richness, of the color you're adding. We don't want to overpower our image with color, so we'll use a low setting.

5 The default Hue value produces a red value that looks more like a deep sepia brown at the 25 percent saturation level. The slider represents movement around a color wheel, with red at the zero point, cyan at the 180 degree point, and yellows and greens in the 180 degree semi-circle to the right, and the magentas and blues in the 180 degree semi-circle to the left. We want a high-tech magenta look, so set the Hue slider to –34.

6 Click on OK to confirm your new settings. We now have a color image to work with.

STEP 3: ADDING TEXT

For our price tag to "talk," we'll need to add some text. Photoshop's text tool can be used to create some very cool effects in your images, and we'll use it extensively here and in later chapters. Just follow these steps to get a quick introduction:

1 Click the type tool in the toolbox (the seventh tool from the top in the right column). Click in the upper left corner of the image, and the Type Tool dialog box appears, as shown in Figure 3-13.

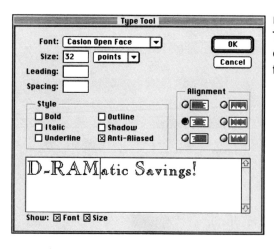

FIGURE 3-13
The Type Tool dialog box enables you to select a type-face and set other parameters.

NOTE The Type Tool dialog box has eight components: In the Font field you'll find all the fonts available on your Mac; in the Size field you can type in the height of the typeface, either in points (72 points equal an inch in the Macintosh world) or pixels (in case you need an exact number of pixels in height). The Leading field lists the amount of space devoted to each line of type measured from baseline to baseline. The Spacing field controls the spacing between characters. From the Style area, you can select Bold, Italic, Underline, Outline, Shadow, or Anti-Aliased (most text looks best when anti-aliasing is applied, as it smoothes out the appearance of the characters). In the Alignment field you can choose various forms of horizontal alignments (left column) or rotate the text 90 degrees clockwise and then align it toward the top, middle, or bottom of the page (right column). Finally, the scrolling text window at the bottom of the dialog box enables you to type in your actual text. You may use carriage returns, but not tabs. Check boxes underneath the text window enable you to specify whether you want the text you type to be shown in the actual typeface that will be used and/or in the actual size.

2   Move the cursor to the top left corner of the text window and type: D-RAM atic Savings!

3   Choose a font that is big and bold. We used Caslon Open, but you can select any other typeface available on your system.

4   Set the type size to 32.

5   Make sure that you check the Anti-Aliased box, and the Align Left radio button is selected.

6   Click on OK. Your first line of text appears on the screen. Photoshop has placed it in its own layer. Drag it with the move tool and position it at the top of the image.

7   You'll notice that we didn't specify a foreground color before we added this text. You can add that now. Make sure the text's layer is active in the Layers palette.

8   Choose light and dark colors from the Swatches palette that match the overall tone of the image, such as a dark red and a lighter magenta. Then apply a linear gradient, starting at the upper left corner of the selected text, and progressing to the lower right, using the techniques you learned earlier in this book. Your image will now look like the own given in Figure 3-16.

FIGURE 3-14
The text with the
gradient applied

9   Add another line of text, using the same font, but decreasing the font
    size to 16 points, and setting the leading to 16. Check the Centered
    radio button. Type in On Kitchen Table [Return] International
    RAM chips. Then click on OK to add the text. You can drag and
    position it with the move tool.

10 Add the next line of text, using the same font, but with a font size of 20.
    Move the cursor to the bottom of the image, click, and type Bet you can't
    add just one! Click on OK, and position the text with the move tool.

11 Move the cursor under the last line you added, click once more, and type
    $10 per megabyte. Use a 30-point font size. Click on OK, and
    reposition the text as necessary. Your image will now resemble Figure 3-15.

FIGURE 3-15
Text has been applied
along the bottom.

12 You can use the line tool to add another graphic element. Select the background layer in the Layers palette, and then choose the line tool from the toolbox (the eighth tool from the top in the left column).

13 Click on the Options palette, and set Line Width to 20 pixels.

14 Click on the cursor at the top left of the image. Hold down the Shift key and drag down to produce a broad, straight line.

15 Repeat across the bottom of the image.

16 Click the curved, double-headed arrow in the color control box to exchange the foreground and background colors.

17 In the Options palette, change the Line Width to 10 pixels.

18 Add a second, thinner line on the left side by holding down the Shift key as you drag. Figure 3-16 shows the final price tag.

19 Select Layers ⇨ Flatten to merge the text and image layers, and save your image to your hard disk.

FIGURE 3-16
The finished price tag.

WHAT YOU'VE LEARNED

In this chapter, you learned a great deal about adjusting the brightness and contrast of problematic images. For example, you know that:

- Images can be captured for manipulation in Photoshop using a scanner or digital camera, or retrieved from a CD-ROM, Photo CD, or other image source.

- TIFF files are a bitmapped file format that can be used by both Macintosh and PC computers.

- Histograms provide a visual representation of the gray tones in an image, with 256 different vertical lines, one for each value from 0 (pure black) to 255 (pure white.)

- You can use Photoshop's Brightness/Contrast sliders to modify these two attributes with a real-time preview on your screen.

- The Brightness/Contrast sliders don't clear up the basic problems with tonal range that you might find in an image. You'll often need more sophisticated tools, such as the Levels dialog box.

- Photoshop's Variations dialog box provides you with a set of images to compare visually. Here you can select the adjustments you want to make for shadow, middle, and highlight tones (for black-and-white images).

- Variations can be applied in Fine to Coarse increments, which you can specify with a slider.

- The Levels control enables you to set the black point, white point, and gamma (midtone contrast) settings for an image.

- The Levels control also provides an Auto button, which has Photoshop attempt to fix the image for you.

- You may also choose black-and-white points directly from your image with the Levels eyedropper tool.

- Color can be added to a grayscale image with the Image ⇨ Adjust ⇨ Hue/Saturation dialog box.

- The text tool's dialog box has eight components: Font selection, Size, Leading (space between lines), Spacing (between characters), Style (such as bold, italic, and so on), and Alignment (centered, flush left, and so on), along with a scrolling text window for entering and previewing text in the actual font and/or size.

- Photoshop enables you to enter text using either point size or pixel measurements.

In Chapter 4, you'll use what you've learned here, plus some new techniques, to create a composite image for the cover of a computer manual.

Designing a Manual Cover

Natural Selection

THE PROJECT

Unbeknownst to KTI's engineering staff, the company's marketing department is still working out the features list for the new KTI Oblivion II computer, built around the world's first 45-bit microprocessor. Although the computer isn't scheduled for delivery for more than a year (the CPU designers still haven't found a use for some of the left-over bits), the manual has been finished, and you need to design a cover, combining several photographs of a prototype model. To assemble the cover, you'll need to learn how to use Photoshop's commands for pasting elements together smoothly, get some real experience with the Layers palette, and sharpen some of the skills you've learned in previous chapters.

THE TOOLS
- Photoshop's Layers palette
- Select ⇨ Modify ⇨ Smooth
- Layer ⇨ Matting ⇨ Defringe
- Quick Mask mode
- Add Noise and Gaussian Blur filters
- Airbrush tool

As art director, you drew up a design for the cover, based on the artwork you knew you'd have to work with, and received approval from KTI's management. The rough sketch appears in Figure 4-1.

FIGURE 4-1
This rough layout will be your guide.

This is a folding cover, so most of the artwork goes on the right side, and the fold will be in the middle. This looks easy, because you already have each component that goes in the picture as a separate file. However, the finished presentation can't look like it was just pasted together haphazardly. We've divided the project into six easy steps.

 manual \man'ual\ *n* Bound volume containing an application's serial number inside the front cover, plus additional extraneous material. *adj* Extremely undesirable, as in manual transmission or manual labor.

STEP 1: ASSEMBLING THE PIECES INTO LAYERS

For the first part of the project, we'll load all the individual pieces and place them in separate layers in a single document. Follow these directions:

1   Insert the CD-ROM that accompanies this book into your CD-ROM drive and copy the following files from the Chapter 4 folder onto your hard disk: background.tif, kti system.tif, kti monitor.tif, and kti keyboard.tif.

2   Open the background.tif file in Photoshop. We'll use it as the basis for our book cover illustration, because it already has the right size and proportions.

3   Open the kti monitor.tif file.

4   Choose the magic wand tool from the toolbox. Then click the Options palette, and make sure Tolerance has been set to 1, and that the Anti-Aliased box is checked.

5   Click anywhere in the image background surrounding the monitor.

6   Use Select ⇨ Inverse (or press Command-Shift-I) to invert your selection, so that only the monitor itself is selected.

7   Press Command-C to copy the monitor.

8   Highlight the background.tif image, and select Edit ⇨ Paste. Photoshop automatically pastes the selection into a new layer of its own. Double-click the layer's name in the Layers palette, and type in a name for it, such as `Monitor`.

9   Open the kti system file, select its background with the magic wand tool, then invert the selection as before. There's one problem with this image. Unlike the monitor, the edges are fuzzy in this picture. Fortunately, Photoshop can fix this problem easily.

10 Choose Select ⇨ Modify ⇨ Smooth. The Smooth Selection dialog box appears, asking for a sample radius within which to provide smoothing. Enter a value of 6. Click on OK. When you do this, you can see that the selection around the system box smooths out. You can use this trick to get rid of rough edges in images where the edge detail is not important, as in this case.

11 Press Command-C to copy the system box, then select the background.tif file again, and paste the image into a new layer using Edit ⇨ Paste as you did before. Double-click the layer in the Layers palette and apply the name `System`.

12 Open the file kti keyboard.tif, select its background, inverse the selection, copy the image, and paste it into background.tif as a new layer named `Keyboard`.

13 Your Layers palette should look like the one shown in Figure 4-2, with the Background image at the bottom, the Monitor image above it, the System unit above that, and the Keyboard layer in front of all of them. If not, grab the misplaced layer's name and drag it up or down to get it in the right position. Photoshop "overlaps" layers according to their order in the Layers palette, so we want to get it right.

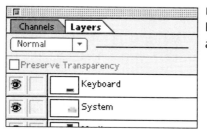

FIGURE 4-2
Layers palette with
all components copied.

STEP 2: RESIZING THE ELEMENTS

Each of the three elements needs to be resized a little so that they are in proportion with each other and fit better on the page. Because the steps to carry out the resizing are identical for each component, we'll provide you with one set of instructions that you can follow for each of the three elements. Just repeat these directions, sizing the elements to correspond roughly to the sketch shown previously in Figure 4-1.

1 Turn on the eyeball icons in all the layers so you can compare the sizes of the objects with each other as you resize them.

2 Activate the layer with the current object you will be resizing by clicking on its layer name. Start with the monitor in the back, then continue with the system unit, followed by the keyboard.

3 Click with the magic wand outside the component you are resizing. Make sure the Anti-Aliasing box is *not* checked in the Options palette. Use Select ⇨ Inverse to invert the selection, so it includes only the object.

4 Choose Layer ⇨ Transform ⇨ Scale. When the selection handles appear around the object, hold down the Shift key (to keep the proportions the same) and drag the handles until the object is the correct size.

5 Press Return to accept the size change.

6 Use the move tool to place the resized object in the approximate location indicated by Figure 4-1.

7 Go back to the first step and repeat with the next object. When you finish, go on to the next section in this chapter. Your resized components should appear as shown in Figure 4-3.

FIGURE 4-3
Resized components
fit better on the page.

At this point, we have all the elements in place, but a lot of work left to do. We need to make each piece look as if it is part of an actual composition, and not just pasted in. Maybe shadows would help.

STEP 3: ADDING REALISTIC SHADOWS

One way to make our composite image more realistic is to add a shadow underneath each component. You can do that as follows:

1 Click the Layers palette, and then click all the eyeball icons except for the monitor to make the other layers temporarily invisible (or, for a short-cut, Option-Click the eyeball in the monitor's layer to make the others invisible). Make sure the eyeball in the Monitor layer remains, and that the layer is highlighted in white to indicate that it's the active layer. Click on the layer name if necessary to make it active.

2 Select the area outside the monitor with the magic wand tool, then invert the selection using Select ➪ Inverse.

3 We want the shadow to appear only under the base of the monitor, and not around its sides; and because the monitor selection itself is going to serve as our shadow template, we'll need to deselect part of it. One easy way to do this is with Photoshop's Quick Mask mode. Click on the right-hand icon in the mask controls box (below the color control boxes), or press Q to activate Quick Mask. Your selection appears in red, which we show in black and white in Figure 4-4 (note that all figures are on the CD-ROM if you want to see this figure in color). Alternatively, you can also double-click on the Quick Mask icon to produce the Quick Mask Options dialog box, as shown in Figure 4-5, which enables you to specify whether the red tone should represent the Selected or Masked Areas. You can also adjust the Opacity of the red tone, making it more transparent so you can more easily see the image underneath, or less transparent so you can view the red mask itself. If you'd rather use some color other than red, double-click in the color box, and choose a hue from the Color palette that pops up.

FIGURE 4-4
A transparent tone representing the selection is placed over the image when in Quick Mask mode.

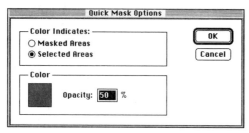

FIGURE 4-5
The Quick Mask
Options dialog box.

4 Next, choose the eraser tool (the fourth tool from the top in the left column of the toolbox), click the Options palette, and then select the 100-pixel brush.

5 Use the eraser to remove the red tone from the monitor screen, leaving the red mask around the base of the monitor.

6 We want a blurry shadow, so duplicate the layer using Layer ⇨ Duplicate Layer, then fuzzy up the selection a bit by selecting Filter ⇨ Blur ⇨ Gaussian Blur. In the resulting dialog box, choose a radius of 10 pixels, and click on OK. With a Gaussian blur, Photoshop uses a bell-shaped curve to determine the amount of blur applied, producing a more random effect.

7 Press Q to exit from Quick Mask mode.

8 Click the Layers palette again. From the fly-out menu on the right side, choose New Layer. Name it Monitor Shadow. When it appears, drag the layer by its name so that it is positioned underneath the Monitor layer in the palette.

9 Make sure that Photoshop's default black/white foreground/background colors are active (if not, click the miniature color control boxes to restore them), choose Edit ➪ Fill, and type in 80 percent as an Opacity value. This allows some of the surface to appear underneath the shadow. Click on OK to add a black drop-shadow to the selection.

10 Deselect the shadow by pressing Command-D, and then use the arrow keys to move the shadow down and to the right, so that it peeks out from under the edge of the monitor.

11 Repeat steps 1 through 10 with each of the other image layers. Just substitute the system unit and keyboard for the monitor layer. Remember to erase the upper and side portions of the selection, so that the shadow will appear underneath the component rather than surround it. When you're all done, you should have something that looks like Figure 4-6.

FIGURE 4-6
Shadows have been added under each component.

STEP 4: FIXING A PROP

We have a couple of small problems with the monitor. With the shadow applied, it's evident that there's a slight fringe of light pixels around some of the edges of the monitor. In addition, the appearance of the screen doesn't quite match the graininess of the rest of the objects in the picture. Both details are easy to fix. Just follow these directions:

1 Make the monitor's layer active by clicking on its name in the Layers palette.

2 Use the magic wand tool to select the area outside the monitor, then inverse the selection to grab the monitor itself. Use Command-X to cut the image of the monitor, then immediately paste it down again with Command-V.

3 Next, use Layer ⇨ Matting ⇨ Defringe, which is Photoshop's way of trimming a little from the edge of the selection. The Defringe dialog box appears. Type in 1 as the width in pixels of the defringing effect. Click on OK to apply the change. Figure 4-7 shows before and after views of the monitor base.

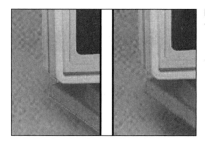

FIGURE 4-7
The fringe around the monitor base has been trimmed away.

4 We can add some texture to the area inside the monitor screen. First, select the monitor screen, and then choose the magic wand tool.

5 Click the Options palette. Because the image area inside the monitor screen is a gradient, the magic wand needs a relatively high tolerance level in order to select everything. You can experiment if you wish to try different tolerance levels. Type in a number, then click in the very center of the monitor screen, and see how much is selected.

6 When you're about to give up, type in 74 as the tolerance level, and click again. The entire screen will be selected.

7 Apply some random pixels by choosing Filter ⇨ Noise ⇨ Add Noise. In the Amount field type in 4, and click the Gaussian Noise radio button before clicking OK to apply the change. When Photoshop uses a bell-shaped Gaussian curve to apply noise, the result is more random-looking and realistic.

STEP 5: ADDING VERY COOL TYPE

To be really effective, our cover needs some cool type. As long as you're experimenting with the Layers command, we might as well look at a very cool type effect you can achieve by playing with the following simple effects:

1 Click the Layers palette, and select New Layer. Name the layer `Oblivion`.

2 Click the type tool (not the Type mask). Add the following two lines of text: `KTI` [Return] `Oblivion II`. We used a 12-point type size, anti-aliased text, and the horizontal centering option. We set the foreground color to black. Click OK to apply the text to the layer.

4 Click on the airbrush tool (the third tool from the top in the left column of the toolbox).

3 Click on the Swatches palette, and select magenta, which should be the sixth square from the left in the top row (if you haven't customized your Swatches palette, yet).

4 Click on the Brushes palette and choose the second brush from the right in the middle row.

5 Position the airbrush on the left side of the text, which should still be selected in its layer. Then, holding down the Shift key, drag the airbrush across the middle of the type. It will leave a glowing magenta stripe. Repeat for each line of text. The result is something that resembles Figure 4-8.

FIGURE 4-8
A glowing stripe added
with airbrush tool.

6   Reposition the text, if necessary, so it overlaps the monitor and the
    background.

7   At the bottom of the image, use the text tool to add the text `User`
    `Manual` in 8-point type, with black as the foreground color. To get the
    best-looking type, you'd usually create text this small in the application
    used to lay out the finished piece (such as QuarkXpress or
    PageMaker), but for this exercise, we're pretending that you're doing
    the whole job within Photoshop.

8   At the left side of the image, add the following text for the back cover:
    ```
    Kitchen Table International
    1 Curdsen Way
    Luna City, IA 67324
    ```

STEP 6: FLATTENING YOUR IMAGE

Our image still consists of a collection of layers, thus you have one final step: To
produce a finished image, we need to combine all the layers into one, a process called
"flattening." To do this, just follow these directions:

1   Save the file under a new name of your choice with the layers
    separated, in case you want to work with it later on. It's always a good
    idea to keep a copy of the unflattened image, because once the layers
    are merged, you can no longer separate them.

2   Make sure all the eyeball icons are visible next to each layer in the
    image. When Photoshop flattens an image, it includes only the layers
    that can be seen, and ignores those that you have hidden.

3   Use the fly-out menu on the Layers palette, as shown in Figure 4-9,
    and select Flatten Image.

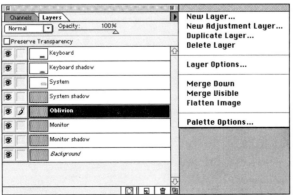

FIGURE 4-9
The Layers palette's
fly-out menu includes
the Flatten Image command.

Our manual cover is finished, and looks like Figure 4-10.

FIGURE 4-10
The finished KTI Oblivion II
manual cover.

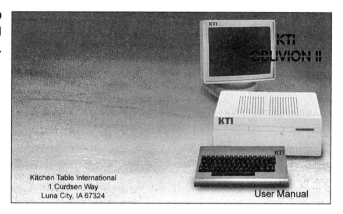

4 Now, you can save the image. Use the File ➪ Save a Copy command
   to store the flattened image on your hard disk, leaving the last version
   you saved (with all the layers intact) undisturbed.

WHAT YOU'VE LEARNED

This chapter is a little shorter than the previous ones, but actually covered as much
ground, because it repeated quite a few steps and you did some work on your own. You
know that:

- ☐ You can use the Layers palette to build a collection of components
  that you can work on separately, then merge when you're finished.

- ☐ Selections can be evened out using the Select ➪ Modify ➪ Smooth
  command. It's one of several options in the Select menu that modify
  the way a selection grabs a portion of an image.

- ☐ Paste Layer puts a selection down into a new layer of its own.

- ☐ Layers can be given names and shuffled around to appear in a different
  stacking order.

- ☐ Selections can be modified using paint-like tools when in Quick Mask
  mode. Pressing Q is a shortcut that toggles this mode on and off.

- ☐ A red tone usually indicates the selection in Quick Mask mode, but
  you can double-click on the Quick Mask mode icon to produce a
  dialog box to change or modify the color and transparency of the mask.

- ⊡ Filters and other effects can be applied to the selection while in Quick Mask mode.

- ⊡ When you create a new layer, the current selection remains active in the new layer.

- ⊡ The fringe around a selected item can be removed with the Layer ⇨ Matting ⇨ Defringe command.

- ⊡ Add Noise is a filter that can put random textures in an image.

- ⊡ The airbrush tool paints a fuzzy image.

- ⊡ Once you finish working with the individual layers, all the visible layers can be flattened to produce a finished image.

In the next chapter, you'll learn more image editing techniques, as we try and fix an unintentional bug in the KTI software manual.

Updating a Screen Shot

Basic Variations and Channels

Kitchen Table International is the only firm to offer a combination program development tool/image editor, which is called Random Basic +++. It's the one program available for the Macintosh that enables you to use fuzzy logic to create partially running software while editing fuzzy TIFF files at the same time. Although the program is a slow seller, KTI plans to upgrade it from Version .09.1.4 to Version 1.0.0.1. No significant new features will be added, but KTI wants to enhance the program's image. All research and development efforts have been concentrated on improving the user's manual. Accordingly, you've been asked to fix some of the screen shots and replace the "pennies" image used in the image editor preview window with a more expensive graphic—quarters. You're also free to add a few buttons to the illustration of the user interface, because most of them don't actually do anything.

THE TOOLS

- ⊡ Photoshop's rectangular marquee
- ⊡ Select ⇨ Modify and Paste Into commands
- ⊡ Save Selection
- ⊡ Channels
- ⊡ Sizing and scaling
- ⊡ Variations

This is your opportunity to learn more about Photoshop's tools for performing transformations on photographic images, including sizing, cropping, rotating, and reversing parts of images, as you update the screen shot showing the Random Basic +++ software.

screen shot \skren shät\ *n* **1:** An image placed in a user's manual representing how the program would theoretically appear if you'd followed all the steps correctly. **2:** In magazine reviews, a single image of the software being evaluated, with a photograph of the author's spouse or companion included somewhere in a document window for no discernible reason.

STEP 1: MAKING AN UPDATE

Photoshop makes it easy to cut and paste between two different image documents, which is exactly what you'll be doing in this case. First, we'll load the original image from the user's manual, delete the old image from the editing window of Random Basic +++, then drop in the new one. Just follow these directions:

1 Find the image random.tif in the Chapter 5 folder of the CD-ROM accompanying this book. Load the image into Photoshop.

2 Save the image onto your hard disk. (Saving to the hard disk enables you to quickly save your work, or revert to the last stored copy if you goof up, in which case you should check out Photoshop's File ⇨ Revert command.) The image you'll be working with appears in Figure 5-1, and shows the Random Basic +++ software interface. Your job is to replace the image of the pennies with an image of quarters. But first, we need to select the image area and delete the old image.

3 Click the rectangular marquee tool and zoom in so the penny image fills as much of your screen as possible, and then select the black border that surrounds the image. It's exactly one pixel wide, so you'll have to be careful. Figure 5-2 shows what the selection should look like.

4 Zoom in closer and examine the upper right and lower left corners to make sure you've selected the black border evenly. If you've grabbed too much or too little in any direction, it's likely to be only a pixel or two off. Use the Shift or Command keys, plus the rectangular marquee tool, to add or subtract from the selection until the borders resemble the close-up shown in Figure 5-3.

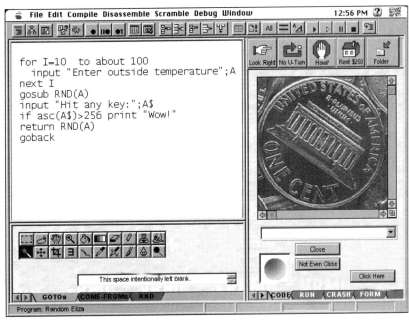

FIGURE 5-1
The Random Basic +++ window that you'll be modifying has a few
nonstandard Macintosh features.

FIGURE 5-2
The penny image has
been selected with the
rectangular marquee tool.

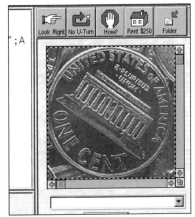

FIGURE 5-3
The image has been
selected at the black border
around the pennies.

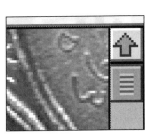

5 Next, choose Select ⇨ Modify ⇨ Contract. The Contract Selection dialog box appears (see Figure 5-4). Make sure the Contract By field entry is 1. Click on OK. The selection shrinks by one pixel-width all around, so that it encompasses only the pennies, and no longer includes the black border. Use Contract Selection and shrink by one pixel whenever the border of an image is easier to see and then select the image itself. Figure 5-5 shows what your image should look like when the selection has been contracted by 1 pixel.

FIGURE 5-4

Contract Selection shrinks the current selection evenly by the number of pixels you specify.

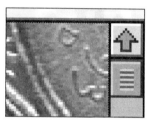

FIGURE 5-5

After the selection is shrunk, only the image area is included inside the marquee.

6 Choose Select ⇨ Save Selection and click on OK in the resulting dialog box. Photoshop saves the coordinates of the boundaries of your current selection as something called a *channel*. You can save these channels with the file itself if you use Photoshop's native PSD or TIFF format. You can reload a saved selection at any time and work with it exactly as if you had just made the selection. When you save a selection, Photoshop assigns a number and deposits it in the Channels palette, which you can view by clicking on its palette tab. Figure 5-6 shows the Channels palette with your new selection at the bottom.

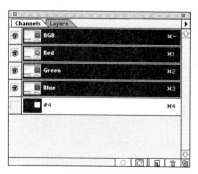

FIGURE 5-6

The Channels palette stores information about a selection or other type of channel.

CHANNELS AND SELECTIONS?

Channels are comparable to layers, which you've already used very briefly. However, while a layer can be a full-color version of an image (an exact duplicate of an image, in fact), a channel is, with one exception, strictly a grayscale version. As you can see in Figure 5-6, Photoshop reserves four channels for the color components of a full-color RGB image. Channels 1, 2, and 3 are versions of the red, green, and blue color information, displaying only grayscale information. That is, the gray tones represent how much of that particular color is present in each area of the image. If you're familiar with color separations, they work the same way, except that they represent the cyan, magenta, and yellow inks used in the printing process, and a fourth separation, representing the black ink, is also made. If you happen to convert an RGB image to CMYK (cyan, magenta, yellow, black) you'll see the same four channels numbered 1 to 4 in Photoshop.

The exception just mentioned is Channel 0, which Photoshop uses to represent the combined image of Channels 1, 2, and 3. When Channel 0 is highlighted in the Channels palette, all your work in the main Photoshop window is carried out on these combined channels. If you happen to select one of the other channels of a color image, Photoshop's editing window changes to a grayscale view, and your work deals with that color channel only. Sometimes interesting effects can be achieved by editing color channels individually.

Selections are a special kind of channel. When you save a selection, a new channel is created, starting with #4, and stored along with the color channels. If you make a simple, hard-edged selection, as we did in this case, the channel will be a stark black-and-white image, with the selected area shown in white. As you'll learn, selections can also be "fuzzy," which means they fade out or are partially transparent, using grayscale information to represent how "strongly" the area is selected. That is, an area covered by a black pixel is fully selected, and any operation you carry out will be applied 100 percent to that pixel. One that is covered by a lighter gray pixel will be given a proportionately smaller effect when the selection is copied, filled, or given some other special effect.

7 While Photoshop assigns numbers to channels, you can give them names. Double-click on the #4 icon in the Channel palette. The Channel Options dialog box, shown in Figure 5-7, appears. Type in a name like `Penny Window`, as we did, and click on OK. Your new name should appear in the Channel palette.

FIGURE 5-7
Channels can be
given custom names.

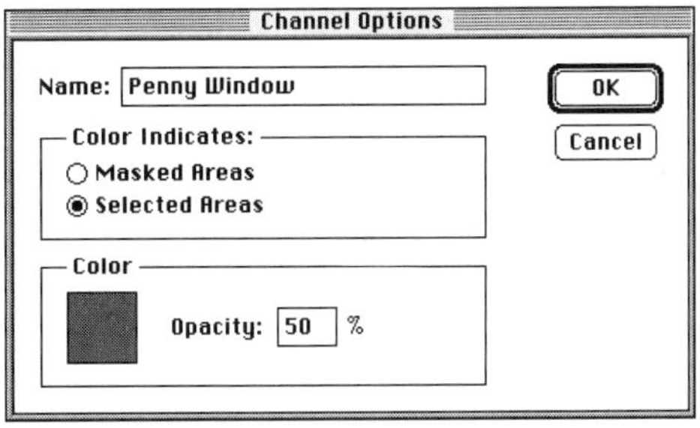

Channel Options

Name: Penny Window

— Color Indicates: —
○ Masked Areas
● Selected Areas

— Color —
Opacity: 50 %

OK
Cancel

8 Click the Layers palette to return it to view. Then, make sure Photoshop's default black/white colors are chosen for the foreground and background colors, then press the Delete key to remove the penny image from the screen shot. The area remains selected, as you can see in Figure 5-8.

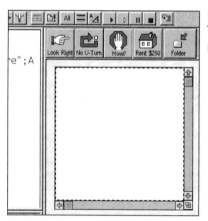

FIGURE 5-8
The penny image has been removed from the screen shot.

TIP You can do several cool things with the Select ⇨ Modify command. In addition to contracting the selection, as you've just done, you can:

- Use Smooth on a rough selection (such as one created with the magic wand tool) to create a more even selection of an image component.

- Create a selection that follows the path of the current selection, using the Border option. If your selection were rectangular, for example, Border would create a selection in a picture frame shape; if you had a circular selection, you'd end up with a ring. You can specify the width of the border created by the selection.

- Choose the Expand option, which operates in the opposite way as the Contract command, widening your selection by the number of pixels you specify.

STEP 2: PASTING IN A FIGURE

Next, we need to work with the image of the quarters, which will give you the opportunity to learn more about pasting, sizing, and rotating images. Follow these directions:

1 Find the quarters.tif file in the Chapter 5 folder on the CD-ROM, and load it into Photoshop. You'll see the image shown in Figure 5-9—one that happens to be both too dark and too large for our screen shot. But, with Photoshop, we can easily fix that.

FIGURE 5-9
The unmodified image of quarters needs a little work.

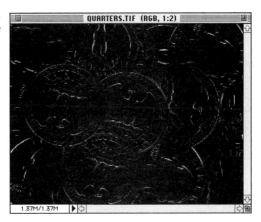

2 Choose Image ➪ Adjust ➪ Levels. The Levels dialog box appears (see Figure 5-10).

FIGURE 5-10
The Levels dialog box works with color as well as grayscale images.

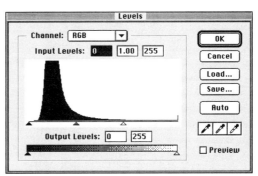

3 You can use the Levels controls both to modify grayscale images as well as to change each of the individual red, green, and blue channels of a full-color image. You'll find that the histograms produced by each colored layer might vary somewhat; advanced users can work with

Levels in this way to adjust colors individually. However, for neophytes in a hurry to get a screen shot finished for a client, it's probably best to work only with the RGB channel. Move the white point triangle over to the left to where the lighter tones actually reside. Click on OK to see your improved image.

4 Next, use the rectangular marquee tool to select part of the quarters image, as indicated in Figure 5-11. While this is actually larger than we need to fill the available space in the screen shot, it contains the image information we want to use. Use Command-C to copy the area you've selected.

FIGURE 5-11
Grab a section of the image
with a rectangular selection.

5 Next, switch to the Random Basic +++ screen shot, and make sure the program's editing window is still selected. If not, choose Select ⇨ Load Selection, and pick Channel 4 or whatever you've named it.

TIP When you choose a channel from Load Selection, if you've only saved one selection so far, it will be shown as the default. If more than one selection has been saved, you'll need to use the drop-down list box to find the one you want. If a selection is already made, pay close attention to the radio buttons in the dialog box. If you want your selection to be a new selection, make sure that button is clicked. Otherwise, Photoshop may default to Add or Subtract from Section (which appends or removes the channel selection you are choosing from the current selection). A fourth choice, Intersect, creates a new selection based on where the current selection overlaps with the one you are choosing.

6 Choose Edit ⇨ Paste Into to paste the quarters image into a window created by the current selection. Even though the image is larger than the selection, only the portion that can be shown in the selection itself appears. The rest is represented by a marquee outside the selection

area, as you can see in Figure 5-12. You can move the image around in the window until you see the portion you want to use. Or, you can do other transformations on it, including changing its size.

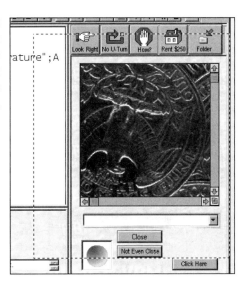

FIGURE 5-12
A marquee represents the extra image area of the selection being pasted in. Only the image that appears in the original selection is shown.

7 Select Layer ➪ Transform ➪ Scale to resize the image of the quarters. Hold down the Shift key to retain the same proportions (you don't want the quarters elongated in a horizontal or vertical direction), grab the sizing handles, and resize it as shown in Figure 5-13. You can see the sizing handles have been positioned just outside the selection area.

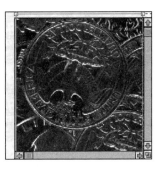

FIGURE 5-12
The image has been resized to fit the window.

8 While the image is still selected, use Image ➪ Adjust ➪ Variations to pop up the Variations dialog box, as shown in Figure 5-14. This version is much like the one you used in Chapter 3, except that options for various color corrections (More Green, More Yellow, and

so forth) appear. You can also lighten or darken the whole image, but Shadows, Midtones, and Highlights are controlled with a single column at far right. You may switch between these three options by clicking the radio buttons at the top of the dialog box. In addition, a Saturation radio button gives you control over the richness of the colors. Use any of these controls to modify the image of the quarters in any way you please. For example, to produce an interesting effect, you can make it more golden in tone and lighter.

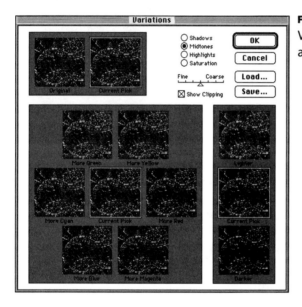

FIGURE 5-14
Variations can also be applied to full-color images.

9   Select Layer ➪ Transform ➪ Flip Vertical to flip the image of the quarters, so they are no longer upside down.

10   Keep the quarters image selected and use Filters ➪ Sharpen ➪ Unsharp Mask, and move the Amount slider until you have made the coins stand out a little more. There, you've finished the screen shot for the manual. Your final results should look like Figure 5-15.

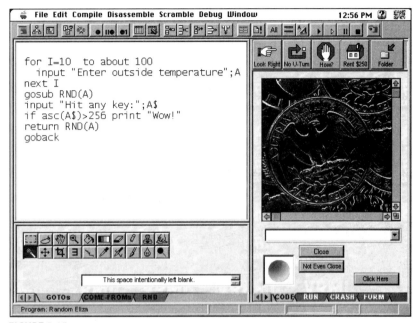

FIGURE 5-15
The final screen shot image for the user's manual looks like this.

WHAT YOU'VE LEARNED

In this chapter, you've learned more about working with selections and modifying images you've copied. By now, you have some fairly sophisticated Photoshop skills under your belt. You now know that:

- Selections can be contracted, expanded, converted into a border, or smoothed out using the Select ⇨ Modify options.
- Selections can be saved and reused if the file is stored in Photoshop's native PSD or TIFF format.
- Selections can be assigned names in the Channels palette.
- Channels are like grayscale versions of layers.
- Separate channels are assigned to the red, green, and blue channels of an RGB image, or the cyan, magenta, yellow, and black channels of a CYMK image.

☐ Copied images can be pasted into a selection. If the pasted image is larger than the selection, the rest will be cropped out after you've finished modifying the selection.

☐ Variations can be applied to full-color images, with extra options available for adjusting color casts and saturation.

In the next chapter, we're going to do some serious work with Photoshop's rubber stamp (or cloning) tool, significantly retouching a valuable but flawed image of KTI's chief executive officer.

Retouching a Photograph

Rubber Stamp Basics

THE PROJECT

Some would say that KTI's CEO, Scott Hollerith, has a face that only a mother could love. Then, his mom, Amy, the company's chairperson of the board, brought you a photograph of her son that she'd like to use in an upcoming annual report. It's not very good, but Scott's put on more than 200 pounds since the last board of director's meeting, and the company wants to use this photo as a way of shaming him into losing some weight. You'll need to remove some dust spots, fix an unruly hair lock, and do some other easy stuff. Oh yes, if you can, would you remove those glasses, which Amy feels makes Scott look like an owl? You decide that this would be an excellent time to learn about Photoshop's rubber stamp (or cloning) tool.

THE TOOLS
- Rubber stamp tool
- Toning tool (Dodge)

Every picture tells a story, but even the best stories can benefit from a little editing. One of the many differences between very good amateur pictures and most of the professional photographs you see published is that the latter probably had some retouching done sometime during the production process. Subtle tweaking here and there can yield dramatic improvements.

 retouch \re-touch'\ *v* **1:** In portraiture, to correct the unfortunate tendency of photography to portray male and female subjects accurately. **2:** In advertising, to enhance an image of an inanimate object so that it resembles something you might actually want to own.

The goal of simple retouching is to remove defects from a photograph. Of course, a defect is often in the eye of the beholder (if not in the bags underneath). In the old days, nearly all retouching was done using the photographic media—negative, slide, or print. But any of the old-time techniques can be duplicated—and surpassed—digitally, even by a Photoshop Instant Expert. Just follow these steps:

STEP 1: GIVING SCOTT THE DUST-OFF

Our first challenge is to remove those nasty dust spots from Scott's picture. The rubber stamp tool will do an excellent job, so follow these directives to see how it's done:

1 Find the scott.tif file in the Chapter 6 folder on the CD-ROM bundled with this book, and load it into Photoshop.

2 Save it to your hard disk as you did in the last chapter. The image you'll be working with appears in Figure 6-1.

3 Select the rubber stamp tool from the toolbox (the fifth tool from the top in the left column). The rubber stamp tool duplicates part of an image, pixel by pixel, in a location of your choice. The stamp analogy isn't very good, however, because you're actually drawing with a brush that you can size and control with your image editor (controlling, for example, the transparency of the image laid down, or some other behavior). Cloning can be used to copy portions of an image to another location in the same or a different image.

4 Zoom in 4× so you can work comfortably with a portion of the image. Here we'll remove the spot from Scott's right cheek to start with, so zoom in on his cheek.

FIGURE 6-1
Our unmodified picture
needs some help.

5 You'll want to set the rubber stamp tool to copy pixels from a fixed place in the current image. Double-click on the rubber stamp tool and make sure the Clone (aligned) option is selected. Choose the smallest brush size, and set the Opacity (or transparency) of your clone brush to 100%, as shown in Figure 6-2.

FIGURE 6-2
Set the Rubber Stamp Option
to Clone (aligned) and choose
a small brush size.

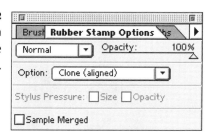

6 Place the cursor near a portion of the image having similar tones to what should have been in the area obscured by the dust spot or other defect, hold down the Option key, and click the mouse button to set that selection as the area to copy from.

7 Next, click on the dust spot area. Work inward from the edges, changing only a pixel or two at a time. Change the point of origin for the cloning from time to time as required to maintain a good match of tones. Figure 6-3 shows what your image should look like.

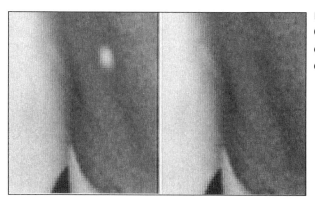

FIGURE 6-3
Cloning can remove dust spots and other defects from an image.

8 Repeat Steps 5 and 6 for each spot, blemish, scar, or other area you want to cover up. The image should look like Figure 6-4.

FIGURE 6-4
All the dust spots have been removed.

RUBBER STAMPS

The rubber stamp has three optional modes: Clone (aligned), Clone (unaligned), and Clone (From Saved). Once you determine the point of origin by pressing Option-click in the Clone (aligned) mode, the rubber stamp tool reproduces that point in the place you next click in your image, and then copies adjoining pixels as you move in one direction or another. For example, if you selected the center of a circle, the place you next click in your image would become the new center of the circle you are cloning. As long as you kept painting, the circle would be reproduced in the new location around the point you originally chose for cloning. That is, if you moved the tool an *inch to the right* and started painting again, you'd apply pixels copied from an area an *inch to the right* of the point of origin. Cloning an aligned image makes it easy to duplicate objects from one portion of an image (or from a different image), because you can use multiple brush-strokes to copy the same object. If you make a mistake, just select Undo, and reapply only the most recent strokes.

After you set the point of origin in the Clone (unaligned) mode, each new click somewhere else in your image starts painting with pixels from *that* point in the original, until you release the mouse button. You'd use this option to apply a pattern to an image, rather than to copy an object in multiple strokes.

Finally, the Clone (From Saved) mode can save your neck when you discover you've cloned too much of an image, or have made any sort of other error that needs correction. The point of origin is automatically set to the equivalent pixel position in the last saved copy of the file; thus, in effect, you can paint over a changed portion of the image with the original version. Use this option when you have done considerable work on a file since you saved it, and only want to cancel out some of the changes you've made. The so-called magic eraser (hold down the Option key while using the eraser) can also change portions of an image back to its previous state, albeit not with the flexible brush sizes and effects of the rubber stamp tool.

STEP 2: DODGING SHADOWS

When color or black-and-white prints are made by exposing photosensitive paper under an enlarger, the darkroom worker can modify how the image appears. That's done by holding back some areas of the print so it doesn't receive as long an exposure, and giving extra exposure to other areas. This is called *dodging* and *burning*.

Our portrait needs some judicious dodging to lighten some shadows under and above our subject's eyes. We can also use dodging to create larger, lighter catchlights in the eyes, and to brighten up the white part of the eye. To dodge the picture, follow these directions:

1 Select the dodge/burn/sponge tool, also known as the toning tool. It shares a palette button with the burn (represented by a cupped hand icon) and sponge tools. Double-click the icon in the toolbox (sixth icon from the top in the right-hand column), and, in the Options palette, change to Dodge (if necessary). Figure 6-5 shows the Toning Tools Options.

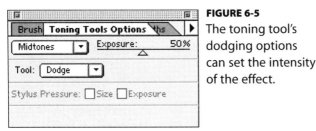

FIGURE 6-5
The toning tool's dodging options can set the intensity of the effect.

2 Set Exposure to 50%, and then choose a small brush from the first row of the Brushes palette. The Exposure parameter controls how much the dodge tool will lighten an area with each application, and the brush size determines the size of the area to be modified.

3 Zoom in at least 4×, and then dodge the catchlight in each eye. Click on the catchlight and, holding down the mouse button, drag to lighten that area of the pupil. Repeat for the other eye.

4 Next, select a slightly larger brush size (four to six pixels). We want to affect a broader portion of the image for the next step to produce a subtler result. In the Options palette, change the Exposure setting to 15%.

5 Use the dodge tool to lighten the white part of both eyes so the blood vessels and dark shadows are no longer visible. Try not to remove all the tone and details from those areas. Because the exposure has been reduced, you may have to go over an area two or three times to produce the desired effect.

6 Next, select an even larger brush size (one about the size of the pupils in Scott's eyes), and use it to remove the shadows under his eyes and beneath the eyebrows. Don't go overboard: dodge a little at a time using broad strokes. Stop and look at your results, and then apply more lightening until the image looks good. Figure 6-6 shows the finished portion of the image after dodging has been applied.

TIP Photoshop enables you to open a second view of the same image, through a New Window or New File command. Select a 1:1 magnification ratio for one version, and then zoom in to 4:1 or greater in the second window. Any changes you make in the close-up view will be immediately reflected in the full versions. It's an easy way to check your work as you go.

FIGURE 6-6
Dodging lightens portions
of an image selectively.

STEP 3: PERFORMING MAJOR SURGERY

Many of the photographs you'll need to retouch won't be in as "good" shape as Scott's. Frequently, you'll be asked to salvage a real dog of a photo that absolutely must be resurrected from snapshot hell for one reason or another. Perhaps it's the only picture available of someone (or something), or it has some importance for historic reasons.

We're going to do further repairs on this photo by removing that unruly lock of hair from Scott's forehead. Perhaps we can even convince him to take off his glasses. You'll be surprised at how easy it is. Here's how:

1 Select the rubber stamp tool and copy areas of the cheek over the rims of the glasses. Set new origin points constantly to maintain a good match of skin tones. For example, the rims of the glasses at the left side of the photo can be replaced by the cheek edge immediately below. In Figure 6-7, we've already replaced part of the lower rim of the glasses at the right side with surrounding cheek tones.

FIGURE 6-7
Replace the glasses with portions
of surrounding skin tones, using the
rubber stamp tool.

2 The portion of the left eyebrow that is obscured by the glasses is more
   tricky. Clone portions of the *other* eyebrow, as shown in Figure 6-8, to
   provide the missing portions.

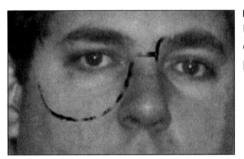

FIGURE 6-8
Use portions of the eyebrow
on the left to replace missing
parts of the eyebrow on the right.

3 Next, you'll want to smooth out the rough edges around the eyes
   where the skin tones don't match exactly, and then follow up with
   some dodging and burning to match skin tones around the face. Select
   the focus tool, which includes both blur and sharpen (the sixth icon
   down in the left-hand column) and make sure that blur is active. It's
   the tear-drop-shaped icon.

TIP   The focus tool enables you to apply sharpening and blurring effects to
portions of an image using brush-like tools. Normally, sharpening and blurring is
applied in filter mode, which means you can perform the transformation on a
selection, but not individual pixels. The focus tool is a way of selectively blurring
only limited parts of an image, which lets you keep the effect from being too
obvious. In practice, blurring decreases the contrast between adjoining pixels,
while sharpening increases the contrast.

4 Finish up by using what you know about the rubber stamp tool to
   remove the hair lock, using portions of Scott's forehead as a source to
   clone. The final image is shown in Figure 6-9. Compare it with Figure
   6-1 to see the image before and after changes.

FIGURE 6-9
Some minor adjustments
produced this image.

WHAT YOU'VE LEARNED

In this chapter, you picked up some skills that will be useful for retouching a broad array of photographs, both portraits and other subjects, in color or black and white. You know that:

- The rubber stamp tool duplicates part of an image elsewhere in the same image or a different one.

- You can select the source area to be cloned by pressing the Option key as you click in the area you want to copy.

- Aligned cloning duplicates an image in a new location, no matter how many different strokes of the tool you use.

- Unaligned cloning produces a new copy of the original whenever you release the mouse button and restart in a new position.

- You can also clone from the last saved copy of an image, which is a way to restore parts of the image that you may have damaged by accident.

- The toning tool can be used to lighten (dodge) or darken (burn) areas of an image.

- You may set an "exposure" for the toning tool to modify the strength of its effects.

In the following chapter, we're going to work with type some more, and learn how to use Photoshop's built-in filter effects.

Creating Fancy Text

More Type Tricks and Layers

Kitchen Table International's Webmaster just emerged from his dungeon. Those fancy buttons and rules you dreamed up in Chapter 2 make the rest of KTI's current Web page look rather anemic. Your next assignment is to dress up the site with some fancy type, including an introductory image for the company's new Organic Programming compiler, a logo, and some text that will highlight the amazing content of the Web site. This is your big chance to learn about layer masks, and gain more experience with the selection and type tools.

THE TOOLS

- ☐ Layer Mask
- ☐ Adjustment layers
- ☐ Gradient Editor
- ☐ Free Transform tool
- ☐ Type tool

Photoshop differs from most applications in the way it handles type placed into an image. To work effectively with text in, say, a desktop publishing program, you need to learn lots of typography terminology and agonize over things such as leading, kerning, and tracking. While Photoshop does use the same fonts available to your other applications, once you've pasted text into an image, it's simply another kind of graphic. As far as Photoshop is concerned, there's not a lot of difference between the word "cat" and an actual feline photograph: they're both just bitmaps to manipulate.

So, while you do need to pay attention to letter spacing and other typographic fine points, once your text is merged with the rest of the image, there's no way to separate it out without using the lasso or other selection tools. Pasted text can't be edited to fix a typo or to vary the style without removing it entirely and replacing it with new text.

typography \ti-pog′-gra-fi\ *n* **1:** Any confusing or over-used feature related to the application of text or type in desktop-published documents. **2:** A technology responsible for the most numerous variety of computer error, called the *typo* for short.

One really cool thing about Photoshop's treatment of type, however, is that Photoshop actually offers two type tools: one creates type filled with the foreground color, and the other creates a selection. With the latter, you're not stuck using the background or foreground color to fill your text. You can add textures and other interesting effects quite easily. In this exercise, you'll learn some techniques that enable you to add an image or texture rather than just a simple color and gradient to your text.

STEP 1: ADDING A WOODY TEXTURE

Make sure you have a fat, sans serif font installed on your system, and the wood.tif and foliage.tif files located in the Chapter 7 folder of the accompanying CD-ROM.

1 Copy the wood.tif file to your hard disk and load it into Photoshop. Zoom out so it's shown at 50 percent of its full size.

2 Click the type tool, and keep holding down the mouse button so both the standard type icon (right) and the type mask icon (left) are visible, as shown in Figure 7-1. Move the cursor to the right to select the type mask icon.

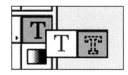

FIGURE 7-1
The type mask icon is represented by a dotted outline.

3 Move the cursor to roughly the center of the wood.tif image, and click. Doing so produces the Type Tool dialog box, as shown in Figure 7-2. Choose a fat font from the Font drop-down list (you can use Palatino Bold if you don't have one similar to the font we used), and then enter 42 points for the Size, and 32 points for Leading (leading is the amount of vertical spacing between lines of text from baseline to baseline). A leading setting less than the height of the font compresses the two lines of type together more closely.

FIGURE 7-2
You can specify the amount of space between two lines of type in the Type Tool dialog box.

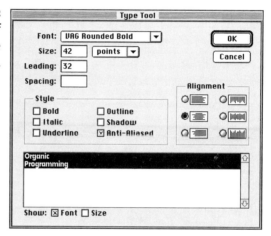

4 In the Alignment box, click the horizontally centered alignment button; in the Style box, check Anti-Aliased, and then type in `Organic Programming`. Press Return between the words to place the text on separate lines.

5 Click on OK to deposit your text into the image as a selection. It will be centered around the point where you positioned the mouse cursor and clicked earlier. Figure 7-3 shows what the image should look like.

FIGURE 7-3
The type has been entered into the image as a mask.

6 Move the cursor inside the selection and reposition the mask until you have a surface showing through the text outline that you like. Then press Command-C to copy the selection.

7 Copy foliage.tif to your hard disk, load it into Photoshop, and press Command-V to paste the characters down into a new layer.

STEP 2: CREATING A GLOW

Our text will be more distinctive if we surround it with a blurry, glowing shadow. The following procedures show you how to add a shadow quickly, using techniques we've already explored.

1 Use the Layers palette's fly-out menu to select Duplicate Layer. Name the new layer Shadow.

2 Click the Shadow layer so that the paintbrush icon appears (indicating that it is the active layer). Your Layers palette should now look like Figure 7-4.

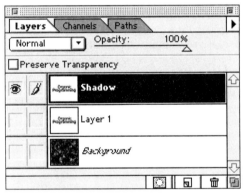

FIGURE 7-4
The new Shadow layer is active in the Layers palette, as indicated by the paint brush icon.

3. Select Filter ⇨ Blur ⇨ Gaussian Blur and set the Radius to about 7 pixels, as Figure 7-5 shows.

4 In the Layers palette, check the Preserve Transparency box, so that only the image portion of the layer will be affected by the next step, which is to fill the blurred text with a hue. (Without this box checked, the entire layer would be filled.)

5 Choose a bright yellow color from the Swatches palette.

6 Now, use Edit ⇨ Fill to fill the blurred text with the yellow hue. You can also use the Option-Delete key. Where Delete removes a selection and replaces it with the background color, Option-Delete replaces a selection with the foreground color.

7 In the Layers palette, grab the layer with the woody text with the mouse, and drag it so that it is above the yellow, blurry shadow. Your image should look something like Figure 7.6.

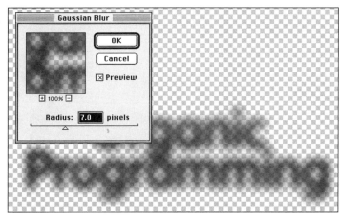

STEP 3: USING A LAYER MASK

A layer mask is a special grayscale channel that can be applied to any of the layers of an image, and used to control how much of the image "shows through." For example, if the layer mask were all black with a white circle in the middle, only the portion in the circle would be visible. Similarly, a mask that took the form of a gradient, from black to white, would enable the entire image to be seen in the white sections, gradually fading to none at all as the gradient becomes black. Figure 7-7 gives you a better idea of how a layer mask can affect an image.

The image on the left of Figure 7-7 is the unaltered photograph. In the middle, we've created an off-beat layer mask using a circle cut-out and a gradient, just to give you a simple, if atypical, mask to use for comparison. At right is the same photograph as viewed through this layer mask.

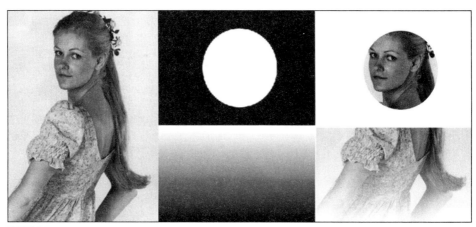

FIGURE 7-7
At left is the original photo; in the middle, a layer mask created with a circular cutout and a gradient; at right, the original image with the layer mask applied.

This same principle can be applied to our current project to create a more interesting effect. To do so, we first need to activate our background image (the foliage) and create a duplicate, because a layer mask cannot be applied to the background. Follow these directions:

1 Click on the background image (the foliage). Select Duplicate Layer from the Layer palette's fly-out menu (or choose Layer ⇨ Duplicate Layer from the menu bar).

2 Activate the copy of the background layer, and select Layer ⇨ Add Layer Mask. Select Reveal All from the fly-out choices that appear, as shown in Figure 7-8.

3 Go to the Layers palette. A mask icon next to the eye icon indicates that the layer mask is now activated, as shown at left in Figure 7-9. (When the layer itself is active, the mask icon is replaced by the familiar paintbrush icon, as you can see at right in the same figure.)

NOTE Reveal All allows everything in a layer to show through. Hide All (surprise!) covers everything up. Depending on the amount of work that needs to be done, you'd select one over the other. For example, it's easier to add a little to a Reveal All mask than to remove almost everything from a Hide All mask.

FIGURE 7-8

Photoshop 4.0's new Layer menu includes the Add Layer Mask choice.

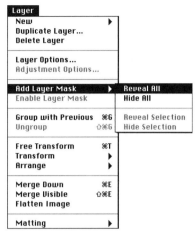

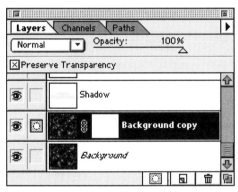 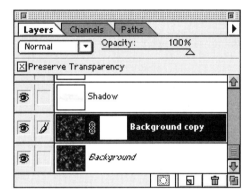

FIGURE 7-9

At left, the layer mask is the active, paintable layer; at right, the image itself is active.

4 Choose the gradient tool, and make sure that the standard black/white foreground/background colors are selected. We're now going to show you how to create a custom, reusable gradient.

5 In the Gradient Options palette, make sure Linear is checked, and then click Edit. The Gradient Editor appears.

6 Click the New button, type in B/W Gradient 25%, and click on OK.

7 Define the starting and beginning colors that you want to use to create the gradient. Click the Adjust: Color button (if it isn't checked already). The Gradient Editor window will now look like Figure 7-10.

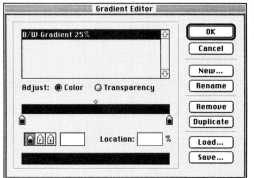

FIGURE 7-10
The Gradient Editor is being used to define the gradient's colors.

8 The bar immediately below the two Adjust buttons (Color and Transparency) displays the properties you'll be adjusting next. First, you use the icons at either end of the horizontal bar to define the beginning and ending colors. You can use the icons below the bar (with the F and B inside them) to select the current foreground or background color for either of the bar's icons. Click the left-hand house-shaped icon when you want to define the end color of the gradient. Because we want to use the current foreground color, click in the icon with the "F" inside just below the icon you just selected.

9 Next, click the icon at the far right of the adjustment bar, and then click the icon below it with the "B" inside (which represents the background color) to define the beginning color of the gradient, as we will be using the current background color. The adjustment bar will now look like Figure 7-11.

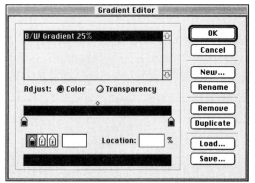

FIGURE 7-11
Use the house-shaped icons to define the beginning and ending colors of the gradient.

10 Click the Adjust: Transparency button to adjust the opacity of the gradient. As you did before, click the left-hand icon to define the end value. Type 25 in the Opacity box that appears after you select the

Transparency radio button. Then click the right-hand icon, and type 0 in the Opacity box. The Gradient Editor dialog box should now look like the one shown Figure 7-12.

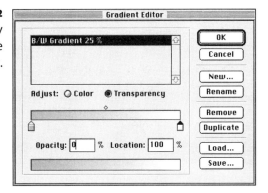

FIGURE 7-12
You can type in opacity figures to determine the transparency of the gradient.

11 Click on OK to save your gradient. You can reuse this particular gradient at any time by selecting it by name from the Gradient Tool Options' Gradient drop-down list box.

12 The layer mask should still be active (if not, you can activate it again by Shift-clicking on the mask icon). Apply the new gradient to the layer mask by clicking in the upper left of the image window and dragging to the lower right.

FIGURE 7-13
The finished image, with a light-to-dark diagonal gradient applied to the foliage background.

13 Merge the layers by selecting Layer ⇨ Flatten Image from the menu bar. The background foliage will be given an interesting light-to-dark variation that may not be apparent on the printed page, but which looks very good in the finished file (which you can review on the CD-ROM). Your finished image looks the one we showcase in Figure 7-13.

14 You can now save the file using the JPG format for display on KTI's Web page devoted to its new Organic Programming compiler. To do this, use the File ⇨ Save As command, and then select JPEG as the file format.

STEP 4: CREATING A 3D SHADOW

As long as we're on a roll, why not create an interesting 3D shadow effect using KTI's acronym? This process will introduce you to Photoshop's new Free Transform tool. We'll look at transformations in much more detail in Chapter 11. Meanwhile, here's how to create a 3D shadow:

1 Create a new, blank document measuring 400 × 400 pixels. In the Contents area of the New dialog box, click the Transparent button so we can enter our text on a transparent background (this makes some of the next steps a little easier).

2 Using the type tool, add the letters KTI in 84 point size, using a font of your choice. (We chose Times Roman because it's a standard font that everyone has.)

3 Use the Layers menu to create a duplicate layer. Turn off the original background layer so you are viewing only the duplicate.

4 Select Filter ⇨ Blur ⇨ Gaussian Blur from the menu bar. Set the pixel radius to 2.5 (this time we want less of a blurry effect than in our last exercise). You've just created a "shadow" for the top layer's text, as you can see in Figure 7-14. (By this time you should be getting fairly adept at creating blurry shadows!)

FIGURE 7-14
A blurry shadow for the KTI logo looks like this before the transformations begin.

5 For our purposes the shadow needs to be flipped, as we want to give the impression of backlighting. Select Layers ⇨ Transform ⇨ Flip Vertical from the menu bar.

6 Turn the background layer back on and reposition your flipped shadow so it mates with the baseline of the original text, as shown in Figure 7-15.

FIGURE 7-15
The reversed shadow has been positioned underneath the original text.

7 Now use the Layers menu again to select Free Transform. Selection handles will appear around the shadow. Hold down the Shift and Command keys to activate the Skew mode. You can then drag the two outer sizing handles down and toward the sides of the image to produce a lengthened, widened shadow like the one shown in Figure 7-16. Press Return to accept the change.

FIGURE 7-16
The Free Transform tool created this dramatic, lengthened shadow effect.

8 With both the original text and the shadow visible, merge the two layers by selecting Layer ⇨ Merge Visible from the menu bar.

9 Make the new, merged layer active so we can create a transparent GIF file using the techniques from Chapter 2.

10 Select File ⇨ Export ⇨ GIF89a Export and choose Adaptive palette, and then 255 colors in the dialog box that pops up.

STEP 5: INTRODUCING THE AMAZING BACKLIT TEXT TRICK

Backlighting black letters against a black background produces a dramatic effect, especially on a Web page that has a black background. We'll finish off our Web page dress-up by creating a great-looking backlit effect that gives you the opportuinty to learn about Photoshop 4.0's new adjustment layer capabilities. Follow these directions:

1 Create a new, empty document that is 400 × 300 pixels in size, with white as its contents.

2 Set Photoshop's foreground and background colors to their default values of black and white.

3 Use the paint bucket tool to fill the document with black.

4 Select the type mask tool. In the Type Tool dialog box, select a fat font of your choice, set (letter) Spacing to 2 and (font) Size to 72, and then enter AMAZING in the text box

5 Choose Selection ➪ Save Selection from the menu bar to save the mask you produced.

6 Choose Selection ➪ Feather from the menu bar, and specify a 4-pixel radius to feather the selection.

7 Choose a purple color as the foreground from the Swatches palette and select Edit ➪ Fill from the menu bar to fill the feathered selection with a bright purple. Make sure the Preserve Transparency box is *not* checked. Your text so far will look pretty cool on its own, as shown in Figure 7-17.

FIGURE 7-17
The blurry text on a black background has a fluorescent effect of its own.

8 Open the selection you saved in step 5. Fill it with black. You'll produce the vivid back-lit effect shown in Figure 7-18.

FIGURE 7-18
The whole image is black,
except for the blurry
shadow we created.

9 Next, select Layer ➪ New ➪ Adjustment Layer from the menu bar, and use the default Hue/Saturation choice. The new adjustment layer will appear at the top of the Layers palette, as Figure 7-19 shows. You can tell an adjustment layer from other layers by the circular icon (half black, half white) to the right of the layer's name.

FIGURE 7-19
The circular black/white
icon at the right designates
an adjustment layer.

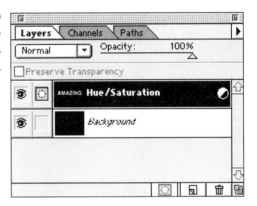

10 Double-click on the new Adjustment Layer's name in the Layers palette. Use the sliders on the Hue/Saturation dialog box that appears to adjust the colors displayed by the background layer you created earlier. Even though you used a purple shade for the backlighting, using the adjustment layer you can change the hue to a red, green, or any other shade, and modify the saturation level and brightness as well. When you get an effect you want to save, store the file on your hard disk using File ➪ Save As.

NOTE Adjustment layers are grayscale masks like the layer mask you created earlier in this chapter, except that their effects apply to all the layers below them, and don't become permanent until you flatten the image. Adjustment layers are a great way to experiment with various effects without actually changing the underlying pixels until you're ready. In addition to Hue/Saturation, you can create adjustment layers that enable you to experiment with Levels, Curves, Brightness/Contrast, Color Balance, and other parameters that you'll become more familiar with as you work with Photoshop. You can return to an adjustment layer at any time by clicking on its name in the Layers palette, or by selecting Layers ➪ Adjustment Options from the menu bar.

WHAT YOU'VE LEARNED

You've picked up three useful techniques for manipulating type in this chapter, and learned a lot more about Photoshop's layers commands. You know that:

- Photoshop, like many image editors, treats type as just another kind of bitmap once you've merged it with other parts of the image.

- Photoshop's type mask mode enables you to create type in the form of a mask that you can save and manipulate like any selection.

- The Preserve Transparency option of a layer enables you to ensure that an effect you are applying operates only on the image area, and not the transparent background.

- Layers can be repositioned in the Layers palette to change the stacking order in which they appear in the image.

- A layer mask is a special grayscale channel that can be applied to any of the layers of an image, and used to control how much of the image "shows through."

- You can create two types of layer masks: one by default reveals all of the image in the layer, while the other hides everything. You may then paint on either of these layers to change how they mask the image.

- Gradients can be custom-designed and saved for reuse with the Gradient Editor.

- The Free Transform tool may be used to flip, rotate, skew, or scale an entire image or selection.

- Two or more visible layers can be merged into one with the Layer ⇨ Merge Visible command.

- Adjustment layers are grayscale masks that can apply various editable effects such as Hue/Saturation, Levels, Curves, Brightness/Contrast, Color Balance, and other parameters to the layers under them without actually changing the underlying pixels until you're ready.

In Chapters 8 and 9, you're going to learn how to use one of Photoshop's most powerful tools for changing the way an image looks—filters.

Rescuing Bad Photos

The Brighter Side of Filters

THE PROJECT

The brass at Kitchen Table International want to feature a photograph of the company's new Research and Development lab on the cover of next year's annual report. In keeping with one of the company's mottoes, "Bringing You Yesterday's Technology Tomorrow," the R & D staff has been ensconced in a 15th century fortress that was transplanted from Europe, brick-by-brick, in numerous shipments over ten years (the bricks were used instead of plastic peanuts as a cost-saving measure). Your job is to add a more dramatic flair to KTI's photograph. This is your chance to explore Photoshop 4.0's considerably enhanced filtering capabilities.

THE TOOLS
- ☐ Magic wand and gradient tools
- ☐ Clouds filter
- ☐ Layer mask
- ☐ Ocean ripple filter
- ☐ Zig-Zag filter

Like all the other photos KTI has asked you to work with, this one is particularly bad. It's a picture of the new R & D center taken from the back, showing the decrepit parking lot, which looks like a Roman ruin, except that its condition is worse. The building itself, as you can see in Figure 8-1, is perched on a hill, and there's little about it that would give it away as a research facility—you'd think it was secret! The plain, unadorned sky in the background is featureless and a little boring. Fortunately, the judicious application of a few filters can help.

FIGURE 8-1
KTI's research lab stands majestically on a hill, with the remains of the company's parking lot in the foreground.

 filter \fil'ter\ *n* **1:** In automotive mechanics, a container filled with a porous substance through which a liquid such as motor oil is passed to separate out suspended matter until the device becomes clogged through neglect and/or the liquid metamorphoses into a solid. **2:** In image editing, a small application that improves a photograph by rendering it unrecognizable.

WHAT ARE FILTERS?

Every time you make coffee, drive your car, or turn on an air conditioner, you're using a filter. Filters do nothing more than let one thing pass through—air, water, motor oil, or drip coffee—while holding back something else, such as dirt or coffee grounds.

In the computer world, filters do something similar, particularly in the case of image-processing filters such as those in Photoshop. These processes take the pixels in an image or selection, and process them, discarding some, changing the brightness or color values of others, or moving pixels from one place to another. For example, a sharpen filter looks at each pixel and its tonal relationship with the pixels that surround it, then increases the contrast between them so the image looks sharper. A blurring filter reduces the contrast.

The only other "technical" things you need to know about filters is that they are actually mini-applications in their own right, which interface with Photoshop through a special "window" called an application programming interface (API) that Adobe has built into the program. Filters are installed into a single folder (and its subfolders), and Photoshop looks for them every time it loads. Information in these plug-ins tells Photoshop how to arrange them in the Filter menu, and you can activate any of the dozens of filters included with the program (or that you've added from third parties) by selecting an image, and then activating the desired filter from the menu. All the dirty work is handled by the dialog box that pops up in response, although some filters have fixed parameters and do their work without input from you as soon as they are activated. Figure 8-2 shows five different filters applied to a single image.

FIGURE 8-2
The original photo at upper left has been processed through the Sharpen (upper center), Blur (upper right), Spherize (lower left), Find Edges (lower center) and Dry Brush (lower right) filters.

The results of filters can range from subtle to dramatic. You've already used blurring, sharpening, and a few other filters in earlier sections of this book. In this exercise, we're going to put a whole clutch of them to work, adding a new sky, disguising the ugly foreground, and dressing up the building.

STEP 1: MODIFYING A VISUAL ELEMENT

So, let's fix up the KTI photo. First, we need to select the sky, add some better-looking clouds, and perhaps make it brighter and cheerier looking. The following directions will get you started:

1   Open the file research.tif from the accompanying CD-ROM and copy it onto your hard drive.

2   Select the magic wand tool from the toolbox. (Because the sky in this photo has roughly the same tone throughout, the magic wand tool will do a good job of grabbing it.) Double-clicking the magic wand tool brings the Magic Wand Options palette to the front. You can experiment with various tolerance levels to find one that captures most of the sky, or just use the value of 32 that worked best for us.

3   Click in middle of the sky, about halfway between the building and the top of the frame. Most of the sky will be selected, as shown in Figure 8-3.

FIGURE 8-3
The magic wand tool can select most of the sky with a single touch.

4   Shift-click in the lower left corner of the sky once or twice to add those pixels to the selection. If you happen to click in exactly the right area, one click will grab the other sky pixels. Don't worry if that doesn't happen; you might click in an area that's slightly too dark, leaving some lighter pixels unselected. Shift-click again in the remaining area of the sky, and you will grab the lighter pixels also.

5 If necessary, use the lasso tool to capture any stray pixels that might not be selected in the sky area. Then choose Select ⇨ Save Selection to save the current selection so you can reuse it later if you want to. We'll be needing this selection later, so do save it.

6 Use the Swatches palette to choose a dark blue as the foreground color. Make sure white is still the background color. Then select Filter ⇨ Render ⇨ Clouds from the menu bar to activate Photoshop's Clouds filter. You'll have no parameters to worry about, because this filter has no dialog box or options. A dramatic cloud effect will be applied to the sky selection, as shown in Figure 8-4.

FIGURE 8-4
These clouds are a little more eye-catching, although they look a little phony.

TIP Any Photoshop filter can be reapplied using the most recently used parameters by pressing Command-F. In this example, Photoshop provides a slightly different type of cloud effect every time you use the Cloud filter. You can press Command-F a few times to reapply the filter until you get a look that you like. If you'd rather go back to the filter's dialog box (should it use one), press Command-Option-F instead.

7 Because real skies aren't quite entirely uniform, the one that materialized in Figure 8-4 looks a little fake. We can give it a more realistic look by using a layer mask, which you learned about in Chapter 7. Make a duplicate of the background layer (because you can't create a layer mask for the background).

9 Now, return Photoshop's default foreground/background colors to black and white by clicking on the miniature color control boxes in the toolbox.

10 With the copy of the background layer active, select Layer ⇨ Add Layer Mask from the menu bar.

11 Reload the selection you saved in Step 5 so only the sky will be subject to the next step.

12 Click the gradient tool and set Opacity to 80% in the Gradient Tool Options palette. Make sure that Gradient is set to Foreground to Background, and the type is Linear. Then, apply a black/white linear gradient from the top of the image to the base of the building. The layer mask will filter out the clouds near the skyline, and allow them to show through as a deeper blue higher in the image, exactly as you might expect in a real scene. The image so far should look like Figure 8-5.

FIGURE 8-5
The gradient applied with a layer mask gives the sky a more realistic appearance.

13 With only the layer you've been working on visible, choose Flatten image from the Layer palette's fly-out menu to merge your work.

STEP 2: DISGUISING THE FOREGROUND

We have several approaches we could take to disguise the ugly foreground. We could always find a picture of a more attractive hillside, and cut and paste it in, trying as hard as we could to make it blend in. However, doing effective compositing so that what you've done isn't apparent to the casual viewer can be time-consuming. Filters can give you a shortcut. In this section, we'll turn those old foreground ruins into a neutral setting that won't be obvious in the finished picture. Just follow these directions:

1 First, we need to select the foreground. Because we've already selected the sky earlier, selecting the foreground is easy. Load the selection you saved before, and then choose Select ⇨ Inverse from the menu bar. Everything except the sky will now be selected.

2 Double-click the lasso tool, and make sure the Anti-Aliased box is checked in the Lasso Tool Options palette. Type in a value of 4 in the Feather box.

3 Next, hold down the Option key and use the lasso tool to deselect the building itself. The remaining selection will be the hillside, with a fuzzy, unobtrusive border between the building and the foreground (because you feathered the lasso tool by four pixels).

4 Select Filter ⇨ Distort ⇨ Ocean Ripple from the menu bar, and select a Ripple Size of 9, and a Ripple Magnitude of 9 in the Ocean Ripple dialog box (see Figure 8-6). Selecting higher or lower values in the Ripple Size and Ripple Magnitude fields produces larger and steeper ripples, respectively. We chose these particular values because we liked the effect.

FIGURE 8-6
The typical filter dialog box has a preview window and slider controls.

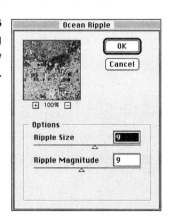

NOTE   Photoshops' filter dialog boxes include a preview window that can be zoomed in and out by clicking the plus and minus keys. You can adjust the view by placing the cursor inside the window, and dragging the image. Below, sliders and text boxes can be used to enter values for the effect's parameters.

5 Click on OK to apply the filter. Then select Filter ⇨ Sharpen ⇨ Sharpen More to add some craggy texture to the hillside. Your image should now look like Figure 8-7.

FIGURE 8-7
Texturizing the foreground makes it look more like a rocky hillside.

6 Use the Image ⇨ Adjust ⇨ Brightness/Contrast control to make the hillside darker and a little less contrasty. Set the Brightness slider to −100, and the Contrast slider to −40. We can use Brightness/Contrast here instead of the Levels command because the adjustments are not critical. We just want to darken the image. When you're finished with this step, the hillside should blend in more smoothly.

STEP 3: ADDING SOME WATER

As long as we're using image editing magic to deceive, we can get as outrageous as we like. It's no great trick to change that broad expanse of lighter-colored foreground into an attractive pond or lake. Just follow these directions to work some more magic:

1 Double-click the magic wand tool, and set Feather to 25 pixels.

2 Next, select the lighter area in the lower right corner with the magic wand. The selection will automatically be blended in with the darker area.

3 Select Image ⇨ Adjust ⇨ Hue/Saturation, and set the Hue to –160, Saturation to –32, and Lightness to +13. Click on OK to apply the change.

4 Change the magic wand tool's tolerance to 40 pixels, and then select the lower right portion of the pond, a short distance from the "shore," as shown in Figure 8-8.

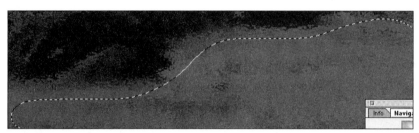

FIGURE 8-8
A feathered selection creates a gradual shoreline.

5 Select Filter ⇨ Distort ⇨ ZigZag. Make sure to enter the settings shown in Figure 8-9 in the resulting dialog box (Amount: 91%; Ridges: 18%; Style: Pond ripples). Click on OK to apply the filter.

Your finished photo of the KTI research center looks quite different from the original, as you can see in Figure 8-10. Compare Figure 8-10 with Figure 8-1 to make a before-and-after comparison.

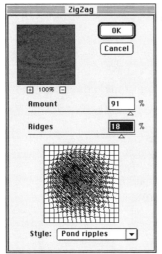

FIGURE 8-9
The ZigZag filter's dialog box adds a wire-frame representation of the ripple effect, and a drop-down list box with a series of several variations from which you can choose.

FIGURE 8-10
The finished image, with craggy hills and pond in place.

WHAT KINDS OF FILTERS EXIST?

As you learn more about filters, you may be hard-pressed to sort out all the different kinds that Photoshop puts at your disposal. After all, nearly 100 filters are built right into the program, and you can add dozens more such as Kai's Power Tools from third-party suppliers. To help you sort out this plethora of options, we've put together a list of the nine major filter categories, grouped together largely by function.

Acquire/Import/Export Modules

Strictly speaking these plug-ins are filters, too, because they process pixels, even though they appear in the File menu under the Import and Export entries. In this group, you'll find plug-ins such as the TWAIN scanner modules that help you introduce images into Photoshop, as well as those that enable you to export files in other formats, such as transparent or interlaced GIF. You generally apply this kind of filter to an entire image rather than just a selection.

Production Filters

These are somewhat specialized filters for sophisticated prepress applications that help you make color corrections or separations, or generate files for Scitex imaging equipment. Photoshop doesn't include any plug-ins of this type, which are typified by third-party add-ins such as Alaras Tropix and Second Glance LaserSeps. This is another type of filter that is applied to a whole image.

Image Enhancement Filters

These filters improve the appearance of images without making fundamental changes in the content. Image enhancement filters make an existing image look better, rather than drastically different, although some of the changes can be significant. This group includes sharpening and blurring filters, which remove dust or scratches, or improve the contrast, brightness, or tonal range of an image. You may find that this kind of filter produces the changes you need when applied to the whole image, or it may make sense to apply it only to a section of a picture.

Distortion Filters

These filters move pixels from one place to another in an image, producing some kind of distortion. You'll find filters in this category that map a flat image onto a spherical surface, rip it apart in a whirlpool (like the ZigZag filter we used in this chapter), or make the image appear as if you are viewing it through glass.

Texturizing Filters

These filters act as if you've placed a piece of canvas, frosted glass, or grainy sheet of photographic film between the original image and your eye, providing an attenuating effect that combines the texture of the filter with the pixels of the original image. Photoshop's Noise filter, or those that add canvas, sandstone, or other rough surfaces to an image, work in this way. They do little to the image other than give it a texture.

(continued)

WHAT KINDS OF FILTERS EXIST? *(continued)*

Pixelation Filters

Like texturizing filters, these plug-ins interpose a texture between your eye and the image, but also take into account the size, color, contrast, or other characteristics of the pixels underneath. Instead of showing the image through a textured filter, the surface becomes part of the image itself, as with Photoshop's Dry Brush, Crystalize, Fragment, or Mezzotint filters.

Rendering Filters

As you might guess from the name, rendering filters create something new, either using elements of the image (as with Photoshop's Chrome or Lens Flare filters) or simply from scratch, as with the Clouds filter we used in this chapter.

Contrast Enhancing Filters

Some filters work with the differences in contrast between pixels at the boundaries between two colors or tones in an image. By intelligently making light pixels brighter and dark pixels darker, these edges are emphasized. The differences can be de-emphasized as well, reducing the apparent sharpness. We already lumped Sharpen and Blur filters into the Enhancing Filters category, because plenty of other filters use edge enhancement, such as Find Edges, Glowing Edges, Poster Edges, Ink Outlines, Emboss, and Bas Relief.

Other Filters

All the filters that don't fit into the previous eight categories go into the "other" bin. These include Photoshop's Video filters, such as the De-Interlace filter (which removes every other line of pixels from an image), as well as the Offset filter, which doesn't distort an image as much as it simply moves the pixels in a fixed direction, according to parameters you type in.

You'll learn more about these filter categories and how Photoshop's near-100 plug-ins fit into them in the sidebar included in the next chapter.

WHAT YOU'VE LEARNED

In this chapter, you learned quite a bit more about how filters work, and ways you can use them, including key points such as these:

- Some image-processing filters operate a little like the filter in your coffee-maker, retaining the good pixels, and removing the nasty ones that represent dust, scratches, or other artifacts.

- Other filters change the value of pixels, altering the contrast, brightness, or color balance of an image.

- Still other filters move pixels around, providing a degree of distortion to your image.

- Filters are mini-applications that work smoothly with Photoshop and its images.

- The Cloud filter creates a puffy cloud effect, obliterating any image that was there before.

- You can reapply a filter to the same selection or a new selection by pressing Command-F. If you want to pop up the same filter's dialog box (if it has one) to make changes in its parameters, use Shift-Command-F.

- When you use the lasso tool's feathering option, a fuzzy selection boundary is created.

In the next chapter, we're going to explore more of Photoshop's built-in filters, and learn what kinds are available.

Variations on a Theme

Enhancing an Image with Filters

C H A P T E R

N I N E

THE PROJECT

KTI's president, Scott Hollerith, wants to include a classy-looking painting of the company's founder and chairperson of the board—his mom—in a brochure you're working on. He likes the photograph hanging in the boardroom, but doesn't want to hire an expensive artist to copy it as a painting. Scott figures that because you work cheap, you ought to be able to transform the picture using your magic image editing tools. He's given you half an hour to do the job—and wants to see as many variations as you can come up with, so he can choose one.

THE TOOLS
- Diffuse Glow filter
- Filter Fade control
- Dry Brush and Underpainting filters
- Facets filter
- Chrome and Note paper filters
- Lighting Effects filter

Luckily for you, Photoshop comes with almost 100 filters, many of which can apply the painterly look that KTI's president wants. In this chapter, you'll gain some valuable experience in using these filters, and get a quick overview of available plug-ins and some of their typical uses. By working on the same image with different filters, you'll learn through comparison how their effects differ.

The picture you'll be working with is the photo shown in Figure 9-1, a semi-formal portrait of KTI's founder, Amy Hollerith. It's a good picture, but doesn't have the artsy quality her son Scott wants to see. A few filters will fix it up nicely, however. For each of the projects that follows, load a fresh copy of the file, and perform your changes on the new version.

FIGURE 9-1
The original photo,
ready for modification,
is a formal portrait.

 diffuse \di-fuse'\ *n* **1:** The thing that ignites dibomb. **2:** An artistic effect achieved through expensive photographic image attenuators or complex computer devices or applications, except when seen in an amateur's photograph, in which case it was probably caused by a peanut-butter fingerprint on the lens.

VARIATION 1: ADDING A GLOW

Amy's a handsome woman in her late 40s, but the glamorous pose of the photo you were given leads you to believe she might be interested in taking 10 or 20 years off for this arty portrait. After all, if the Holleriths really wanted the picture to be a faithful rendition, they would have used the photograph, right? So, your first transformation will involve adding a romantic glow to the picture. To do that bit of cosmetic photo-surgery, follow these directions:

1 Load amy.tif from the CD-ROM that accompanies this book. You'll need to load a fresh copy for each of the following exercises, too, but we won't tell you again to do it. You can also select Image ⇨ Duplicate from the menu bar to create a copy that you can use in each exercise, if you have enough memory to keep more than one loaded at a time, that is.

2 Make sure the default black/white Photoshop colors are active. This filter uses the current background color as the color for the glow that is added; if your background is a dark shade, the image will look very strange.

3 Select Filter ⇨ Distort ⇨ Diffuse Glow from the menu bar. The Diffuse Glow dialog box appears, as shown in Figure 9-2.

FIGURE 9-2
The Diffuse Glow dialog box has sliders to control an image's graininess and the amount of glow and clear.

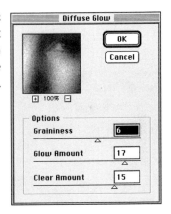

4 Set Graininess to 6. This is the amount of rough texture that the filter will add to your image, obscuring unwanted detail and adding to the dreamy look of the image. Graininess can be set as high as 10, but we'll use this intermediate setting instead.

5 Set Glow Amount to 17. This parameter controls the strength of the glow, as if you were turning up the voltage on a light source; the higher the setting, the more the glow spreads into your image.

6 Set Clear Amount to 15. This setting controls the size of the image area that is not affected by the glow.

7 Click on OK to apply the change.

8 The effect is a little harsh, so we'll use a very neat trick that was added to Photoshop 4.0. Open the Filter menu. There you'll find a new choice: Fade Diffuse Glow. Click on it and the Fade dialog box appears, as shown in Figure 9-3.

FIGURE 9-3
The Fade slider enables you to mix the filtered image with the original.

9 Set the Opacity slider to 67%. This control enables you to mix the effect you just applied with the original image in proportions you specify. It's exactly the same as if you created a copy of a layer, applied the effect, and then adjusted opacity and merged with the original background layer. Photoshop enables you to do it in one step; even after you've played with the fader, you can still go back to the Undo menu and remove the whole effect. Figure 9-4 shows how the resulting image should appear.

FIGURE 9-4
Diffuse Glow has added a glamorous effect to the image.

VARIATION 2: APPLYING A BRUSH

The version we just prepared doesn't look much like a painting, so we'll do one next that gives Scott that starving artist look he wants so badly for his mom's picture. Here's how to do it:

1 Select Filter ➪ Artistic ➪ Dry Brush from the menu bar. The Dry Brush dialog box appears, as shown in Figure 9-5.

FIGURE 9-5
The Dry Brush dialog box has controls for brush size, detail, and texture.

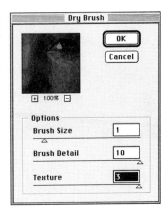

2 Set Brush Size to 1. The larger the brush, the broader the strokes, and we want some fine detail in this image.

3 Set Brush Detail to 10. This setting controls the roughness of the edges of the brush strokes, with a value of 10 giving you a great deal of detail.

4 Set Texture to 3. Doing so specifies a heavy texture that gives a sort of posterization effect.

5 Click on OK to apply the effect.

6 Use the same Filter ➪ Fade control you used in the previous variation to set the mixture of this modified image with the original to 60 percent. The result of these effects appears in Figure 9-6.

FIGURE 9-6
The Dry Brush filter makes
the image look like a painting.

VARIATION 3: UNDERPAINTING

The Underpainting filter gives an effect you might get if you texturized an image, and then placed an unaltered version on top of it. It looks a little as if the image were applied to the front of a sheet of glass, and the texture painted on the back side of the glass. To experiment with this filter, follow these directions:

1 Select Filter ➪ Artistic ➪ Underpainting from the menu bar. The Underpainting dialog box appears, as Figure 9-7 shows.

2 Set the Brush Size to 1, to give us a fairly fine amount of detail in the final image.

3 Set Texture Coverage to 16. Texture Coverage controls the amount of the image that will be obscured by the texture. A medium setting of 16 minimizes the effect and enables most of the original image to show through.

4 From the Texture drop-down list box select the default Canvas texture. (Other built-in textures include Sandstone, Brick, or Burlap.) You can also create a custom texture, save it as a PICT file, and load it from the Load Texture entry that appears in this list, shown in Figure 9-8.

FIGURE 9-7
The Underpainting filter is a useful way to add texture to an image.

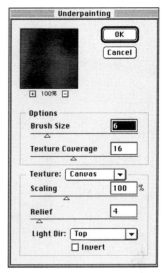

FIGURE 9-8
You may select the texture of your choice, or load one from the hard disk.

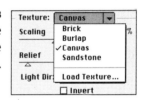

5   Leave Scaling at the default 100% setting. Scaling controls the size of the texture, compared to the image. If you wanted a finer texture, you'd set the slider to less than 100 percent. Moving it above 100 percent makes the texture larger and grosser.

6   The relief slider adjusts the 3D effect of the texture. We want to make the effect quite pronounced, so set it to 4.

7   From the Light(ing) Dir(ection) drop-down list box, select Top Left. The lighting direction control enables you to specify the position of the light source that's casting the shadows of the embedded texture. In our example, we want the light source to coincide with the one used to make the original picture.

8   Click on OK to apply the effect, and use the Filter ⇨ Fade control to adjust the image to a 60 percent mixture. Your finished image should look like Figure 9-9.

FIGURE 9-9
Underpainting
produces this effect.

VARIATION 4: FILTER OF FEW FACETS

If you're in a hurry and your photo has a variety of defects, ranging from dust spots to graininess to unsharpness, the Facets filter can quickly turn a bad shot into an interesting, artsy image. Follow these two steps to see how easy it is:

1 Select Filter ⇨ Pixelate ⇨ Facet from the menu bar. This filter has no dialog box and is applied to your image immediately.

2 Press Command-F four or five times to reapply the filter. Each time, the effect gets stronger. Stop when you have a version you like. The finished image should look like Figure 9-10.

VARIATION 5: BURNING CHROME

Photoshop's Chrome filter is often dismissed because it produces a smooth, swirly image that bears little resemblance to the original picture. We're going to show you how to overcome the plug-in's shortcomings and create an interesting image with it. Just follow these steps:

1 Select Filter ⇨ Sketch ⇨ Chrome from the menu bar. The Chrome dialog box appears, as shown in Figure 9-11.

FIGURE 9-10
The Facets filter is a fast way
to add a painterly effect.

FIGURE 9-11
The Chrome filter
has only detail and
smoothless options.

2 Set Detail to 10, and Smoothness to 1. This gives us the most detailed image possible with the Chrome filter, which tends to dissolve most of the image information in a pool of melted silver metal.

3 Click on OK to apply the changes. Your image should look like Figure 9-12. We're not done yet, but you might like to check out the intermediate version.

4 Use the Filter ➪ Fade control, and set the level to 50 percent.

FIGURE 9-12
The intermediate version looks like this with the Chrome filter applied: interesting, but not outstanding.

5 Apply the Filter ➪ Sharpen ➪ Sharpen More filter to the image. The picture looks like the one in Figure 9-13, which is a different effect, indeed.

FIGURE 9-13
The Fade slider enables us to end up with an image that looks like this.

VARIATION 6: USING LIGHTING EFFECTS

The Lighting Effects filter is a versatile plug-in with a broad range of controls. You may place up to 16 different light sources to illuminate your image, select from spotlights or broad lights, add textures that are lit by those sources, and do other cool things. You can actually achieve dozens of different effects with this filter, but we'll try just one. We'll explain what each control does, but, in practice, your best bet is to play with each one and watch the effect in the thumbnail preview. Unless you have a photographer's experience with lighting in the studio, it's difficult to achieve an exact effect with this plug-in: Your best results will come from happy accidents. Follow these steps as your introduction to this filter:

1 Select Filter ⇨ Render ⇨ Lighting Effects from the menu bar. The Lighting Effects dialog box appears, as shown in Figure 9-14.

FIGURE 9-14
The Lighting Effects dialog box bristles with controls.

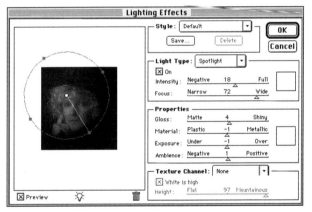

2 We want a shiny, plastic-like appearance for this image (trust me on this), so you should set the Properties sliders so that the Gloss control is shiny, Material is plastic, and Exposure is set to –62 (to produce a darker effect.) Ambient light—which is the nondirectional light that bounces around a room—should be set to –100. That will make the shadows darker in our finished image.

3 We'll apply a texture to the image, so, in the Texture Channel drop-down list box, choose the blue channel (actually, you could use any of the three for this image, but you must choose one, so use blue).

4 To make the texture as obvious as possible, move the Height slider to the Mountainous setting.

5 Now, we need to choose a light source. You can select from Directional (like a flood light), Spot (a narrow, focused light), or Omni (a broad, multi-directional source.) Choose Omni.

6 A circle appears on the thumbnail preview. Drag it so the center is in the upper left corner, then drag the boundaries of the light so they cover the whole image, as shown in Figure 9-15.

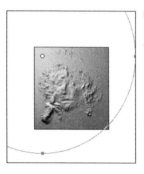

FIGURE 9-15
Positioning the light with the Lighting Effects filter.

7 Click on OK to apply the effect, and use the Filter ⇨ Fade slider to adjust the mixture to about 67 percent. You'll end up with a very nice etched-metal effect like that shown in Figure 9-16.

FIGURE 9-16
This etched metal effect is the final result.

VARIATION 7: TAKE NOTES

We'll try one last effect so you'll have a good overview of Photoshop's key filters. This one produces an interesting embossed effect that looks like note paper. Just follow these steps:

1 Choose a dark blue color as the foreground, and leave the background color as white.

2 Select Filter ➪ Sketch ➪ Note Paper from the menu bar. The Note Paper dialog box appears, as shown in Figure 9-17.

FIGURE 9-17
Use the Note Paper dialog box to set contrast (Image Balance), Graininess, and Relief parameters.

3 Set Image Balance to 11. The Note Paper filter changes your image into a high-contrast version of itself, and the balance control adjusts the relationship between the dark and white areas. You can play with the slider to get an effect you like in the preview window, but we preferred the look with this control set to 10.

4 Set the Graininess slider to 10 to provide a good grainy effect.

5 Set the Relief slider to 22 to make the grain really stand out.

6 Click on OK to apply the effect.

7 Although the image looks good as it is, we moved the Fade slider to 40 percent to produce the image you see in Figure 9-18.

FIGURE 9-18
An arty paper-embossed
effect is the final result.

WHAT FILTERS DOES PHOTOSHOP HAVE?

With around 100 filters built right into Photoshop, the toughest task you may encounter is deciding which one to use for a particular purpose. The very best path toward experience is to experiment with as many filters as possible until you learn what each can do. The second best way is to examine the filter samples in Appendix C of this book and the color insert. For a quick overview, you can skim through the descriptions in this sidebar.

For Photoshop 4.0, Adobe completely rearranged its Filter menu, combining the filters used in Version 3.05 with those included in Adobe Gallery Effects, which were formerly available as an extra-cost add-on. Here we'll describe the broad categories of filters in the order Adobe has arranged them in its revamped menu.

Artistic

This section contains 15 filters that make your images look as if they had been drawn or painted by an artist, or otherwise rendered in an artistic way. The most painterly of these filters include the following:

- ⊡ Dry Brush, Fresco, Paint Daubs, Palette Knife, Sponge, Watercolor

A second group makes more drastic changes on your image, but still produces an interesting effect—especially Underpainting, which adds texture as if it were applied to the back side of a piece of glass, with your image painted on the front. This group includes the following:

- ⊡ Colored Pencil, Cutout, Rough Pastels, Smudge Stick, Underpainting

The final group creates effects of their own that more closely resemble other graphic arts techniques, rather than painting or drawing effects. These include the following:

- ⊡ Film Grain, Neon Glow, Plastic Wrap, Poster Edges

Blur

This section contains six filters that desharpen your image dramatically:

- ☑ Blur, Blur More, Gaussian Blur, Motion Blur, Radial Blur, Smart Blur

The first three filters are standard blurring effects, while Motion Blur smears your image as if it were captured while in motion by a camera with a slow shutter speed. Radial Blur duplicates the image you get when you zoom in on a subject during an exposure. Smart Blur is an update on Gaussian Blur, with additional parameters you can set, such as image quality and edge/overall blurring.

Brush Strokes

These eight plug-ins are more painterly filters, generally with a stroke-like quality to their effects. We find all of the following less useful than those in the Artistic category:

- ☑ Accented Edges, Angled Strokes, Crosshatch, Dark Strokes, Ink Outlines, Spatter, Sprayed Strokes, Sumi-e

Distort

The 12 filters in this category generally move pixels around in outrageous ways, although Diffuse Glow (one of our favorite filters) is more of a blurring/grain filter than a distortion plug-in. The filters in this category include the following:

- ☑ Diffuse Glow, Displace, Glass, Ocean Ripple, Pinch, Polar Coordinates, Ripple, Shear, Spherize, Twirl, Wave, ZigZag

You can tell what most of these do by their names, although ZigZag, as we saw in the previous chapter, is actually a better water-type filter than Wave, Ripple, or Ocean Ripple. You might want to experiment with the strange Polar Coordinates filter, which takes an image and wraps it around a central point.

Noise

The following four filters either add random noise, or remove it from your image:

- ☑ Noise, Despeckle, Dust & Scratches, Median

Pixelate

Seven more great painterly filters, most of which use a dot motif rather than broad strokes to work their magic. The Facet filter is especially appropriate for breaking up an image into a dramatic, blocky-looking picture. The filters in this group include the following:

- ☑ Color Halftone, Crystallize, Facet, Fragment, Mezzotint, Mosaic, Pointillize

Render

Several of these five are among the most versatile filters in the Photoshop batch. Lighting Effects, for example, enables you to place multiple lights in an image to give a dramatic effect, as demonstrated in this chapter, while Texture Fill uses a set of supplied textures, or those you import, to add a rough surface to an image. Included in this group are the following filters:

- ☑ Clouds, Difference Clouds, Lens Flare, Lighting Effects, Texture Fill

(continued)

WHAT FILTERS DOES PHOTOSHOP HAVE? *(continued)*

Sharpen

Here are four standard sharpening filters, three with no parameters. Unsharp Mask uses a dialog box that enables you to specify degree and kind of sharpening to be applied. The Sharpen filters include the following:

- ▣ Sharpen, Sharpen Edges, Sharpen More, Unsharp Mask

Sketch

Still more artistic filters, with the Chrome, Note Paper, Photocopy, and Plaster plug-ins being the most successful of the 14, we think.

- ▣ Bas Relief, Chalk & Charcoal, Charcoal, Chrome, Conté Crayon, Graphic Pen, Halftone Pattern, Note Paper, Photocopy, Plaster, Reticulation, Stamp, Torn Edges, Water Paper

Stylize

This group includes some outstanding filters. You'll want to experiment with Find Edges, Trace Contour, and Wind a lot if you need to stylize some images in an artistic way. This group includes the following nine filters:

- ▣ Diffuse, Emboss, Extrude, Find Edges, Glowing Edges, Solarize, Tiles, Trace Contour, Wind

Texture

You'll find a little overlap here with filters from other categories (for example, Grain versus Film Grain, and Texturizer versus Texture Fill). Of the six, we like Patchwork the best. Craquelure produces a deep, cracked-canvas effect that's interesting but a little heavy-handed, while Stained Glass usually obliterates so much image detail that you end up with a completely different mosaic-like picture. This group includes the following:

- ▣ Craquelure, Grain, Mosaic Tiles, Patchwork, Stained Glass, Texturizer

Video

Just two filters here. De-interlace removes every other line (odd or even—your choice), which may improve some video captures. NTSC changes an image's color palette to one compatible with National Television Standard Code requirements.

- ▣ De-Interlace, NTSC Colors

Other

You can create your own filter here with the Custom plug-in, offset an image, or filter out pixels with brightness or darkness values you specify. "Other" filters include the following:

- ▣ Custom, High Pass, Maximum, Minimum, Offset

WHAT YOU'VE LEARNED

In this chapter you were able to jump in and tackle some sophisticated filter effects, using seven of Photoshop's most popular plug-in modules. We also referred to some of the major classifications of filters that Photoshop builds into the program. The key points covered include:

- ▣ The Diffuse Glow filter is a good way to add a fuzzy, romantic look to a picture.

- ▣ If you want a brush-like effect, the Dry Brush filter can convert an image to a quasi-painting, while masking many small defects that might exist in the original.

- ▣ Underpainting applies a paint-like texture to an image without obliterating the original picture's detail.

- ▣ The Facet filter, which has no dialog box or parameters to worry about, can convert an image into a more artistic picture quickly.

- ▣ The Chrome filter doesn't have to overpower any image to which you apply it: enough detail can be preserved to let the original picture remain recognizable.

- ▣ Lighting Effects is a versatile filter that can reproduce some of the effects of a photographer's studio lighting system, plus add texture to an image.

- ▣ The Note Paper filter produces a high-contrast image that looks as if it were embossed on a rough paper surface.

In the next chapter, we're going to look at ways you can work with outlines in Photoshop documents, using the Pen tool and Paths palette.

Recycling Text

From Bitmap to Outline via Paths

Kitchen Table International has scrapped its most recent advertising campaign, based on the slogan, "Dedicated to Reinventing the Wheel" in favor of a new theme, "Better Products than You'd Expect from a Company Like Ours!" The firm would like to reuse a typeface from an old brochure, and combine it with a bright, cheery cloud background. Unfortunately, the typeface was created especially for the previous brochure by an artist who is now selling aluminum siding in Italy. You'll have to recycle the type you have, somehow, using some Photoshop tools you've been meaning to try.

THE TOOLS
- Drag and Drop
- Rulers, Grids, and Guides
- Snap to Guides
- Pen and airbrush tools
- Paths palette
- Stroke Paths
- Make Selection

As you might know, electronic artwork exists in two basic forms: bitmaps such as those Photoshop can manipulate, and outline/object-oriented art usually created with illustration packages such as Adobe Illustrator or Macromedia FreeHand. Each kind of art (pixels or vectors) has advantages and limitations of its own (see sidebar).

Although Photoshop does a better job with bitmap-based images, the program does include some tools that enable you to work with outline-oriented objects, such as text, and you'll need to learn about them in this chapter. While parts of this project might have gone easier with an illustration program, you're about to find out that Photoshop is flexible enough to handle such a job well.

We're going to grab copies of the K, T, and I that make up Kitchen Table International's abbreviated name from the original text, reproduce it in outline form, then create a new set of characters that we can drop into the cloud background. As always, we've divided the project into simple steps.

pixels \pix'els\ *n* Picture elements. One of the few image components that everyone wants a lot of, but nobody wants to be able to see.

BITMAPS VERSUS OUTLINES

Bitmapped images (*pixels*) can be captured with scanners or digital cameras, created from scratch or modified with painting tools, and manipulated pixel by pixel. However, when you enlarge or reduce a bitmap or any portion of such an image, the pixels don't scale well, producing jaggy diagonal lines and other unpleasant artifacts. Such image files also tend to be very large, because you must store density and color information about every picture element. Even with compression schemes that ignore redundant image information (for example, broad expanses of the same color) or use shorter codes to represent groups of pixels, Photoshop users often find themselves working with multimegabyte files that load slowly, and handle awkwardly.

Outline or *vector* artwork treats each object in an illustration as a set of numbers (basically, mathematical instructions) representing the curves and lines needed to reproduce that object, plus information on how to fill that object with tones or textures. Because the objects are all laid one on top of another (with the ones in front obscuring part of the view of those they overlap), a stacking order is also important.

Because vectors use outlines instead of bitmaps, a vector object can be scaled up or down to any desired size without losing sharpness. A circle looks just as sharp on your screen with a one-inch diameter as with a six-inch diameter. It's easier to change the shape of such objects smoothly, rearrange the stacking order, or replace one kind of fill with another. Vector art files tend to be much smaller than bitmaps, too.

STEP 1: DRAGGING AND DROPPING THE INITIALS

We're going to open the image file containing the text, move the characters to a new file, and use Photoshop's Guides commands to arrange them evenly. Just follow these directions:

1 Open the clouds.tif file from the Chapter 10 folder of the accompanying CD-ROM.

2 Open the kitchen.tif file from the same folder. Make sure that clouds.tif and kitchen.tif are both visible on the screen at the same time. The kitchen.tif file is shown in Figure 10-1.

FIGURE 10-1
The unaltered text characters look like this.

3 Use the rectangular marquee to select the letters KIT. These happen to be the exact letters we need, even if they're in the wrong order.

TIP Dragging and dropping portions of images from one document window to another is faster and more efficient than copy and pasting between them. You save several series of key presses, and Photoshop can copy between windows without first copying to its Clipboard. This is important on three counts: 1) Because the Clipboard isn't used, whatever you've already copied there remains on the Clipboard and can be pasted down after you've finished dragging and dropping another portion of the image; 2) moreover, avoiding the Clipboard can be a blessing when you're short of memory, and 3) copying to the Clipboard takes extra time.

4 Switch from the rectangular marquee selection tool to the move tool, and drag the selected area over to the clouds.tif file, as shown in Figure 10-2. Photoshop places the characters in a new layer.

FIGURE 10-2
After they are dragged to the new window, the characters are placed in their own layer.

NOTE If you drag a selection between windows with a selection tool active, only the selection itself, not its contents, are moved between the windows. You might want to do this if you've created a selection and want to reuse it on a similar object in another window. When you drag a selection between windows using the move tool, the contents of the selection itself are copied, leaving the original image undisturbed.

STEP 2: REALIGNING THE LETTERS WITH GUIDES

Next, we're going to rearrange the characters KIT into the correct order, KTI, and learn how to use Photoshop's grid and guidelines feature at the same time. Here's how:

1 Turn off the background layer so only the layer with the pasted KIT characters is visible. Zoom in to 200 percent, so you can view the characters clearly.

2 Select View ⇨ Show Rulers (or press Command-R) to turn on the rulers (if you haven't done so already).

3 Select Preferences ⇨ Guides & Grid. The Preferences dialog box appears, as shown in Figure 10-3. We're going to make sure Photoshop's Guides and Grid are set up to be easily visible.

FIGURE 10-3
Use the Preferences dialog
box to set up Photoshop's
guides and grid.

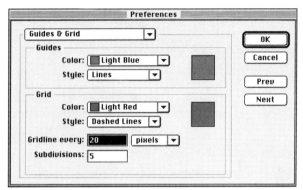

4 Set the Guides color to Light Blue, and Style to Lines.

5 Set the Grid color to Light Red, and Style to Dashed Lines.

6 Set the measurement used for gridlines to pixel, and specify one line every 20 pixels.

7 Specify subdivisions every 5 pixels. Click on OK to make your adjustments permanent. The image should now look like Figure 10-4.

FIGURE 10-4
With the grid turned on, lines
like these are displayed.

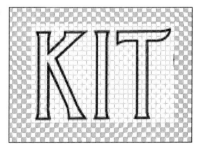

8 Use the View menu and make sure Snap to Guides and Snap to Grid are turned on.

9 Move the cursor up into the horizontal ruler, press the mouse button, and drag downward. A blue-colored guideline will follow. Position the guide as closely as you can under the baseline of the text, as Figure 10-5 shows.

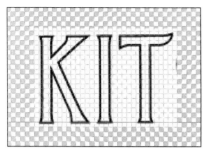

FIGURE 10-5
The guideline has been placed
under the baseline of the text.

10 Select View ⇨ Snap to Guides. Doing so causes the grid and guides to "attract" selections to them, making it easier to align objects to the guideline.

11 Using the rectangular marquee, select the letter K. Notice how the selection aligns itself with the red gridlines.

12 Using the Move tool, move the selected K over to the left. Notice how easy it is to align the selection to the guide you dragged to the baseline of the text.

13 Next, select the letter T, and move it next to the letter K, and then position the I at the end of the row of characters, giving you the KTI initials we were looking for, as shown in Figure 10-6. Because Photoshop snapped each selection to the guide, the characters are in precisely the same vertical position they were before.

FIGURE 10-6
The letters have snapped
to the guideline.

TIP You can also set up grids and guidelines using inches or other measurements, even though in this case pixels were the most convenient unit.

STEP 3: CREATING A PATH

In addition to the KTI initials we've already produced, we need a set of larger characters. We can use the monogram we've already created as a starting point, using Photoshop's Paths capability to produce the outline. Just follow these steps:

1 Select the KTI initials with the rectangular marquee tool, and press Command-C to copy them.

2 Select File ➪ Open to open a new, empty file. Photoshop automatically inserts the dimensions of the selection on the Clipboard as the size for the new file.

3 Press Command-V to paste the initials into the new file.

4 We need text that is three times larger than what we have. Select Image ➪ Image Size and enter 300 percent in the Pixel Dimensions box. The new file will now look like Figure 10-7.

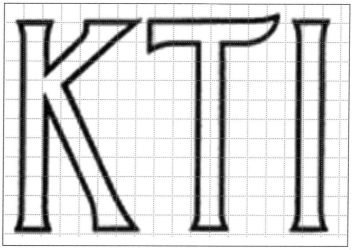

FIGURE 10-7
The file has been made three times larger.

5 Unfortunately, this blown-up text is too fuzzy to use, because we're working with a bitmap instead of an outline. Fortunately, we can turn it into an outline. Double-click the Pen tool in the toolbox (the seventh icon from the top in the left column) to pop up the Pen Tool Options palette shown in Figure 10-8.

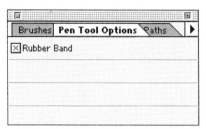

FIGURE 10-8
The Pen Tool Options palette
has only one choice: the
Rubber Band checkbox.

6   Click the Rubber Band checkbox. This tells Photoshop to show you
    the path being created as you move the Pen tool from one point to
    another. Each time you click the mouse button, the path from the
    previous point to the new position is locked in.

7   Start in the upper left corner of the letter K, and draw a path that
    follows the center of the character fairly closely, clicking the mouse to
    set various points along the way. The gridlines will help you position
    each point precisely. When you've returned to the start point, your
    new path will look like Figure 10-9.

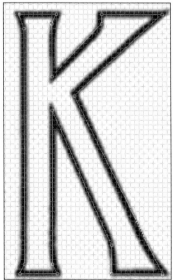

FIGURE 10-9
The new path should
look like this.

8   Repeat this step for the letter T. However, this letter doesn't have all
    straight lines like the K. Don't try to follow the curve of the T's
    crossbar. Just click from a point at the beginning of the curve to the
    upper corner, then move down again, and back to your point of
    origin, creating a closed outline, as shown in Figure 10-10.

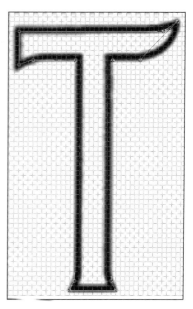

FIGURE 10-10
The closed path doesn't match the curved corner of the crossbar—yet.

9 Click the Pen tool in the toolbox, moving the cursor over to the right to select the pen with the plus sign in it. This tool is used to add points to a path.

10 Click in the center of the straight line that spans the crossbar's curve; a new point with selection handles on either side of it appears. If you've worked with illustration packages such as Illustrator, you'll know this type of handle represents Bézier curves. You can drag the outer handles to adjust the direction of curve, or the center point to control the position of the curve.

11 Drag the center point until the curve matches that of the crossbar as closely as possible, as shown in Figure 10-11.

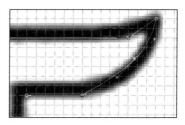

FIGURE 10-11
Now the path curves to match the crossbar.

12 Finally, outline the letter I, as shown in Figure 10-12.

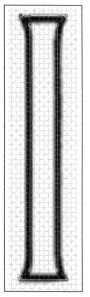

FIGURE 10-12
The letter I has
been outlined, too.

STEP 4: USING A PATH

Now that we have a path that recreates the text, we can use it to produce some new text in the larger size. Follow these directions:

1 Photoshop creates a path and by default calls it Work Path. If you want to save and reuse a path, give it a new name and save it. Double-click the path's name in the Paths palette. The Rename Path dialog box, shown in Figure 10-13, pops up. Call the Path KTI Initials.

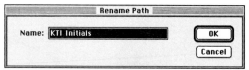

FIGURE 10-13
Rename a path using
this dialog box.

2 You might also want to use the path you've created as a selection, so use the Paths palette's fly-out menu and choose Make Selection. The Make Selection dialog box appears, as Figure 10-14 shows. Select a path and press the Return key to create a selection from the path.

FIGURE 10-14

A path can be turned
into a selection.

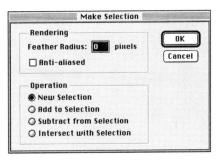

ABOUT PATHS

When you draw paths in Photoshop, you're not really drawing in the sense that pixels are being created in a layer. All you're actually doing is defining an outline that Photoshop can save for later reference, stroke with pixels to produce a real line, fill to create a shape, or change into a selection. In other words, paths are a convenient way of creating an object that contains straight lines or smooth curves (because both kinds of paths can be drawn) to trace the outline of an existing shape, as we're doing in this chapter, or to create a very precise selection.

You'll use both the path tool on the toolbox as well as the Paths palette. The tool has several modes: a Pen that defines a path as you click with the mouse; tools marked with plus and minus signs to add or remove points from an existing path; and a convert-anchor-point tool (that looks like a diagonally oriented caret), that changes a curve's point into a straight line, or corner point on an existing path.

The Paths palette provides a list of paths you've created, a trash can into which you can drag paths you no longer need, and icons that enable you to fill or stroke a path with pixels. You'll also find a fly-out menu that you can use to save a path as a selection, duplicate, or save a path, and perform other functions.

Creating and adjusting paths is definitely nonintuitive if you're used to working with pixels rather than outlines. If you haven't used an illustration package, your best bet is to follow up the exercises in this chapter with a few of your own, until you are comfortable working with paths. Practice these skills introduced in this chapter:

- Drawing straight-line paths
- Adding and removing points from a path
- Creating curved paths
- Changing curves to a different shape

Also, try out these additional capabilities:

- Copying and moving paths, which is done exactly as with other objects in an image
- Filling a path with a tone
- Erasing and deleting portions of a path by selecting a segment and pressing the Delete key
- Deleting a whole path by dragging it to the Paths palette's trash can

3 This exercise shows you how to stroke a path. You can choose several different tools to stroke a path, and we'll use the airbrush. Double-click the airbrush tool in the toolbox, and make sure Pressure is set to 50 percent in the Airbrush Options palette.

4 Select the 35-pixel brush in the Brushes palette. If you use brushes a lot, you might want to drag this palette to the desktop so it will always be visible. You may then use the right and left bracket keys to switch back and forth from one brush size to another.

5 Select a bright red as the foreground color.

6 Choose Stroke Subpaths from the Paths palette's fly-out menu. You'll see the Stroke Subpaths dialog box, as shown in Figure 10-15. Notice that, in contrast to when you're stroking a selection, you can choose from about a dozen different painting tools when stroking a path.

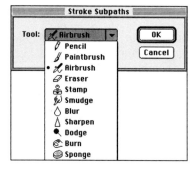

FIGURE 10-15
About a dozen painting tools are available for stroking a path.

7 Select the airbrush, and then click on OK to apply the airbrush strokes to the path. You'll notice that this technique is much faster and cleaner than turning a path into a selection, and airbrushing inside the selection manually.

8 Next, choose a purplish-magenta as the foreground color.

9 Reduce the size of the brush by three or four sizes using the left bracket key.

10 In the Airbrush Options palette, change the pressure to 25 percent.

11 Use Stroke Subpaths again and apply the airbrush one more time. An interesting highlight effect in the contrasting color is applied, as is shown Figure 10-16. (You really need to load the file from the CD-ROM to see exactly how it looks.)

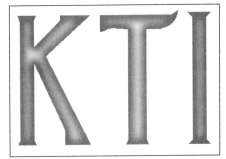

FIGURE 10-16
An interesting highlight
effect has been added
in a second color.

12 Turn off the paths by using the Paths palette's fly-out menu, and selecting
Turn Off Path.

13 Now, make sure the layer with the modified text is active, and click the
Preserve Transparency box. This ensures that when we copy the whole
layer, only the image and not the transparent background will be copied.

14 Use the Move tool to drag the KTI characters from the window to the
clouds.tif window. Position the text in the upper left corner of the clouds,
as you can see in Figure 10-17.

FIGURE 10-17
Arrange the text in the
corner of the clouds.

STEP 5: ADDING ORIGINAL TEXT

Now we can copy the original text into the clouds.tif file, and make a few final changes,
as follows:

1 Return to the kitchen.tif file.

2 Double-click the magic wand tool, and set its Tolerance to 32.

3 Click outside the text, and then Shift-Click inside the closed areas inside such characters as A, B, R, and O.

4 Inverse the selection, and then drag it onto the clouds.tif window. Photoshop places the selection in its own layer, and the image will look roughly like Figure 10-18 at this point.

FIGURE 10-18
The text is positioned in its own layer.

5 Double-click the gradient tool, and set the Opacity to 80 percent. Our characters are white with a dark border, so using this setting allows some of the border to show through even after color has been added.

6 Select Radial gradient, and then choose a red background color to go with the magenta-purple foreground you selected earlier.

7 Make the layer with the Kitchen Table International text active, if you haven't done so already.

8 Move the cursor down to the middle of the O in International and drag to the upper left toward the K.

9 The final effect should look like Figure 10-19.

10 Save a copy of this image under a new name in Photoshop's PSD format, flatten it, and save it again; this time, select File ⇨ Save a Copy from the menu bar, and choose TIFF as the format. Rename your file to create a souvenir of all your hard work.

FIGURE 10-19
The final image looks like this.

WHAT YOU'VE LEARNED

In this chapter, we looked at vector-oriented artwork, and how Photoshop can work with outlines. Among other things, you learned that:

- Two basic kinds of electronic artwork exist: bitmaps such as those Photoshop can manipulate, and outline/object-oriented art usually created with illustration packages such as Adobe Illustrator or Macromedia FreeHand.

- Enlarging or reducing a bitmap produces unpleasant jaggy effects, and bitmap files can be very large.

- Vector artwork uses only mathematical representations of the outlines and fills, so that images of this kind can be scaled up or down to any size without losing resolution. Vector-based files are smaller and easier to store, too.

- ⊡ Dragging and dropping portions of images from one document window to another is faster and more efficient than selecting the Copy and Paste commands between them. You save time, and ease the amount of memory required for these operations.

- ⊡ If you drag a selection between windows with a selection tool active, only the selection itself, not its contents, moves between the windows. When you drag a selection between windows using the move tool, the contents of the selection itself are copied, leaving the original image undisturbed.

- ⊡ Grids can be set up using measurements you define as a way of lining up objects more accurately. Guidelines can be placed anywhere you like and used to align objects horizontally or vertically. Either can be turned on or off at will, and they don't show up when the file is printed.

- ⊡ The Pen tool creates paths using straight lines or curves.

- ⊡ Paths can be named, saved with the file, converted into selections, or stroked using a variety of painting tools.

In the next chapter, we'll learn how to twist and distort type using Photoshop's transformation tools. This is a "free" assignment for you to explore on your own. KTI has given you the day off.

Twisting Type

Distortions and Contortions
with Transformations

You're more than halfway through the book, so we decided it's time to give you a breather and create your own project. You've had fun working with text in the last few chapters, and decide that now is a good time to learn about the new Free Transform tool in Photoshop 4.0. Anything included at no cost has to be worth investigating for a budget operation like yours. Your goal for this project is to take the Kitchen Table International text from the last chapter, and come up with as many variations as you can.

THE TOOLS
- ☐ Scale, Rotate, Skew, Distort, and Perspective tools
- ☐ Numeric transformations
- ☐ Rotate in increments
- ☐ Flip Horizontal/Vertical
- ☐ Actions palette
- ☐ Free Transform tool

Often, you'll need to change the size of an object to match more closely other objects in a composite image. At other times, you'll want to add a slant, rotate all or part of an image, or distort the image. Photoshop can perform six different transformations of this type on 2D objects. You can start with a layer or just a selection, and use one of the following tools or commands:

- ⊡ **SCALE** Changes the size of the object, either in all directions evenly (making it larger while keeping the same proportions), or stretching its width or height alone.

- ⊡ **ROTATE** Turns an object around its center point, as if you were spinning it on a phonograph record turntable.

- ⊡ **SKEW** Slants a selection vertically or horizontally.

- ⊡ **DISTORT** Changes the shape of a selection.

- ⊡ **PERSPECTIVE** Adds a 3D effect to an object by making it appear that the flat image is being seen from an elevated or depressed viewpoint.

- ⊡ **FLIP HORIZONTAL** Reverses an image along its vertical axis.

- ⊡ **FLIP VERTICAL** Reverses an image along its horizontal axis.

For this project, you'll experiment with all of these options, and learn about some new Photoshop tools that enable you to streamline and automate the transformation process.

phonograph \fon-o-graf'\ *n* **1:** An instrument used to reproduce sounds prior to the invention of magnetic media and the laser. **2:** An archaic device used chiefly today by those over 40 years of age who need an analogy for something that goes around and around.

STEP 1: CHANGING THE CANVAS SIZE

First, we'll change the size of the canvas we're working with, without changing the size or the resolution of the text image itself. Here's how:

1 Open kitchen.tif, located in the Chapter 11 folder of the companion CD-ROM.

2 Because the text has been tightly cropped, we should add a little breathing room by enlarging the window, or canvas, on which it resides. First, make sure Photoshop's default black/white colors are

the foreground and background colors by clicking on the default colors icon in the color control area of the toolbox, or by pressing D on your keyboard.

3 Select Image ⇨ Canvas Size from the menu bar. The Canvas Size dialog box appears, as shown in Figure 11-1.

FIGURE 11-1

You can adjust the size of the window in which an image appears with the Canvas Size dialog box.

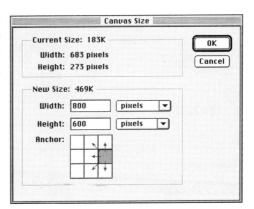

4 The Current Size area shows the size of the file in bytes, as well as its width and height. The New Size area has several controls you can use to create a larger canvas. Select pixels as the unit of measurement for both width and height from the drop-down list boxes, if pixels isn't already selected.

5 Type in 800 for the new width, and 600 for the new height.

6 The Anchor box is a grid of nine squares that shows the current image in gray in the center square. You can drag this square to one of the other eight locations, or just click the destination square, to adjust where the original image will appear in relation to the new canvas area. For example, drag the image square to the left, and the original image will be located at the left side of the new, larger canvas. In this case, drag the gray scare to the center right position, so we can add white space to the left of the original image.

7 Click on OK to expand the canvas of kitchen.tif to the new size. The image will look like Figure 11-2.

8 Save this file under a new name, and reload it as required to have a fresh copy for each of the remaining steps in this exercise.

FIGURE 11-2
The text now has extra
white space around it.

STEP 2: USING SCALE

To warm up, we'll change the size of the text using the Layer ➪ Transform ➪ Scale command, as follows:

1   Use the lasso to trace closely around the outside of the Kitchen Table International text. We could have used the rectangular marquee because the text appears on a plain white background, and we don't really care how much of the image outside the text is affected by the transformation. However, doing it this way demonstrates that any selection tool can be used to define the area to be affected by a transformation.

2   Select Layer ➪ Transform ➪ Scale from the menu bar list, shown in Figure 11-3.

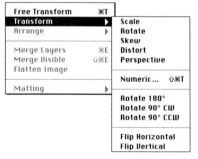

FIGURE 11-3
These are the commands available
from the Transform menu.

3   Even though the selection is irregular, a rectangular box with selection handles appears around the area you've defined, as you can see in Figure 11-4. Hold down the Shift key and grab the handle in the upper left corner (notice that the cursor changes to a pair of diagonally-pointing

arrows). Drag the handle. Notice that you can only drag in a diagonal, 45-degree direction while the Shift key is depressed. The selection gets smaller or larger while retaining its original proportions. This is the method you'd use to change the size of a selection in a freeform way without distorting it vertically or horizontally.

FIGURE 11-4
The selected area has selection handles around it.

4 Next, release the Shift key and drag the same handle. Notice that you can now drag either horizontally (to make the image wider without making it taller), vertically (to make it taller, but not wider), or diagonally at any angle you wish, making the image larger or smaller without retaining the original proportions. You'd use this method to enlarge or reduce an image to fill a specific space, especially with textured or abstract images in which the proportions aren't critical.

5 Press Escape to cancel the effect. (If you had pressed Return instead, the scale change would have been applied to the image.)

STEP 3: ROTATING THE TEXT

Next, we'll learn about rotating the image of the text. Follow these directions for an instant education:

1 Select the KTI text with the lasso tool, as before.

2 Select Layer ➪ Transform ➪ Rotate, and the selection handles appear around the image once more.

3 Move the cursor to the upper left corner handle again. Notice that this time the cursor changes into a pair of curved arrows, indicating that you can rotate the selection by dragging the handle.

WHAT'S INTERPOLATION?

As we explore transformations, it's helpful to understand how Photoshop handles changing images using a process called *interpolation*. At the very least, knowing about interpolation will help you appreciate why manipulating images in these ways can degrade the quality.

You already know that the bitmapped images that Photoshop works with are based on individual picture elements or pixels. Whenever you enlarge an image or selection, Photoshop must create the added pixels that produce the bigger image. Reduce an image or selection, and the program must decide which pixels to discard. Rotate, skew, or otherwise distort the same image, and some calculations must be done to figure out what new arrangement of pixels is needed to reorient the selection in its new configuration. All of this magic is done by the process called interpolation.

Interpolation uses mathematical algorithms to create or delete pixels as required based on the values of the pixels in the original image. The process is relatively simple if you're just enlarging or reducing an image, particularly if even-number magnifications or reductions are involved, say, from 600×600 pixels to 1200×1200 or 300×300 pixels.

Photoshop does not, as you might guess, just duplicate every pixel to enlarge an image, or discard every other pixel to reduce an image. Instead, it uses a more sophisticated method. To double the size of an image, the eight pixels that border each pixel are examined to get an accurate image of the four pixels needed to replace it. To halve the size, clumps of four pixels are averaged to determine the value of the one that will replace them. This works great when you're changing the size in multiples or fractions of 2, but not so great by any other factor. For this reason, Photoshop does a great job if you want to increase the size of an image by 200 or 400 percent, or reduce it by 50 or 25 percent with optimum results. But it doesn't do quite so good a job if you want to enlarge an image by 173 percent or reduce it to 31 percent of the original size.

In these cases, Photoshop has particular difficulty reproducing objects with diagonal lines, which are difficult enough to represent using square pixels without throwing unevenly added (or subtracted) picture elements into the mix. For the same reasons, rotating images (especially in increments other than 90 degrees) and slanting or skewing selections can produce rough-looking, jaggy results.

The most important thing you should remember about interpolation is that it's always just an approximation of the pixels that should be in an image, so you should minimize the number of times Photoshop has to put your image through this wringer.

4 Drag the handle to see how the image can be rotated. It doesn't matter which of the eight selection handles you drag. All of them simply rotate the image around its center point. If you hold down the Shift key, rotation will be constrained to 15-degree increments.

5 Press Escape to return the image to its original state.

STEP 4: SKEWING THE TEXT

We can now experiment with an effect that you might want to apply to your own work. Skewing is a way of slanting the selection in one direction or another. The following steps show you how skewing works:

1 Select the text using the lasso tool, as before.

2 Choose Layer ⇨ Transform ⇨ Skew, and the selection handles will appear.

3 Next, drag the handle in the upper left corner. Notice you can move it up, down, left, or right, and the other corner handles remain in place. Each time you grab one of the corner handles (but not the handles in the center of each line in the bounding box) you can drag vertically or horizontally, but not a combination. This has the effect of slanting the image, as you can see in Figure 11-5.

FIGURE 11-5
Skewing produces a slanted effect.

4 Grab one or more of the other corner handles, and drag to either side to produce an interesting effect, like the one shown in Figure 11-6. Photoshop uses interpolation to adjust the pixels of the selection so they fit in the new area you've defined with the Skew tool.

5 Press Escape to cancel the transformation, or press Return to make it permanent, and then save the file to disk (if you'd like to save the effect).

STEP 5: DISTORTING THE TEXT

Distortion is like skewing, but with some added features, as you'll see by following these directions:

1 Select the text using the lasso tool, if it isn't still selected from the previous exercise.

2 Choose Layer ⇨ Transform ⇨ Distort, and the selection handles will appear again.

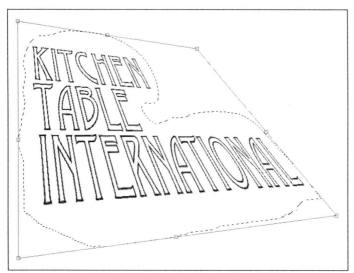

FIGURE 11-6
Several changes can produce a slanted effect like this one.

3 Grab our old friend, the upper-left selection handle, and drag it.
Notice that when Distort is active, you can drag the handle freely,
vertically, horizontally, and diagonally, while the other corner handles
remain in place. You can even drag the handle inward, toward the
interior of the original selection (which isn't possible with Skew) to
produce an effect like the one shown in Figure 11-7.

FIGURE 11-7
The Distort tool lets you twist the selection freely.

STEP 6: CHANGING THE PERSPECTIVE

The Perspective tool creates a 3D effect by moving two of the selection handles in opposite directions, making the outer borders of your selection converge on an imaginary vanishing point elsewhere in the image. To learn how this works, try the following:

1   Select the text using the lasso tool, if required.

2   Choose Layer ⇨ Transform ⇨ Perspective, and the selection handles appear.

3   Grab the upper-left selection handle, and notice how the upper right handle moves in the opposite direction when you drag horizontally. When you drag vertically, the handle in the lower left has been moved in the opposite direction, as Figure 11-8 shows. This is a great technique for producing images that look as if they were printed on a piece of paper that is laid out in front of the viewer.

FIGURE 11-8
Dragging any corner handle produces a perspective effect.

STEP 7: ROTATING IN INCREMENTS/FLIPPING

You learned how to rotate a selection freely in Step 3. Photoshop also enables you to rotate images in fixed increments of 180 degrees, 90 degrees clockwise, and 90 degrees counterclockwise, and to flip a selection horizontally or vertically. While the techniques are simple enough that it hardly deserves an exercise of its own, you might want to follow these directions to see how the process works:

1   Select the text using the lasso tool.

2   Choose Layer ⇨ Transform ⇨ Rotate 180 Degrees. The text rotates in a half-circle. Press Escape to cancel.

3   Choose Layer ⇨ Transform ⇨ Rotate 90 Degrees CW (or 90 Degrees CCW) to watch the image rotate one-quarter turn. Press Escape to cancel.

4   Choose Layer ⇨ Transform ⇨ Flip Horizontal (or Flip Vertical) to reverse the image. Press Escape to cancel.

STEP 8: USING NUMERIC TRANSFORMATIONS

Numeric Transformations are a very cool way of applying sets of transformations to selections using fixed amounts, because you can "dial in" the exact movements you want. This is also our chance to learn how to use the great new Actions palette. Here's what to do:

1   Select the text using the lasso tool.

2   Locate the Actions palette (use Window ⇨ Show Actions if it's not visible), and choose New Action from the palette's fly-out menu. This palette enables you to record sets of actions—called a *macro*—and play them back at any time, which can be a tremendous time saver if the list of steps is long or complex. The New Action dialog box appears in Figure 11-9.

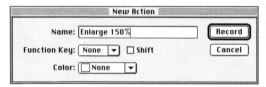

FIGURE 11-9

Use the New Action dialog box to set up a macro for the Actions palette.

3   In the Name field, type in `Enlarge 150%`. Note that you can assign a shortcut key to actions you plan to reuse often. For now, though, you can just click Record to start capturing the steps you will put in this macro. The name of the action you are recording appears in the Actions palette, and a red button at the bottom of the palette appears, showing that recording has begun.

4   Select Layer ⇨ Transform ⇨ Numeric. The Numeric Transform dialog box appears, as shown in Figure 11-10.

FIGURE 11-10
You can use the Numeric Transform
dialog box to apply several different
effects at once.

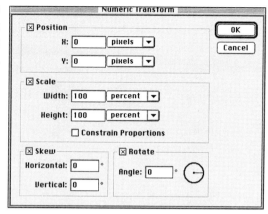

5 Note that four effects are available in this dialog box. Use the Position fields to enter the coordinates of a selection (in case you want to perform the operation on a specific location of your image, rather than the area you have currently selected). You can use the Scale section to enter enlargement or reduction values, using percent, pixels, inches, or other units of measurement. Use the Skew section to enter degrees of horizontal or vertical tilting, and use the Rotate section's Angle field to store the amount of rotation you want. By entering any or all of the values available for these effects, you can apply several kinds of transformation, using numeric values, from this single dialog box.

6 Make sure Percent is chosen as the unit of measurement in the Scale area in the drop-down list box to adjust the value displayed, if necessary.

USING ACTIONS

Once you work with Photoshop for awhile, you'll find the Actions palette a useful tool for doing repetitive tasks. In this chapter, we recorded a simple macro that enlarges a selection by 150 percent. You can capture much longer series of actions, such as applying a set of filters and then saving a file in a particular file format. Some of the other commands you'll want to learn include the following:

- ⊡ Associating a shortcut key with an action.
- ⊡ Saving groups of actions to disk, and loading them as required, so you can keep only those macros you need for a particular project on your Actions palette.
- ⊡ Using the Actions palette's batch mode that enables you to apply a macro to groups of files.
- ⊡ Setting up actions as a group of buttons you can press to start their playback.

7 Check the Constrain Proportions box, then type in 150 in the Width field. Note that the Height field will be changed to 150 percent to match.

8 Click on OK. The selection will be enlarged by 150 percent.

9 Next, select Stop Recording from the Actions palette's fly-out menu. The macro you have captured will be displayed in the palette, as shown in Figure 11-11. You can apply this macro to any selection in the future by making your selection, then highlighting the action in the palette, and clicking the "play" button (the right-pointing triangle) at the bottom of the palette.

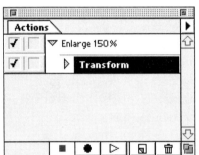

FIGURE 11-11
The new macro is shown in the Actions palette.

STEP 9: USING FREE TRANSFORM

Now that you've learned about the various transformation options in Photoshop, the final step is to become acquainted with the Free Transform facility, which puts the scale, rotate, and skewing commands at your disposal all at once. Try it out, as follows:

1 Select the text with the lasso.

2 Choose Layer ➪ Free Transform (or press Command-T).

3 Selection handles form around the image, as noted previously. However, you can now perform several different transformations, depending on what you do next. Move the cursor inside the selection, and drag. Note that the selection moves.

4 Move the cursor to a corner handle and drag. You can scale the image just as if you had used the Scale command. Shift-drag rescales the image proportionately, as you might expect.

5 Move the cursor outside a corner handle, and it will change into the curved double-arrow of the Rotate tool. You can now drag to rotate the image. Hold down the Shift key to constrain the rotation to 15-degree increments.

6 Hold down the Command key and drag a handle to distort the image.

7 Hold down the Option key and drag a center handle to distort the image symmetrically.

8 Use Command-Shift to drag a handle and skew the image.

9 Try Command-Option-Shift and drag a handle to apply perspective changes, using either corner or center points

10 If you want to save any of these transformations, press Return. Otherwise press Escape to cancel.

WHAT YOU'VE LEARNED

While this chapter was something of a "breather" from your client, Kitchen Table International, you probably still found it packed with useful new techniques that you can apply to your work. These include the following basic tricks:

- You can change the size of the canvas that an image appears on, using the Layer ⇨ Canvas Size command.
- Images can be scaled proportionately, or either horizontally or vertically alone.
- Interpolation is the process Photoshop uses to represent images that have been enlarged, reduced, or distorted.
- Images can be rotated freely, or in fixed increments.
- Images can also be flipped left or right and vertically.
- Skewing slants a selection or image.
- Distorting can change the shape of an image radically.
- The Perspective tool gives a 3D effect to an otherwise flat-looking image.
- Numeric transformations can be used to enter changes in fixed units, and to apply multiple changes of this type simultaneously.
- The Actions palette can record macros that you can apply to individual files or batches of files.
- Free Transform can apply scaling, rotating, and skewing effects.

In the next chapter, you'll learn some more sophisticated techniques for restoring a damaged photograph.

Restoring a Damaged Photo
More Sophisticated Retouching Techniques

THE PROJECT

Kitchen Table International is preparing to unleash its new writeable CD-ROM drive, codenamed WORIL (write once, read if lucky) and would like to avoid the expense of having Scott's brother-in-law, the wedding photographer, buy a new single-use camera just to make a product shot. Would it be possible for you to reuse a photo of KTI's original CD-R drive? This model, which never sold very well because of an unfortunate tendency to explode unexpectedly, is basically the same. The chief difference is an indicator light on the front panel, which was modified because its main function was to flash brightly just before the unit exploded, and the engineering staff has the MTBE (mean time between explosions) up to 100,000 hours. The indicator light should be green now, instead of red. You'll also have to change the background and remove some faded and darkened spots, as Scott had been using the picture as a mouse pad. You've wanted to explore some more sophisticated retouching techniques, so this is your chance.

THE TOOLS
- ☐ Rubber Stamp, Clone (aligned), Clone (non-aligned)
- ☐ Darken, lighten calculations
- ☐ Select, Color Range
- ☐ Noise filter

You learned to use the rubber stamp tool in Chapter 6, but we intentionally kept the techniques simple so you'd become comfortable with this cloning tool. Now the gloves are off, and you are ready to learn some more advanced ways of putting this tool to work. We're going to fix the picture by using the rubber stamp's Clone (aligned) and Clone (non-aligned) modes, then darken and lighten areas using calculations, and finish up by selecting the background using the Color Range commands.

The rubber stamp is actually one of the most flexible tools in your arsenal. The secret is in the Rubber Stamp Options palette, shown in Figure 12-1.

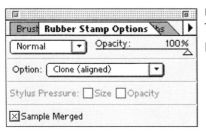

FIGURE 12-1

The Rubber Stamp Options palette has three main options.

There are three main options for the rubber stamp that we'll explore in this chapter are as follows:

- ⊡ **OPACITY**   This option controls the transparency of the cloned area you place on your image. With the slider set to 100 percent, the cloned portion completely obscures the underlying image. A lower opacity setting allows more of the original image to show through.

- ⊡ **BLENDING OPTION**   This drop-down list includes seven choices: Clone (aligned), Clone (non-aligned), Pattern (aligned), Pattern (non-aligned), From Snapshot, From Saved, and Impressionist. These settings control what image or portion of an image the rubber stamp tool uses as its source.

- ⊡ **MODES**   Although unlabeled, the drop-down list box just to the left of the Opacity slider contains the available calculation modes for merging your cloning source image with the destination image you are overpainting. You'll find almost one and a half dozen choices here, so we won't list them now. You'll learn a little about calculations in this chapter, and more later in the book.

The other options in the Rubber Stamp Options palette include the following:

- ⊡ **STYLUS PRESSURE (SIZE AND OPACITY)** Photoshop supports pressure-sensitive tablet-style pointing devices from Wacom and other vendors, and if you have one installed, two checkboxes will appear that enable you to activate the stylus size and opacity settings you have defined in the tablet's control panel.

- ⊡ **SAMPLE FROM MERGED** This checkbox is easy to understand. If you're cloning an image with the rubber stamp, check this box if you want Photoshop to clone image information from all the layers that happen to be visible. Uncheck it if you'd like Photoshop to clone only from the active layer.

Find the cd-r.tif file on the accompanying CD-ROM and copy it to your hard disk. As you work through the exercises, save the file from time to time so you'll have intermediate stages to examine later on. Now, get started working on this picture.

CD \see-dee'\ *n* Compact Disc. A technology created by Philips and Sony that replaced the phonograph record, most video game cartridges, and that huge stack of 32 floppy disks required to install minuscule software applications. The "disc" nomenclature was implemented to differentiate the CD from computer floppy disks, a convention that all computer users and their spell checkers ignore when referring to them.

CD-R \see-dee-ar'\ *n* Compact Disc–Recordable. A technology that empowers individual users to place incorrect data, defective images, and other computer files in immutable form onto a CD-ROM, where it cannot be changed and will theoretically reside for all eternity in commemoration of the user's error(s). In practice, the archival life of CD-R disks ranges from 10 to 30 years, which will be much longer than there are CD-ROM drives available capable of playing them.

STEP 1: FIXING BACKGROUND DEFECTS WITH CLONE (ALIGNED)

At times you'll want to copy an image from one place to another, but at other times you won't care about duplicating the exact image in the new location. We'll see why when we try to fix a dust spot in the background of our image. Just follow these directions:

1 Open the cd-r.tif file, as shown in Figure 12-2. You'll notice it has darkened and faded spots, a splotchy background, and other defects that need to be corrected.

FIGURE 12-2
The cd-r.tif file is full of defects.

2 Zoom in on the faded spot in the background at the right of the drive itself in the photo. You have two ways to correct this image. In Chapter 6, you used the Clone (aligned) mode to copy pixels from an area that was similar to the portion of your image you wanted to cover up. You'll recall that you positioned the cursor in the source location and Option-clicked. The next time you clicked in the area to be fixed, Photoshop started copying pixels centered around that source area. That is, if you moved the rubber stamp up, pixels from above the original source spot were copied. Move it to the right, and pixels to the right of the original area were duplicated. You can repeat the technique with this image.

3 In the Brushes palette, choose the smallest brush in the middle row of brushes.

4 Next, click the rubber stamp tool to activate it. Make sure Clone (aligned) is showing in the Option field.

5 Move over an area of the background just a little to the right of the CD-R drive, and Option-click to define a new source area. The arrow in Figure 12-3 shows where you should click.

FIGURE 12-3
Click here to define the rubber stamp's source location.

6 Move the cursor over to the center of the white faded spot, and click a few times. As you'd expect, pixels from the source spot, marked with a cross-hair (if you've set brushes and cursors to their precision setting in the Preferences box as Chapter 2 directed), are copied over the white pixels in the destination. Figure 12-4 shows what's going on.

FIGURE 12-4
Cloning from the source point we selected copies pixels over those in the defect.

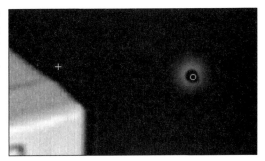

7 You can stop clicking at any time, and resume at any point. The source location stays the same, and your clicks with the rubber stamp always copy pixels in relation to it. To check that out, start painting on the left side of the white spot. Notice how the cross-hair marker moves left, so that eventually you begin copying pixels from the CD-R drive itself, as shown in Figure 12-5. That's not what we want. There are better ways to do this.

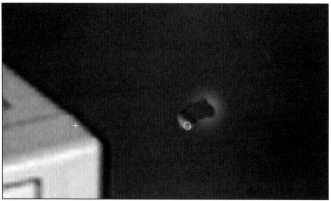

FIGURE 12-5
Now we're copying pixels from the drive itself, as the source
point moves with the cursor.

STEP 2: IMPROVING BACKGROUND FIXES WITH CLONE (NON-ALIGNED)

Clone (aligned) works best when the area you want to use as the source is big enough
to cover the destination area once you start copying. If not, you need to continually
redefine your source and copy more pixels. We could have selected a different source, of
course, that was not so close to the CD-R drive, but we wanted you to see what happens
under problematic circumstances. Next, try Clone (non-aligned) to see the difference.
Here's how to try it:

1   In the Rubber Stamp Options palette, select Clone (non-aligned).

2   Move the cursor to roughly the same point that you used to define the
    source before, and Option-click.

3   Next, move back to the white spot, and start painting. Notice that, as
    you copy pixels, the source point does move around, as before.
    However, as soon as you release the mouse and click again, the source
    jumps back to the original location. Each new set of strokes starts from
    the source you defined with Option-click. Consequently, you can paint
    over the white spot using the same small set of pixels without drawing
    on those in the CD-R drive. The image now looks like Figure 12-6.

FIGURE 12-6
Clone (non-aligned) enables you to copy over pixels from a fixed point.

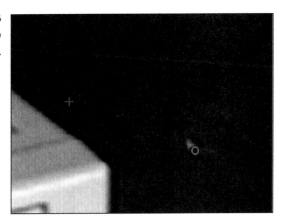

SOME RUBBER STAMP TIPS

Use Clone (aligned) when you have broad expanses to copy from, or you want to copy an entire object (say, to place a duplicate of some ornamentation or a flower in another location). Clone (aligned) also works if you are willing to constantly redefine your origin point, which may be a good idea if you want an unobtrusive effect rather than a straight copy. Clone (non-aligned) works if you're copying from a limited area (say, a small textured surface) and don't want to create a duplicate image at the destination.

One of the dangers of Clone (aligned) is that, because the origin point moves with the cursor, it may eventually be drawn into an area that you've already cloned. What happens then is that you start cloning a clone, producing an unpleasant fish-scaly effect as the same area is duplicated over and over. To avoid this problem, use a larger area and watch the origin cross-hair closely, or use Clone (non-aligned) or one of the other techniques in this chapter.

Photoshop can also clone from a copy of a file you have saved on disk, or from a snapshot that the program saves in a special buffer area. The chief difference between these two methods is that the snapshot is a temporary copy that is lost when you exit the program or take another snapshot, while the saved program is permanent and may be reused. Why would you want to clone from an exact copy of the same image? One reason would be to restore an image that you changed in some unsatisfactory way. You can clone back the parts you want restored, while leaving any other modifications you made to the image alone.

STEP 3: CLONING WITH DARKEN

For this step, we're going to explore Photoshop's calculation modes to discover one way to darken pixels that are too light. Photoshop can perform certain types of calculations when cloning—comparing a pixel in the current image with the same pixel in the copy, and modifying the painted pixels accordingly. Follow these directions to get a closer look at how this works:

1   Zoom in on the light area of the CD-R drive on the left side of the
    device. The target area appears in Figure 12-7. As you can see, much
    of the detail is there, but obscured by the white spot. We could simply
    clone similar detail from elsewhere in the image, but might not get an
    exact match. Instead, we'll use the rubber stamp.

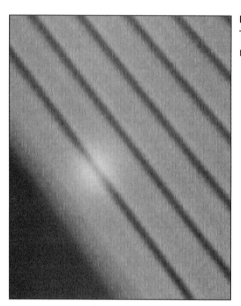

FIGURE 12-7
The area that has been
marred by a light spot.

2   From the Rubber Stamp Options palette, change the calculation mode
    from Normal to Darken in the list box to the left of the Opacity slider.
    In this mode, Photoshop compares each pixel from the source area to
    the destination pixel. The value of the darker of the two pixels is applied
    in either case. So, any pixels that are already darker in the edited area
    will be untouched. If the pixels are lighter, they'll be replaced by the
    cloned pixels. If you choose to clone from an area that is very similar to
    the area being edited, the changes can be quite subtle and pleasing.

3   We need to make the "rib" on the drive and its surrounding area
    darker. Option-click in the image in an area that hasn't been marred
    by the white spot. (We used the next rib over toward the right.) Then
    move to the lighter area and paint. The darkened image is shown in
    Figure 12-8.

4   Zoom in on the area of the CD-ROM (the disk) that is darkened.

FIGURE 12-8
The image has been darkened by cloning with the Darken calculation.

5 Change the clone calculation mode to Lighten.

6 Use the dark area near the darkened area as the source, then paint with the rubber stamp. The image will be lightened, reducing the dark-colored defect. Figure 12-9 shows the before and after images.

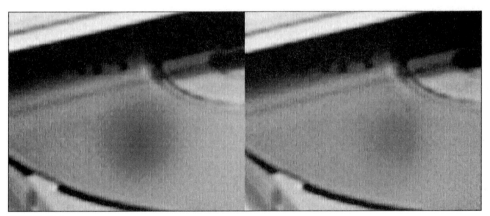

FIGURE 12-9
The dark spot (at left) has been lightened at right.

7 Use what you've learned in this step to remove any of the other light spots you see in the image. It will look like Figure 12-10 when you're finished.

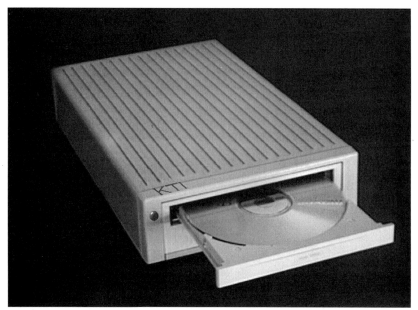

FIGURE 12-10
The image with the dark and light spots removed looks like this.

STEP 4: SELECTING THE BACKGROUND WITH COLOR RANGE

The folks at KTI don't like the background of this image. It's a little motley, for one thing. Unfortunately, that quality makes it harder to select the background using the magic wand tool, because a very broad range of pixels must be selected. It's likely the magic wand will grab a portion of the CD-R drive along with the background. Using the pen tool to outline the drive would take a long time. We can try another technique, and learn a new way to select—by color range. Just follow these directions:

1   Choose Select ⇨ Color Range. The Color Range dialog box pops up, as shown in Figure 12-11. The window in the center shows the portion of the CD-R image that has been selected, which, at the moment is nothing. So, the window will be mostly dark. We can select parts of the image using one of several tools.

2   In the Select field, make sure Sampled Colors is showing from the drop-down list box. From the list you can also select ranges of colors—from reds, yellows, and greens, to cyans, blues, and magentas, as well as highlights, midtones, and shadows. Or, you can choose only colors that are out of gamut (beyond the ability of your current color model to reproduce).

Getting Maximum Use from an Image

COLOR 1-1
These images were created simply by selecting areas of a blank Photoshop document, and then filling them with linear and radial gradients, as you can see in the three images here.

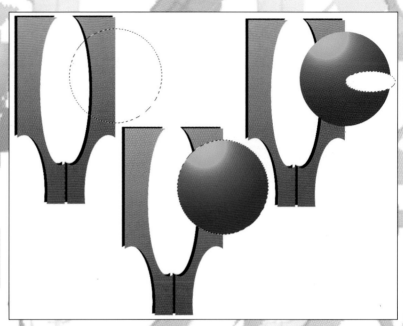

COLOR 1-2
The large, square image in the figure was recycled by using it as a brush and various colors of "paint" (see Chapter 2). Then, at lower right, a part of the same image was used yet again by applying the Spherize filter to turn it into a button.

Touring Photoshop's Variations Dialog Box

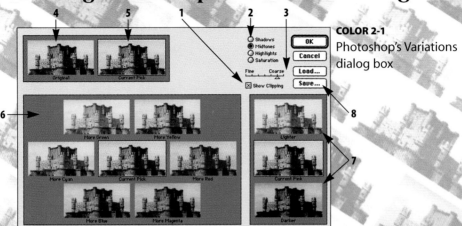

COLOR 2-1
Photoshop's Variations dialog box

1. If you check the Show Clipping box, hues that can't be represented by a particular variation will be displayed in bright neon colors.

2. You can adjust Shadows, Midtones, Highlights, and Saturation separately with these radio buttons.

3. Adjust this slider to select fine or coarse adjustments.

4. This is your unaltered image.

5. This is a preview of your image with the current modifications applied.

6. These six variations surround your original image, so you can select a color correction by comparing the different possibilities.

7. Click on the Lighter or Darker previews to lighten or darken your image.

8. When you're finished making modifications, click this Save button to apply the changes.

Compositing Images

COLOR 2-2
Each of the elements you see here was created in a separate layer and then carefully merged to produce these composite images.

Applying Special Effects

COLOR 3-1
The Diffuse Glow filter produced this soft effect.

COLOR 3-4
The Plastic Wrap filter coats the image with a glossy surface.

COLOR 3-2
Photoshop's Note Paper filter can create interesting embossed effects like this.

COLOR 3-5
The Facets filter is a quick way to produce a painterly effect.

COLOR 3-3
The Dry Brush filter transforms the image into a painting.

COLOR 3-6
Lighting Effects with the texture option created this etched metal look.

Using Sample Filter Effects

COLOR 4-1
The original, unaltered image

COLOR 4-2
Lens Flare filter

COLOR 4-3
Unsharp Mask filter

COLOR 4-4
Find Edges filter

COLOR 4-5
Lighting
Effects filter

COLOR 4-6
Wind filter

COLOR 4-7
Emboss filter

COLOR 4-8
Radial Blur filter,
Zoom setting

COLOR 4-9
Trace contour,
inverted

Using More Sample Filter Effects

COLOR 5-1
The original, unaltered image

COLOR 5-4
Ink Outlines filter

COLOR 5-7
Solarize filter

COLOR 5-2
Palette Knife filter

COLOR 5-5
Patchwork filter

COLOR 5-8
Pinch filter

COLOR 5-3
Craquelure filter

COLOR 5-6
Poster Edges filter

COLOR 5-9
Watercolor filter

Restoring a Photo with Cloning

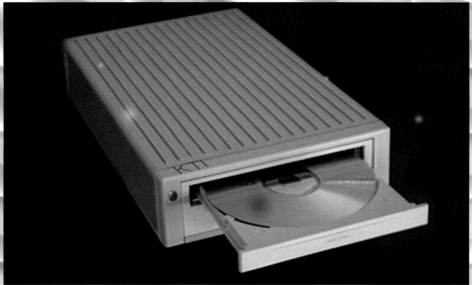

COLOR 6-1
This damaged product shot needs a lot of work.

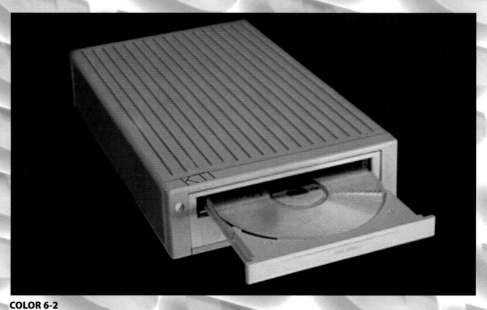

COLOR 6-2
A judicious use of the rubber stamp cloning tool, some Adjustment Layers, and a few other tricks, transforms the picture into this winner.

Combining Images with Calculations

You can use Photoshop's channel calculations to combine two layers, such as this castle and text overlay, using algorithms that control how they blend together.

COLOR 7-1
In Normal mode, the pixel values of the two layers are combined to produce this version.

COLOR 7-4
In Multiply mode, the pixel values of the two channels are multiplied together and then divided by 255, producing a darker color than the original. In this example, the text in both the lighter and darker areas of the image has been made darker.

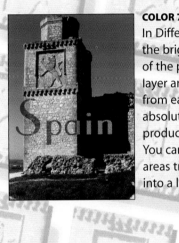

COLOR 7-2
In Difference mode, the brightness values of the pixels in each layer are subtracted from each other, and the absolute value of the result produces the new channel. You can see how the lighter areas transform the text color into a lighter blue tone.

COLOR 7-5
In Darken mode, the darker of the two pixels in the pair of channels is displayed, as in this example.

COLOR 7-3
In Luminosity mode, Photoshop examines the two channels and replaces each pixel with one that combines the hue and saturation values of the base channel with the luminance of the underlying channel. As you can see in this example, the text takes on the brightness properties of both channels.

COLOR 7-6
In Lighten mode, the lighter of the two pixels in the pair is displayed.

Making Color Corrections

COLOR 8-1
This image has some serious color and density problems.

COLOR 8-2
After correction with Color Balance Adjustment layer and levels command, the image looks like this.

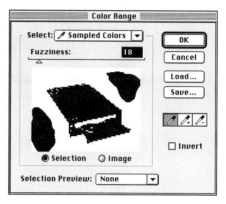

FIGURE 12-11

The Color Range dialog box can be used to make selections by color.

3 The Fuzziness slider controls how closely to the sampled color a hue must be to be added to the color range selection. Move this slider to 18 (this slider operates on the same principle as the Tolerance field in the Magic Wand Options dialog box, first described in Chapter 1).

4 Click the Eyedropper icon in the dialog box, and move the cursor over the image in the preview window, or in the actual document window, which remains visible behind the dialog box. Click anywhere in the background. All the pixels in the image with that color will be selected, as well as those of the same hue within a brightness range of 18 (plus or minus 9). Selected pixels will turn white, letting you see clearly which parts of the background have not yet been selected. The dialog box will look like the one shown in Figure 11-12.

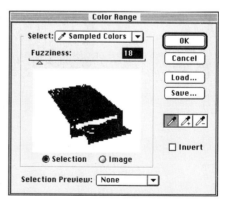

FIGURE 12-12

Some of the background pixels have been selected.

5 Click the Eyedropper icon with the plus next to it, and click again in the preview window on any pixels in the background that have not been selected. Repeat until you've specified a color range that includes the entire background. Because the background is a purple color, and none of that color is included in the CD-R, you should be able to select it in this way without grabbing any of the drive's pixels. You may add pixels by holding down the Shift key as you click with they eyedropper, or subtract them by holding down the Option key, just as you can when making any other kind of selection.

6   Click on OK to view your selection. If you've missed any pixels, you can round them up with the lasso (pressing Shift as you draw to add the pixels to the current selection), or choose Select ➪ Color Range again, and add pixels using the dialog box. Extra pixels you don't want in the selection can be removed with the lasso while holding down the Option key.

TIP Although we worked with the entire image here, in other cases you might want to use Color Range to add or subtract pixels from a selection you already have.

STEP 5: IMPROVING THE BACKGROUND

Now that we have the background selected, we can clean it up a little and add some effects. To do that, follow these directions:

1   Choose Select ➪ Save Selection to save the background selection. This might be a good time to save a copy of the current file to disk, so you'll have it if something goes wrong in the next few steps. (Don't worry, we're not planning anything dangerous!)

2   Next, select the eyedropper tool from the toolbox and choose a color from the image background, and make it Photoshop's current foreground color.

3   Press Option-Delete to replace all the tone in the background with the color you just selected. You'll recall that pressing Delete fills a selection with the background color; Option-Delete is the opposite: It fills the selection with the foreground color.

4   Select Filter ➪ Noise ➪ Add Noise to add a little texture to the background. The Add Noise dialog box pops up, as Figure 12-13 shows.

FIGURE 12-13
You can use the Noise filter's dialog box to add texture.

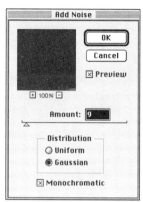

5 Click the Gaussian radio button in the Distribution box, check the Monochromatic box, and set the Amount slider to 9. Click on OK to apply the filter. The image so far will look like Figure 12-14 (please refer to Figure 12-14 on the accompanying CD-ROM to get the full effect in color).

FIGURE 12-14
The image so far looks like this.

STEP 6: CHANGING THE COLORS

If you're working along, you'll notice that the colors are a little drab. Your first impulse might be to play with the color balance to see if you can brighten things up a little. However, that's not the way colors work. Even if the hues are more or less accurate from a color-balance perspective, they may still lack richness or saturation. In the next exercise, we'll show you how Adjustment Layers, which we used in Chapter 7 to modify hue, can be applied to create interesting saturation effects. Just follow these directions:

1 Load the background selection you saved in the first directive of Step 5, previously.

2 From the menu bar, choose Layers ➪ New ➪ Adjustment Layer. The New Adjustment Layer dialog box appears. Change the Type drop-down list box to read Hue/Saturation. Photoshop automatically fills in Hue/Saturation in the Name field. Opacity should be 100% and the mode set to Normal, as shown in Figure 12-15.

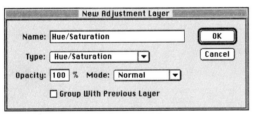

FIGURE 12-15
Create a new Adjustment Layer for Hue/Saturation.

3 We're going to create two different Adjustment Layers of the same type, so we need to rename this one. Move the cursor to the end of the Name field and add the word Background, so that this layer's name is now Hue/Saturation Background.

4 Click on OK once to exit from the New Adjustment Layer dialog box. The Hue/Saturation Layer dialog box immediately appears, but we don't want to work with it yet. Click on OK in the Hue/Saturation Layer dialog box to remove it from the screen. Your new Adjustment Layer appears in the Layers palette. This layer has a mask included, so that only the background will be affected by any of the modifications you make.

5 Select the original background layer of the image once more. Now, use Select ➪ Inverse (or press Shift-Command-I) to invert the selection, so that only the CD-ROM drive is included.

6 From the menu bar, choose Layers ⇨ New ⇨ Adjustment Layer once again. The New Adjustment Layer dialog box appears. The Type drop-down list box should still read Hue/Saturation. Change the name of this layer to Hue/Saturation CD-ROM. Click on OK to exit from this dialog box, and on OK in the next dialog box to remove it from your screen. The Layers palette should look like Figure 12-16. Notice that the mask icons are the opposite of each other.

FIGURE 12-16
The Layers palette has two new Adjustment Layers added.

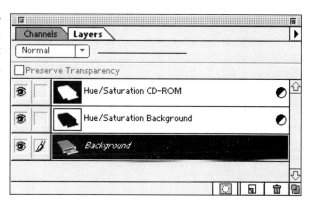

7 Double-click the Hue/Saturation CD-ROM adjustment layer. The Hue/Saturation Layer dialog box, shown in Figure 12-17, appears.

FIGURE 12-17
Use the Hue/Saturation Layer dialog box to add richness to colors.

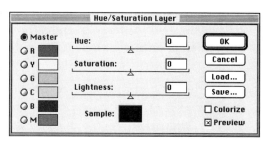

8 Notice that the Master radio button is checked. That means that the changes you make will be applied equally to all three color channels. Click the Red button, then move the Saturation slider to the left or right and watch what happens. Only the red hues become brighter, and the effects are most pronounced in the shadows. You could use this technique to add an interesting cast to the shadows of an image, as a special effect.

9 Click the Master radio button again when you finish experimenting with the individual color channel buttons. Our goal is to improve the richness of all the colors in the image.

10   Move the Saturation slider to the right until the colors become much more vibrant. We moved the control all the way to the +50 mark. You'll notice that the colors are brighter, but haven't changed hue in any way. They are still relatively accurate, if you ignore the richness of the color. Click on OK to accept this change.

11   Double-click the Hue/Saturation Background Adjustment Layer. Move the Saturation control to +50, and adjust the Lightness control by about +8. The background is now brighter and more colorful. Click on OK to accept the modification. Because all of these changes have been made on Adjustment Layers, you can save the file and come back at any time to make additional modifications.

STEP 7: RECOLORING THE INDICATOR LIGHT

Because this KTI product no longer explodes quite so often, you've been asked to change the indicator light from red to green. The Hue/Saturation control is perfect for this, too, and you can use an Adjustment Layer if you think you might need to come back and change the color back to red or some other color if the R&D staff is proved wrong about all those explosions. Just follow these directions:

1   Select the original background layer once more.

2   Choose the elliptical selection tool, and, while holding down the Option and Shift keys, position the cursor as close as you can to the center of the indicator light. Then drag a perfect circle that includes only the light.

3   If the circle isn't perfectly centered, as in Figure 12-18, you can move the selection itself by placing the cursor inside the selection (while the elliptical selection tool is still active), and then dragging to center the selection.

FIGURE 12-18
Create a circular selection around the indicator light.

4 Now, use Layer ⇨ New ⇨ Adjustment Layer to create yet another Hue/Saturation Layer. Name it Hue/Saturation Light. Click on OK to create the layer, which is masked to include only the indicator light.

5 Move the Hue slider to the right to change the color of the indicator light. Move it to about +100 to give the light a rich, green color. Click on OK to apply the change. You can always come back and change the light to another color at a later date.

6 Now, save the file. The finished image appears in Figure 12-19, although you can get a better look at it in the color insert (Figure Color 6-2).

FIGURE 12-19
The finished image looks like this.

WHAT YOU'VE LEARNED

You picked up quite a bit of information about the rubber stamp tool in this chapter, and got a quick introduction to Photoshop's calculation modes. Among the gems you gathered:

- ▫ The rubber stamp tool has three main options: Opacity, which controls the transparency of the cloned area placed on the image; Blending Option, which controls the portion of the image used as the source; and Calculations, which determine what (if any) mathematical operations Photoshop applies to the pixels being painted.

- ⊡ The rubber stamp also has a Stylus Pressure control for those who have a pressure-sensitive tablet pointing device, and a Sample Merged checkbox, which determines whether all visible layers are used as a cloning source, or only the active layer.

- ⊡ Clone (aligned) copies pixels from the source point and points around it to equivalent points in the image being edited, no matter how many times you stop and resume painting.

- ⊡ Clone (non-aligned) copies pixels from the source point, and resumes from that exact point when you stop and resume editing.

- ⊡ You should be careful when cloning images to make sure the source point doesn't stray into an area that has already been painted over with the Rubber Stamp, to avoid creating an unattractive repetitive pattern.

- ⊡ Photoshop can clone from a copy of a file, or a snapshot saved to a special buffer area.

- ⊡ The rubber stamp can use any of nearly one and a half dozen calculation modes, such as Darken or Lighten, that copy pixels only if they are darker or lighter (respectively) than the pixels being painted over.

- ⊡ You can use the Select ⇨ Color Range command to select areas based on their color.

- ⊡ You can create several different Adjustment Layers of the same type, each masked to affect a different portion of an image.

In the next chapter, we're going to learn how to import Encapsulated PostScript files as we create a postcard that KTI marketing types will pass out at trade shows.

Designing a Postcard

Placing an EPS File

THE PROJECT

The Kitchen Table International marketing director wants to pass out postcards at an upcoming trade show. He got this brilliant idea about using a photograph of Scott Hollerith's driveway to symbolize the company's unrelenting drive down the road to the future. You're given a scan that needs a bit of spiffing up, and some files containing Encapsulated PostScript type to place into the image. You'd always thought that Encapsulated PostScript was a time-release cold remedy, like histograms, and decide to sharpen your Photoshop skills with this new challenge.

THE TOOLS
    ▣ Select ⇨ Similar

    ▣ File ⇨ Place

    ▣ Quick Mask

By this time you've had at least a taste of most of Photoshop's key features, so the remaining chapters will cover more advanced capabilities of several tools you've already explored earlier. We're going to look at some more sophisticated selection options and learn how to import vector art and change it to a bitmap.

We'll be working with the road.tif, roadahd.eps, and pathto.eps files from the Chapter 13 folder on the CD-ROM, so you should copy them to your hard disk before we begin.

PostScript \post'skript\ *n* A technology designed to delay printouts from Photoshop through the needless conversion of a bitmapped image into the vector-oriented instructions of this page description language, which an interpreter built into the printer then converts back into the bitmaps used to print a page. From the Latin *postscriptum*, extraneous writing added after everything else is finished. See also *cash cow*.

STEP 1: SELECTING SIMILAR PIXELS

Our first step is to add a little interest to the sky area of the image. You learned how to select by color range in the previous chapter. Now, we'll discover another way of selecting noncontiguous pixels. Follow these directions:

1   Open the road.tif image that you copied from your CD-ROM. The basic picture we'll be working with looks like Figure 13-1.

FIGURE 13-1
The road to the future looks strangely like the driveway to the stately manor of KTI's president.

2 Double-click the magic wand tool. In the Magic Wand Options palette's Tolerance field, enter a value of 24.

3 Place the wand anywhere in the middle of the sky area and click. Shift-click in the other major contiguous areas of sky until a larger group of pixels is selected. Don't worry about the smaller areas. We just want to grab a large chunk of representative sky pixels.

4 Photoshop's Quick Mask feature is a good way to clearly see exactly which pixels have been selected. Click the Quick Mask icon in the toolbox (it's immediately below the color control boxes, and to the right). The screen will now look like Figure 13-2, with the unselected (masked) areas overlaid with a red tone, and the selected pixels left clear.

FIGURE 13-2
In Quick Mask mode, you can clearly see which pixels are selected.

5 Turn off Quick Mask again by clicking the icon to the left of the one you used to activate the mode.

6 Change the magic wand Tolerance to 8.

7 Next, choose Select ➪ Similar. Doing so tells Photoshop to grab pixels anywhere in the image that have values similar to those in the sky area you've already selected. Many of the extra little bits and pieces of sky between the tree branches will be selected, without the need for you to Shift-click with the magic wand to capture them one at a time.

8 Switch into Quick Mask mode again to see the results of your work so far. The image will look like Figure 13-3.

FIGURE 13-3
Select ⇨ Similar has grabbed additional pixels.

NOTE The Select ⇨ Similar command is useful when you want to select many pixels in a color image that may have similar brightness values, but may not be similar in color. Instead of selecting multiple colors, you can choose a range directly from your image, and let Photoshop find the similar pixels.

9 Notice how Photoshop has done a great job of grabbing all the sky pixels between the branches. However, it's also picked up some light-colored areas in the road and surrounding foliage. Still in Quick Mask mode, choose the Paint Brush, make sure the default black/white foreground/background colors are available and the brush's mode is set to Normal, and paint over the nonmasked areas in the road and foliage, so that only the sky itself is selected. Switch back to normal mode and save your selection.

USING QUICK MASK

Photoshop's Quick Mask mode is one of the most useful selection tools available. While in this mode, the nonselected area is displayed in a transparent red that allows the image underneath to show through, unless you toggle the image (using Option-click on the Quick Mask icon) so that the selected areas, instead, are shown in red. The translucent image makes it easy to view the area being masked (or selected).

You can add to the red-tinted area (which, remember, can represent either the masked area or the selection) by painting with any of the painting tools—including the very cool airbrush tool—and using black as your foreground color. The paint you lay down appears as red, instead of black, however.

You may remove part of the red-tinted area (representing either mask or selection) by painting with white or by using the eraser tool. In this case, the "paint" appears as a clear area that shows the image underneath. Choosing an intermediate shade of gray applies a semitransparent mask; that is, the area is partially selected as if you'd used the Feather selection option. Soft-edged brushes and the airbrush produce the same kind of feathered selection: hard in the center and fading off at the edges. Using Quick Mask in this way enables you to create soft-edged masks (or selections) easily, using the painting tools you already know how to use.

Other selection tools work normally while in Quick Mask mode, but they add or subtract from the masked or selected area only if you subsequently fill them with tone before exiting from Quick Mask mode.

When you click on the Standard Mode icon and exit, the red-painted areas will be turned into either a selection or masked area, depending on the mode you chose when activating the Quick Mask.

One thing that's worth repeating (yet again), Quick Mask's red tone can represent either the area that *is* going to be selected when you exit the mode, or the area that is *not* going to be selected. Make sure you know which is which. The best way to tell is to look at the Quick Mask icon: If the red tone represents a selection, the icon will be a gray circle inside a white rectangle, with a gray border around it. If the red tone represents the masked area, the icon will be a white circle inside a gray rectangle with a gray border around it. If you are not currently using Quick Mask mode, the same icon will be a white circle inside a gray rectangle, with a *white* border around it. You may want to switch back and forth a few times with a practice image until you learn to recognize the mode you're in.

STEP 2: ADDING INTEREST TO THE SKY

Now that we've selected the sky—even the little pieces between the branches—we can darken it while leaving the rest of the image untouched. Here's how to do it:

1 With the sky still selected from the previous step, choose Select ⇨ Feather, and type in 2 in the Feather Radius field. This setting allows the sky to blend in smoothly with the foliage after we've darkened it.

2 Next, select Image ⇨ Adjust ⇨ Levels from the menu bar. The Levels dialog box appears, as shown in Figure 13-4. Note that all the tones are concentrated at one end of the histogram.

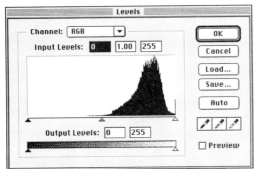

FIGURE 13-4
The Levels dialog box shows the tonal range of the selected sky.

3   Move the black and white point triangles so they correspond more closely to the actual tonal areas in the sky. Adjust the center gray triangle to the right to improve the contrast of the midtones.

4   Click on OK to apply the change. Your image will now look more like Figure 13-5.

FIGURE 13-5
The sky has been darkened using the Levels control.

WHAT'S ENCAPSULATED POSTSCRIPT?

You won't see Encapsulated PostScript spelled out very often; usually, the format is simply represented by its initials: EPS. It's a vector-oriented format that stores objects using mathematical terms rather than bitmap images, and, as such, is able to include objects, such as text, that can be scaled up or down precisely. As you might guess from its name, EPS was created as a format for the PostScript page description language, and is so called because it contains, or encapsulates, instructions for re-creating the image information in the same file that holds other page-formatting information and font instructions.

EPS files used directly by Photoshop must be saved in Adobe Illustrator (AI) or EPS formats. The program can open such files directly in document windows of their own, or you can "place" an EPS file into Photoshop, in which case it will automatically be loaded into a separate layer. You can also open the file in the original application, such as Illustrator, copy it to the Mac's Clipboard, then paste it into a Photoshop document. If you go that route, however, the Clipboard converts the vector image into a PICT bitmap, so you won't be able to resize it effectively in Photoshop after it's been pasted. However, if you drag and drop a vector image from Adobe Illustrator into a Photoshop window, the System Clipboard won't be used, and the image will not be converted to PICT en route.

However, if you select File ➪ Place and place the file instead, it appears with resizing handles that you can use to change its size or proportions before it is *rasterized* (converted into a bitmap). That's an important distinction, because it is often advantageous to resize an EPS graphic without losing resolution before you're forced to work with it as a POB (plain old bitmap).

Vector-oriented applications can save the text included in their files in one of two formats: as Adobe Type 1 outlines (which are editable as text when the file is re-opened by the vector-graphic program) or as curves (which can't be edited as if it were text; that is, you can't change fonts or retype characters even though the curves themselves can often be adjusted).

When text is saved in an EPS file as text, Photoshop must have the same fonts available that were used by the application that created the EPS file, and Adobe Type Manager must be installed on the computer. That won't be a problem if you created the file yourself on the same machine, and have ATM. If not, Photoshop will try to replace the font with Times, Helvetica, or Courier or a TrueType equivalent of the original font (if available).

Under some conditions, you'll get no font replacement at all, so your best choice may be to save the EPS file from the vector editor as curves (in Illustrator, you'd use the Create Outlines option) so Photoshop will be capable of faithfully reproducing the type. Actually, your best choice would probably be to finish your bitmap editing in Photoshop, if possible, and then import the image into Illustrator and add the type there, giving you the sharpest possible text, which you could also edit at a later point.

However, this is a Photoshop book, so this chapter concentrates on the reverse process: getting vector-oriented text placed into a bitmapped image.

STEP 3: IMPORTING A TEXT OUTLINE

The next step is to get those Encapsulated PostScript files into your image. If you must add existing text to a bitmapped image, this way is preferable to the method we used in Chapter 10, but KTI didn't give us that option, did they? You'll see how much easier the process works using this procedure. Follow these directions:

1   Use File ➪ Preferences ➪ General, and make sure the Anti-alias PostScript checkbox is marked, as shown in Figure 13-6. If so, Photoshop will smooth out rough lines that appear when it takes the precise vector outlines and changes them into bitmaps as EPS files are imported.

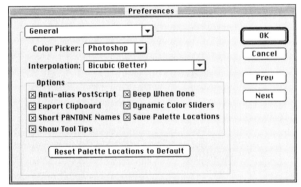

FIGURE 13-6
Make sure the Anti-alias PostScript checkbox is marked.

2   Select File ➪ Place and locate the roadahd.eps file you copied from your CD-ROM earlier. Click the Place button in the dialog box to put the text into its own layer.

3   The file will appear in a new layer, surrounded by a bounding box and selection handles, as Figure 13-7 shows.

FIGURE 13-7
A bounding box surrounds the placed EPS file.

4   You can drag the selection handles to resize or rotate the placed text using the same techniques you learned with Free Transform. That is, drag a handle to make the text taller, wider, or narrower; hold down the Shift key while dragging to preserve the aspect ratio; place the cursor outside the handle to rotate the image instead.

5 Make the text a bit smaller, to fit in the upper left corner of the road image, and then press Return to confirm the size and placement. Photoshop rasterizes the outlines and creates a bitmapped version. We'll provide no screen shot of the image at this point because the black text is difficult to see against the dark foliage, and we can't change it to another color until after it has been rasterized. Photoshop always places an EPS file with close to its original color values as specified in Illustrator. The gamuts may differ, however. We'll show the artwork with text in position at the beginning of the next step.

TIP Keep in mind that you can resize the placed graphic immediately after you've placed it, while the bounding box is still visible. You can cancel the placement if you change your mind by pressing Escape. But once you press Return, Photoshop rasterizes the text, and you can no longer resize it without the usual bitmap interpolation demons taking their toll. However, because the placed text is in its own layer, you can delete it and replace it at any time until it's finally merged with the other layers.

STEP 4: MODIFYING THE TEXT

Now we can change the placed EPS file to the white outline we want, and add the second batch of text from a different EPS file. Just follow these directions:

1 Make sure Photoshop's foreground and background colors are the default black/white (click the default colors icon in the color control box, or press D).

2 Activate the layer containing the placed text.

3 Select Edit ➪ Fill (if you're ready for another shortcut, you can also press Shift-Delete to pop up the Fill dialog box). From the drop-down list box in the Contents area of the Fill dialog box select the Background choice. Check the Preserve Transparency box so that only the text will be filled, and not the transparent background of the layer. The placed text will be changed to white, as shown in Figure 13-8.

4 Select File ➪ Place once more, and place the text file pathto.eps. Resize and deposit it in the lower right-hand corner, as shown in Figure 13-9.

FIGURE 13-8
The placed text has been converted to white.

FIGURE 13-9
The second line of text has been placed in the lower right corner.

5   Choose a bright color as the foreground hue from the Swatches palette. (We chose a bright blue that matched the sky.)

6   Finish by choosing Edit ⇨ Fill again, select Foreground for the contents, and make sure Preserve Transparency is checked.

Here's another trick for you, which lets you select all of something like this text, as long as it has more or less the same color:

7   Double-click the magic wand tool to bring the Magic Wand Options palette to the front. Change its tolerance level to 4, which enables the wand to grab some of the anti-aliased pixels at the edge of an image.

8 Next, with the most recently placed text layer still active, click with the magic wand anywhere inside one of the text characters. All of that character will be selected.

9 Choose Select ⇨ Similar from the menu bar. In most cases, only the pixels within the text will be selected, because you probably don't have other pixels in the image that happen to be that exact color, as you can see in Figure 13-10. This trick works even if you have already merged the layers.

FIGURE 13-10
Only the text has been selected.

10 To check to see if other pixels have been selected by the Select ⇨ Similar command, double-click on the Quick Mask icon, change the Opacity to 100 percent, and then click on OK. The entire image will be hidden, except for the selected text and any additional pixels that might have been selected by mistake, as you can see in Figure 13-11.

FIGURE 13-11
Quick Mask confirms that only the text has been selected.

11 You can perform other operations on the selected text, such as adding a gradient, stroking the outline with another color, or adding noise and a texture. We decided to copy the text layer, blur it using Gaussian Blur set to 4.0 pixels, fill the copied layer with a glowing yellow color, and then move that yellow glow layer so it lies underneath the text layer in the Layers palette. (This technique should sound familiar to you by now!) The final image appears in Figure 13-12.

FIGURE 13-12
The final postcard
image looks like this.

WHAT YOU'VE LEARNED

In this chapter you discovered how to place vector-based images into Photoshop and, more importantly, learned about some of the advantages and disadvantages of doing this. We also covered yet another way of selecting pixels and worked with the Quick Mask. Among the topics covered:

- Select ⇨ Similar is a fast way to select pixels that correspond to those already part of a selection.

- Quick Mask can show you clearly what pixels are or are not selected.

- You may toggle between having Quick Mask show the selected area or masked area with a transparent red tone by Option-clicking on the Quick Mask icon.

- Paint with black to the red-tinted area to add to the selection or mask. Paint with white to remove from the selection or mask. Use gray, and a translucent mask is created.

- ☐ Encapsulated PostScript (EPS) is a vector-oriented format that stores objects using mathematical terms rather than bitmapped images, and, as such, can include objects, such as text, that you can precisely scale up or down in size.

- ☐ Vector files used directly by Photoshop must be saved in Adobe Illustrator (AI) or EPS formats. Photoshop can also open PostScript files that have been printed to disk, although these are not in Encapsulated PostScript format.

- ☐ You can also open the vector file in the original application, copy it to the Mac's Clipboard, and then paste it into a Photoshop document, but it will be converted immediately to a bitmap with no opportunity to resize it.

- ☐ You can also drag vector files directly from an Adobe Illustrator window to a Photoshop window without having the outlines converted to a bitmap, which can be an important time-saver if you have both applications and are creating the vector file just prior to importing it into Photoshop.

- ☐ Vector-oriented applications can save the text included in their files either as Adobe Type 1 outlines or as curves. Photoshop may have some difficulty with the former, if the fonts are not available on your system, but curves are converted smoothly.

In the next chapter, we'll discover ways to create our own filters and effects, using Photoshop's Custom and Displace filters.

Creating Your Own Effects
Custom and Displace Filters

You knew you were in trouble when KTI's aging baby-boomer advertising director called to ask if you could come up with some "really groovy, far out images" for a retro-'60s ad campaign he's dreamt up. Thoughts of solarized, psychedelic images crossed your mind until you realized that Photoshop has several custom filter fabrication tools you haven't had a chance to try out. Even though the program already has nearly 100 filters built in, you figure your résumé could be enhanced if you added "created custom imaging effects for national ad campaign" to your accomplishments, and decide to experiment with Photoshop's Custom and Displace filters.

THE TOOLS
- Custom filter
- Displace filter

Most Photoshop books will tell you that Custom and Displace filters are "too hard" for beginners to handle, because they involve complex math and other stuff that only techies and advanced users enjoy toying with. The simple truth of most custom filters is that the average user probably won't find it worthwhile to learn all the mathematics and programming acumen involved in juggling pixels to be able to go out and intentionally create a specific kind of filter. However, Photoshop makes it easy enough to experiment with your own filters that it is definitely a good idea—and a lot of fun—to simply play around until you get something you like. You can always say, "I meant to do that!" when one of your serendipitous accidents looks terrific. No one ever has to see your mistakes.

This chapter introduces you to filters that enable you to create customized filter effects easily. We're going to take an image, transform it with a few custom filters, and then add a displacement map to really twist things around. You'll want to make a copy of the final CD-R image you created in Chapter 12, because that's going to be our basis for the following exercises.

convolution \con-vo-lu'-shun\ *n* **1:** A prison riot, the result of a conspiracy. **2:** The movement of a pair of satellites in their orbit. **3:** Something really complicated that filters do.

WHAT'S A CONVOLUTION?

A convolution is a series of mathematical operations performed on all the pixels in an image or selection. The process itself is a bit convoluted (hence, the name) because the algorithms are applied in turn to each pixel in an image, based on the values of the pixels that surround it, and which themselves are processed in turn. For example, a particular effect may start with a pixel at coordinates 1,1 (the upper left corner of an image), and then darken or lighten that pixel, depending on the values of its neighbors. Then, the process may move on to the pixel at coordinates 1,2 and adjust it based on the new values of its neighboring pixels. A sharpening filter may use a process like this to locate boundaries between pixels of different shades and darken the darker pixels while lightening the lighter pixels to increase the contrast (and thus the apparent sharpness) at those edges.

Filter convolutions are based on a matrix called a *kernel*. The pixel being transformed is represented by the center box or cell in the matrix, and its surrounding pixels by the cells that border it. Figure 14-1 shows a convolution kernel. The positive and negative numbers in each cell indicate how much the center pixel should be brightened or darkened in relation to the value of the pixel represented by that cell. Sounds confusing, doesn't it?

Fortunately, Photoshop makes it easy to experiment by typing in values and viewing the results. When you get an effect you like, just say to yourself, "I meant to do that!" and save the settings under a name of your choice for reuse at any time.

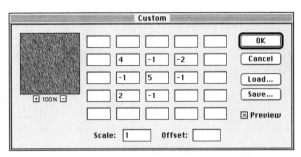

FIGURE 14-1
A typical convolution kernel, displayed in the Custom (filter) dialog box

Several kinds of kernels exist, each relating to a particular property of your image, including the color and spatial location of the pixel. Photoshop's Custom filter works only with the brightness values of pixels in relation to each other, so the effects it generates are limited to things affected by brightness, such as contrast, and 3D effects such as embossing, which are generated by lightening or darkening pixels to create ridges, valleys, and shadows.

STEP 1: EXPERIMENTING WITH CUSTOM FILTERS

The best way to explore the Custom filter's capabilities is to play with the filter and try out several different combinations of numbers to see what happens. First, we'll have you type in some numbers, and then we'll explain a little about what happened. Just follow these directions:

1 Load the final version of the cd-r.tif file you worked with in Chapter 12.

2 Select the background using the magic wand (with Tolerance set to 32), and then inverse the selection so only the drive itself is selected.

3 Choose Filters ⇨ Other ⇨ Custom to produce the Custom filter dialog box, as shown in Figure 14-2.

4 Move the cursor into the preview window area, and drag the view until the CD-R drive itself is visible in the window. This allows us to preview our effects.

5 Type the values shown in Figure 14-3 into the kernel's cells. The preview image takes on a marked embossed effect. We didn't do the math that would tell us we'd get this effect with these particular numbers; we experimented and through trial and error came up with this effect. The sidebar, How Do Custom Filters Work?, explains the process in more detail.

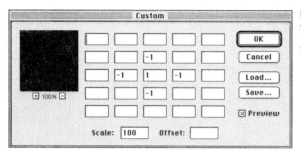

FIGURE 14-2
The Custom filter dialog box's default values look like these.

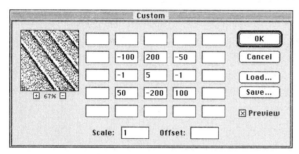

FIGURE 14-3
These settings produce an embossed effect.

6 Click on OK to apply the change. The image looks like Figure 14-4. You'd probably want to reselect the background and lighten it if you planned to use this image.

FIGURE 14-4
The CD-R picture with the custom embossed effect applied.

7 Press Command-Z to undo the effect.

HOW DO CUSTOM FILTERS WORK?

Photoshop's Custom filters simply change the brightness value of all the pixels in your image or selection. How they are modified is determined by the values you type into the kernel matrix, as outlined in Step 1.

The center box represents the pixel currently being processed. If you enter a 1 here, the pixel will remain unchanged. You may also brighten the pixel by typing in a value from 2 to 999, or darken it by typing in −2 to −999. Photoshop will multiply that pixel's brightness by the value you enter.

The rest of the boxes represent the neighboring pixels. You can multiply the brightness value of those pixels by positive or negative numbers to lighten or darken them. Placing a 2 in the box to the right of the center cell tells Photoshop to always multiply that adjacent pixel by 2.

In the Scale field, you may type a positive figure, which determines the strength of the effect: the higher the number, the more the effect is subdued. In the Offset field, you can enter a positive or negative number that is added to the Scale calculation.

Don't let these complex concepts scare you away from experimenting with Custom filters. We've seen Photoshop books that ignore this facility entirely on the (sound) theory that the average reader doesn't care about the math behind convolution kernels. That shouldn't mean, however, that you should shy away from experimenting to see what you get.

If you do get an effect you like, you can click the Save button and save the settings under a name you select. Use a descriptive name, such as "Ultra Sharp," so you'll know what you're getting when you load the filter later on. Photoshop doesn't let you save these filters as stand-alone effects—you must always open the Custom filter first, and then load the settings you previously stored.

STEP 2: TRYING MORE EFFECTS

While you're at it, you may as well try the following experiments:

1 Select Filter ⇨ Other ⇨ Custom to open the Custom filter dialog box, and type in the settings shown in Figure 14-5 for a particularly wild effect. Notice that we're playing with the Offset and Scale fields to see what happens.

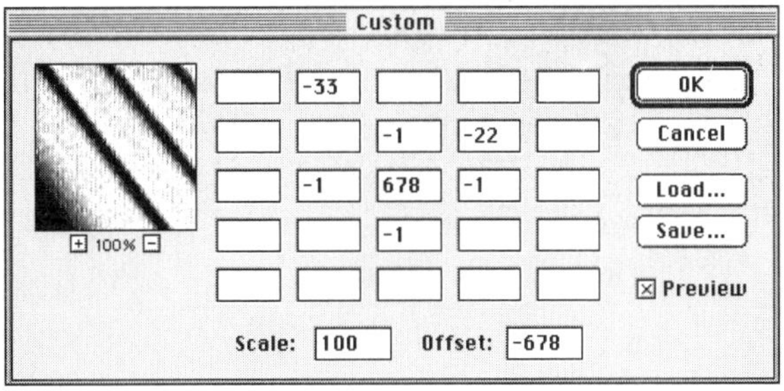

FIGURE 14-5
This filter builds up the color contrast dramatically.

2 Click on OK to see the results, as shown in Figure 14-6. You really need to load the original file (labeled Figure 14ie06.pct) on the CD-ROM to appreciate the interesting effect.

FIGURE 14-6
The final results of the color contrast filter look like this.

3 You can save the file if you like or press Control-Z to undo the effect and try the next one.

4 Select Filter ⇨ Other ⇨ Custom to open the Custom filter dialog box once more, and type in the values shown in Figure 14-7.

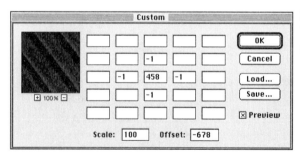

FIGURE 14-7
These settings produce a dramatic effect in the original image.

5 Click on OK to apply the change and view the effect, as shown in Figure 14-8. You can lighten the image a bit if the effect is too dark and dramatic for you.

6 Save this file under a name of your choice, because we're going to use it in the next exercise.

FIGURE 14-8

The photo has taken a darker, more foreboding turn after the filter was applied.

NOTE Custom filters vary in their effect depending on the image that you apply them to. While a filter that decreases contrast or enhances edges will perform essentially a similar function on all the images you try, the effects may be drastically different, because the new image already had lower contrast or fewer sharp edges than the picture you used to create the filter. This is true for all filters, of course, but you can avoid some disappointment if you realize this fact up front. Also, as Custom filters look different with different images, you may find that you use this filter most often to create a customized, one-off filter effect for a particular image, and perhaps not reuse that particular effect again.

STEP 3: USING A DISPLACEMENT MAP

The Displace filter adds a texture to an image by using the color values of a second must be either a color image or a grayscale image with a second channel—to govern how pixels should be moved (or displaced) in a diagonal line. Displacement maps are fun to experiment with. You can generate maps with fairly predictable results, as well as those that do things you never expected. Just follow these steps to see how the maps operate:

1 From the Chapter 14 folder on the CD-ROM, open the Gradient Displacement Map file so you can see the map we'll be working with. It looks like Figure 14-9.

2 From the menu bar, select Filter ⇨ Distort ⇨ Displace, and the Displace dialog box appears, as shown in Figure 14-10.

FIGURE 14-9
The displacement map has two gradients.

HOW DO DISPLACEMENT MAPS WORK?

While special algorithms determine how much and in which direction pixels are moved, the rules aren't particularly difficult to understand, even if the results are hard to visualize.

If the image being used as a displacement map is a grayscale image, the brightness value of the pixel in the map at a particular position is used to move the corresponding image pixel in the same relative position. That is, if the brightness of the map's pixel is 0 to 127, the image pixel is moved southwesterly, with 0 representing the maximum amount of movement, and 127 the least. If the map's pixel has a brightness value of 128, the image pixel stays put. If the map's pixel has a value of 129–255, the image pixel is moved in a northwesterly direction, with 255 representing the maximum amount of movement.

If the image being used as a displacement map is a color image, or a grayscale image with more than one channel, the Displace filter uses the first two channels of the grayscale image or the red and green channels of an RGB image, and ignores the rest. The values of a pixel in the map's first channel are used to determine the amount of horizontal movement, while the second channel's brightness value are used to vary the vertical movement.

The effects of some types of displacement maps are easy to predict. For example, one that includes a smooth dark-to-light gradient performs exactly as you might expect: the portions of the map that are dark produce the most displacement in one direction, with the movement tapering off to the mid-range gray tones (remember, with a brightness value of 128, the image pixel remains in place). Then the pixels reverse to the other direction as the tones get lighter and lighter in the map.

However, create a map that has a texture or random lines, and the effects will be weird. You can experiment with the displacement map provided on the CD-ROM, or search online sources such as America Online or CompuServe. Other Photoshop users have kindly uploaded their own personal favorite displacement maps for you to try out.

FIGURE 14-10

Use the Displace dialog box
to enter the relative amount
of displacement you want.

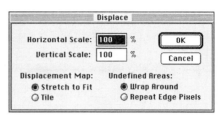

3 Make sure 100% appears in the Horizontal and Vertical Scale fields.
Click the Stretch to Fit button. These options tell Photoshop to
stretch the displacement map so that it is wide and tall enough to
match the image you're processing. Each image pixel must have a
corresponding pixel in the displacement map.

4 Click the Wrap Around button to instruct Photoshop to wrap the
displacement map around to fill any undefined areas with pixels.

5 Click on OK. The Choose a displacement map dialog box, shown in
Figure 14-11, pops up. Select the Gradient Displacement Map file.
Click Open to apply the map.

FIGURE 14-11

You can select a displacement
map from this dialog box.

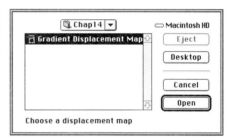

6 Use the Type tool and any serif font (that is, one that has the little
strokes at the ends of the characters, like the font used to print the body
text of this book) of your choice in 72-point size to add the following
text: KTI's new CD-R twists reality!. (Press Return after CD-R
so the text appears on separate lines.) Use a light foreground color so it
stands out. Figure 14-12 shows the finished image.

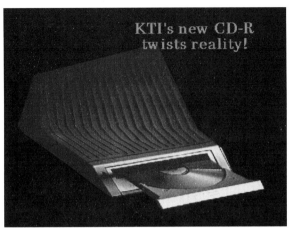

FIGURE 14-12
The finished image looks like this.

WHAT YOU'VE LEARNED

This chapter introduced you to several Photoshop filters that you can play with to create your own custom effects. You know that:

- ⊡ A convolution is a series of mathematical operations performed on all the pixels in an image or selection.

- ⊡ Filter convolutions are based on a matrix called a kernel. Several kinds of kernels exist, each relating to a particular property of your image, including the color and spatial location of the pixel. Photoshop's Custom filters work only with the brightness values of pixels in relation to each other.

- ⊡ Photoshop's Custom filters simply change the brightness value of all the pixels in your image or selection, depending on the values you type into the kernel matrix.

- ⊡ If you do get an effect you like, you can save the custom settings under a name you select.

- ⊡ Custom filters vary in their effect depending on the image to which you apply them.

- ⊡ The Displace filter adds a texture to an image by using the color values of a second image, which must be either a color image or a grayscale image with a second channel, to govern how pixels should be moved, or displaced, in a diagonal line.

In the next chapter, we'll look at how to use paths to trace an original piece of artwork.

Tracing a Logo
Recreating Artwork with Paths

THE PROJECT

Amy Hollerith finally got a computer of her own, and the first thing she did was draw a crude logo for Kitchen Table International, which she then printed out on some sort of dot-matrix printer at about 75 dpi or worse. She wants you to turn it into a more professional-looking logo to be used on KTI's letterhead. One glance at the logo tells you that this project won't be easy in Photoshop, especially with what you've learned so far. Even so, you decide to take a crack at it, because you have a feeling that the application's pen tool has some features you really haven't used to their fullest.

THE TOOLS
- ▫ Pen tool
- ▫ Paths palette
- ▫ Polygon lasso tool
- ▫ Make Work Path command
- ▫ Grids

We'll tell you up front that Photoshop may not be the best tool to use when you need to convert a coarse bitmap image into something smooth and professional. As you've learned, bitmaps don't lend themselves to smooth edges, particularly when diagonal lines or curves are involved, and they're not especially scalable. If you recreate Amy's logo in Photoshop, you'll be stuck with it in that size. Illustration packages such as Illustrator, FreeHand, or CorelDRAW not only are better suited for dealing with outlines, curves, and objects that you may want to reduce or enlarge, they have automatic tracing tools built in.

With that said, we'll concede that you just might get stuck with an assignment like this someday, have only Photoshop at your disposal, and wish then that you'd taken the time to learn more about using the program's pen tool and Paths palette. This is your chance.

We'll show you how to use Photoshop not only to trace existing artwork, but to create more complex objects with outline-oriented tools. After all, Photoshop's built-in selection tools can create only circles and ellipses, and if you want a particular curve you'd probably torture yourself with hours of trial and error. Copy the badlogo.tif file from the Chapter 15 folder on the CD-ROM, and get started with the following exercises.

STEP 1: ROUGH-TRACING AN OUTLINE

First, we're going to trace the outline of the oval that surrounds the logo, so that later in the chapter we can use the Stroke paths command to recreate it. Just follow these directions:

1 Open the badlogo.tif file. Make sure you're seated when you do so, because the image may come as something of a shock. It's rough, but it does at least show what Amy is trying to accomplish.

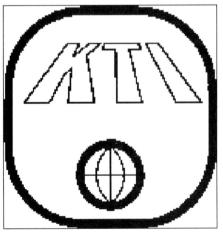

FIGURE 15-1
The rough logo you've been given to work with won't win any design awards.

2 In the Windows menu, turn on Show Grid and Snap to Grid. This makes it easier to place points evenly. As we add points, they will automatically snap to the grid that has been laid out on the screen.

3 From the toolbox, select the polygon lasso selection tool, which resides alongside the lasso icon on the fly-out tool display. Just hold down the Option key when you click on the lasso icon; keep clicking until the polygon lasso appears. You don't actually need to use this tool to accomplish this particular exercise, but, like chicken soup, it won't hurt, and will give us a chance to introduce you to Photoshop's Make Work Path feature.

4 Using the polygon lasso, start outlining the center of the outer oval shape that surrounds the logo. Don't worry about following the curve too closely. Click in any spot along the perimeter to start, and then move the cursor to the next spot and click again. Notice how Photoshop draws a selection border to follow the points you click, as shown in Figure 15-2. You can use the polygon lasso to select complex areas when you don't want to try and make the attempt with a single long drag, as you must with the plain lasso.

FIGURE 15-2
Clicking with the polygon lasso produces a selection border.

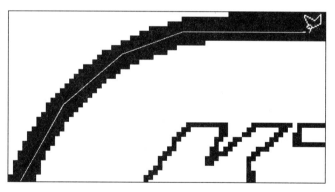

5 Continue on around the oval until you reach your starting point. Click the polygon lasso at the origin point, and Photoshop creates a selection, as Figure 15-3 shows.

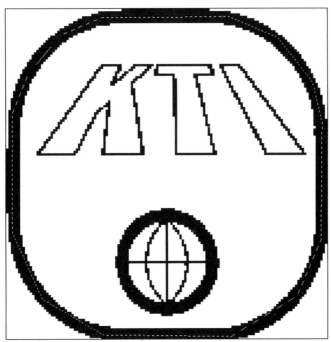

FIGURE 15-3
Photoshop has created a selection in the oval.

6 In the Paths palette, choose Make Work Path from the fly-out menu. The Make Work Path dialog box pops up asking for a tolerance; that is, how closely should the new path follow the selection. If you had a selection with rough edges—for example, if you used the magic wand to select the entire oval—you'd want to use a higher tolerance to smooth out the path and reduce the number of points. However, for this selection, the default value of 2 will do fine, because you didn't create an excessive number of points. Click on OK and the selection will be converted into a path, with points inserted at each place you clicked.

TIP You can convert any selection into a work path. A good way to put this capability to use is when you need to outline an object, but want a smoother outline than you'd get with ordinary selection tools. The Select ⇨ Modify ⇨ Smooth command can even out a rough selection, but doesn't give you the control over the selection's outline that you get by converting the selection to a path, making adjustments, and then converting back to a selection.

STEP 2: LEARNING ABOUT CURVE POINTS

We're going to give you a chance to learn how to manipulate curve (or smooth) points before the serious work begins. You'll need to know how to create curves in Photoshop because the normal painting and selection tools don't do a good job of allowing you to create the exact curves you want. By learning how to use paths, you will be able to develop all kinds of complex and compound curves easily. Just follow these directions:

1 Zoom in on the oval so you'll be able to view the path and its points more clearly.

2 Choose the pointer from the pen tool's icons by holding down the Option key and clicking until the pointer appears. You can also press the Command key to switch to the selection arrow.

3 Click the Work Path in the Paths palette to select it. You may have many different active paths in the Paths palette. Always choose the one you want to work with by clicking its name in the palette. Your current work path is what is called a *closed* path, because it has no beginning or end. Photoshop can also create *open* paths, which may be nothing more than a series of lines, or a figure that may appear to be closed, but actually has a gap at some point so that it has distinct beginning and end points.

4 Click anywhere on the path to make the points appear. Notice that if you click on one of the points, it changes from a hollow box to a filled box to show that the point is selected, and a straight line appears with handles at either end. These handles show the direction line, which you can drag to adjust the curve of the path. You can see a close-up of the path and its direction lines in Figure 15-4.

FIGURE 15-4
This closed path
has multiple points.

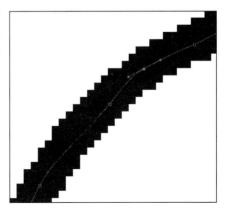

5 Using the pointer, grab one of the ends of the direction line and drag it far outside the boundaries of the oval. Notice how the curve bulges between the points on either side to follow the point you just dragged, as shown in Figure 15-5.

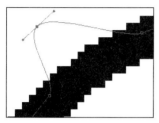

FIGURE 15-5
Drag a point to change the curve.

6 Now grab each end of the direction line in turn and move them farther away from the point. Move one end of the direction line up or down to see how the curve changes to follow. It's important to understand how manipulating a point and its direction lines changes a curve. Figure 15-6 shows what we've done so far.

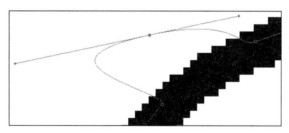

FIGURE 15-6
Dragging the direction lines changes the width of the curve.

7 Drag the point back to its original position, and move the ends of the direction line closer to the point to return the curve to its original orientation. We went through the previous two steps just to let you get comfortable with moving points and direction lines to adjust curves. Now the real work begins.

STEP 3: SMOOTHING THE CURVES

Now we can smooth the curves and reduce the number of points in our path. The reason for doing so is that a smoother curve looks better and has fewer jaggies than one that includes many different points. Follow these directions:

1 We probably have too many points in our path. Any given curve needs only three points: a start point, end point, and center point. You'll need more only to create compound curves, and you can usually judge by eye whether the curve you're creating is a simple curve or a compound one. Option-click on the pen tool until the pen with the minus sign next to it appears.

2 You can remove extraneous points by clicking them with this pen tool. You'll need to look at the path, decide which points aren't needed, and click to delete them.

3 Next, move the remaining points and their anchors with the pen pointer to follow the curve of the oval. Figure 15-7 shows the path after the extra points have been removed and the points adjusted.

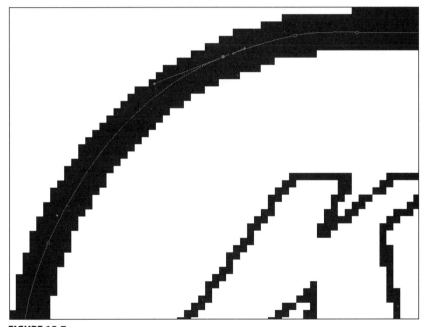

FIGURE 15-7
The extra points have been deleted, and the curve adjusted.

4 Repeat steps 1–3 on each of the other three corners of the path. Don't worry about the straight lines of the path at the sides, top, and bottom right. If you make a mistake and remove a point you decide you need, you can create a new one with the pen tool that has the plus sign next to it. You can also reposition a point by dragging it along the path with the pointer tool. The path will now look like Figure 15-8.

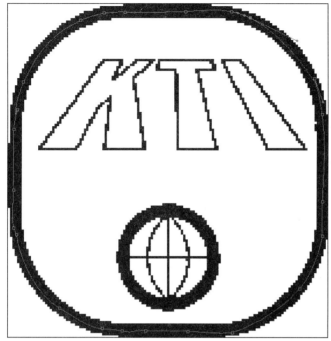

FIGURE 15-8
The curves are smooth even if the straight lines are still raggedy.

STEP 4: STRAIGHTENING LINES

The straight lines on all four sides not only have too many points, they're the wrong kind. Photoshop used curve points to turn your original selection into a path. However, paths also can include corner points, which define a straight line. Here's how to add straight lines to our path:

1   Zoom in on one of the four sides, such as the top of the oval, as shown in Figure 15-9. Notice that the path is crooked and contains too many anchor points.

FIGURE 15-9
The straight lines actually contain curve (or smooth) points.

2 Eliminate the extra points so only one pair remains at either end of the straight line.

3 Option-click the pen tool until the convert-anchor-point tool appears. It looks like a caret symbol pointing toward 11 o'clock on a clock face. You can also press Control-Command and click on a point while using any of the other pen tools to convert the point from curve (smooth) to corner, or vice versa. Convert the two points at the ends of the straight area to corner points. The path will now look like Figure 15-10.

FIGURE 15-10
Corner points have been inserted to create a straight line at the top of the figure.

4 Repeat Steps 1–3 until you've straightened all four sides. The path will now look like Figure 15-11.

FIGURE 15-11
The completed oval path looks like this.

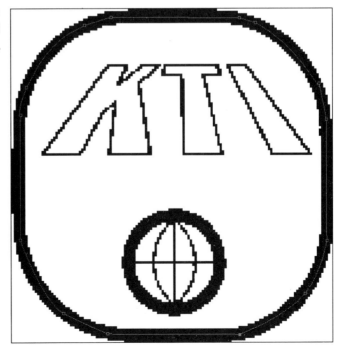

5 Double-click the Work Path in the Paths palette, and enter Oval as the name of this path you've just created.

STEP 5: CREATING THE GLOBE

We can create a separate path for the globe near the bottom of the logo. It's a good idea to create separate paths for each object so you can edit them individually later. Follow these directions to create the globe:

1 Although it is not necessary to create a path for the outer edge of the globe—it's a perfect circle and Photoshop does a good job of creating circles—for future reference we'll show you how to create one now. Select the elliptical marquee tool, hold down the Option and Shift keys, and place the cursor in the center of the globe's "cross hair." Next, drag in any direction as a perfect circle is formed. Keep dragging until the circle is centered in the outer perimeter of the globe.

2 Use Select ⇨ Save selection to store this circle for use later.

3 A circular path helps you position the other lines you'll be creating, so choose Make Worth path from the Paths palette's fly-out menu. Accept the default tolerance level. Your path will look like Figure 15-12.

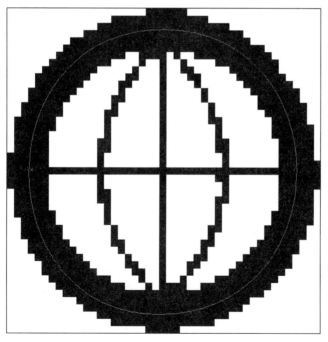

FIGURE 15-12
A circular path is easy to create.

4 Click the pen tool, and click just inside the circular path at the top of the center "longitude" line in the globe. Click again inside the circular path at the bottom of the line to create a straight line.

5 Click the pen tool again to begin a new path, and click at right and left in the "latitude" line to bisect the circle once more. Place the beginning and end points just inside the circle, rather than on the circular path itself. Your new paths should look like Figure 15-13.

FIGURE 15-13
Latitude and longitude lines have been added.

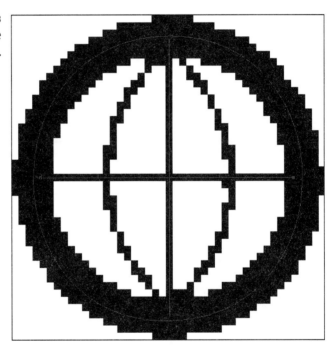

6 Click the pen tool again and create a diamond shape with the four anchors at the intersections of the curved longitude lines with the straight paths you just completed, as shown in Figure 15-14.

7 Use the pen tool with the plus sign and add points to the centers of each of the four diagonal lines of the diamond. (This gives you extra practice in adding anchors.) Drag the anchor, if necessary, to make sure it's centered. Next, use the Pen pointer to move each new point's direction lines so that a smooth curve is created that corresponds to the curved longitude lines on the sample logo. Your image should look like Figure 15-15.

8 Place the pointer tool on the circular path we created as a guide to select it. Then press the Delete key to remove this path.

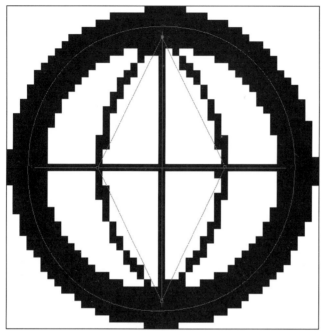

FIGURE 15-14
The diamond path represents
the curved longitude lines.

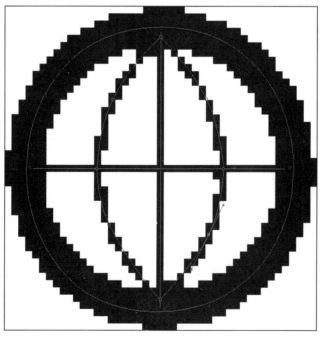

FIGURE 15-15
The lines have been curved
to match the longitude lines
of the original.

9 Click and Shift-click on the latitude and longitude lines to select all of them.

10 Next, double-click on the Work Path in the Paths palette, and name it Globe to save the path.

STEP 6: CREATING THE KTI INITIALS

The initials should be easy—they're nothing but straight lines. You won't need many directives to complete this short section, which completes the basic steps for reproducing this logo. Just follow these directions:

1 In the Paths palette, choose New Path from the fly-out menu. Name it KTI.

2 Using the pen tool, click to trace the outline of the initials. Close the path for each letter, and then start a new one for the next. Your image and the Paths palette should look like Figure 15-16.

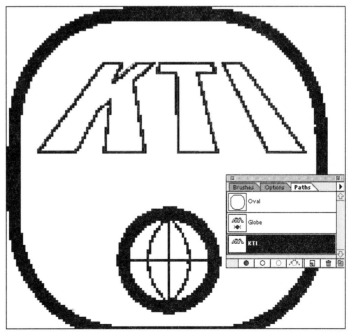

FIGURE 15-16
The Paths palette shows all three of the paths you've created.

STEP 7: STROKING THE PATHS

Now you can stroke the subpaths you've created to produce the smooth outlines you wanted, as follows:

1 Create a new, empty layer.

2 Choose a large, hard-edged brush from the Brushes palette.

3 Select the Globe path from the Paths palette, and Shift-click on the subpaths to make sure they are all selected.

4 From the Paths palette's fly-out menu, select Stroke Subpaths. The Stroke Subpaths dialog box pops up; select Paintbrush from the drop-down list.

5 From the Paths palette, select the Outline path.

6 Repeat Step 4 to stroke the Outline

7 Select the KTI path, and Shift-click on the subpaths to make sure they are all selected.

8 Choose a smaller hard-edged brush.

9 Repeat Step 4 to stroke the initials. Your logo is now complete except for the perimeter of the globe. Your work so far is shown in Figure 15-17.

10 Load the selection you saved earlier.

11 Stroke the circle using the Edit ⇨ Stroke command. Set the width of the stroke to 14 pixels, and click the Center button.

12 Flatten the image using Layer ⇨ Flatten. Your final logo will look like Figure 15-18.

13 Show the finished product to Amy Hollerith and recommend she hire a logo designer next time.

FIGURE 15-17
The paths have all been stroked.

PATH ESSENTIALS

Here are some additional important reminders you should keep in mind as you work with paths:

- ☐ Remember to keep the Rubber Band option on if you want to preview path segments as you draw them.
- ☐ To create a curve with a 45° angle (or any multiple of 45°), click with the pen tool at the point where you want to begin the curve, and then Shift-click while dragging away from that point. Release the mouse button when the curve is set the way you want.
- ☐ Work Paths are always temporary: You must save the path under a name if you want it to be stored on disk with the file.
- ☐ Click on a path segment to select it; Shift-click to select additional segments. To select a whole path, Option-click anywhere on the path.
- ☐ Paths may be moved anywhere in an image using the move tool.
- ☐ Use Command-C and Command-V to copy and paste paths, respectively.
- ☐ Paths can be converted to selections, just as selections can be converted to Work Paths.

FIGURE 15-18
The finished logo looks like this.

WHAT YOU'VE LEARNED

You worked a lot with the pen tool and paths in this chapter, and learned quite a bit about manipulating curves and outlines. You know that:

- ⊡ While Photoshop isn't the best tool for working with outlines, its pen tool and Paths palette do give you the capabilities you need to create paths.

- ⊡ You can use the polygon lasso tool to create odd-shaped selections by a series of clicks.

- ⊡ Selections can be converted to paths, which you may then edit.

- ⊡ If a path has no distinct beginning or end points, it is a closed path. An open path has beginning and end points.

- ⊡ Curve, or smooth points consist of an anchor point and a direction line. These can be dragged to adjust the curve.

- ⊡ Points can be added or subtracted from a path.

◻ Curve, or smooth points can be converted to corner points, which define one end of a straight line.

◻ You can create a perfect circle selection by holding down the Option and Shift keys while dragging with the elliptical selection tool.

In Chapter 16, we'll explore the Actions palette to learn how to create our own macros.

Recording a Macro
Speeding Your Work with Actions

Kitchen Table International's president has taken a liking to you, probably because you don't charge very much. He's come to you with a small personal favor. He had a few photographs scanned from his vacation in Spain—500 to be precise—and wants to send copies to his relatives. Unfortunately, all the images are PICT files, and most of Scott's family own Windows PCs. Others don't have any computers at all. Could you convert all the pictures to the PCX format his non-Mac-using relatives say they need, reduce the images that are too large to a size that will fit on an 800 × 600-pixel screen, and create lower resolution versions that take up less disk space? And can you do it over the weekend? You remember how much fun you had using the Actions palette in Chapter 11, and decide to see just how much mayhem you can make with it.

THE TOOLS
- ⊡ Actions palette
- ⊡ Save As
- ⊡ Image ➪ Resize

We rank Photoshop's new Actions feature as one of the top additions to the program. Once you see how easy Actions are to use, you'll find scores of applications for this macro-like capability. You got only a brief look at its capabilities in Chapter 11, but now we'll devote a whole chapter to Actions so you can see just how versatile this feature is.

Photoshop's Actions are easy to use and can do most of the automation that Photoshop addicts crave. With Actions, you can combine a series of steps into a single command that you can activate by typing a shortcut key, choosing the command from a menu, or by pressing a button. You can even start in the middle of a series of actions, or tell the macro to stop at a certain point so you can perform some step that cannot be automated—such as making a selection, or painting with a tool. Actions can be carried out on large batches of images—such as Scott's 500 vacation pictures—or used on an individual basis to speed up some tedious or repetitious task. While we could list dozens of ways you can use Actions, the best way is to show you. In the following exercises, we'll convert Scott's photos to two different formats, change their size, and perform a couple of other tricks.

 macro \ma'cro\ *n* From the Greek *makro*, very large. In computing, a simple way for an end user to spend hours developing and debugging a series of steps that may then be carried out by the computer in an automated fashion, saving a few seconds here and there that may equal the development time in as little as a decade.

STEP 1: GETTING READY

We'll first have you copy the files to be processed from the CD-ROM, and set up some destination folders. Actions could easily work directly from the CD-ROM, but the process goes much more quickly if the files are available on your hard disk. Here's what you should do:

1 Create a folder on your hard disk called Scott's Vacation.

2 Inside that folder, create two more folders, called JPEG and PCX.

3 Drag the Spain folder from the Chapter 16 folder on the CD-ROM, and place it inside the Scott's Vacation folder. This arrangement will make it easier to keep everything straight as we work.

STEP 2: STARTING TO RECORD A MACRO

Now we can start recording the macro. Just follow these directions to get underway:

1 Open the PICT file called Giralda in the Spain folder you just copied from the CD-ROM to your hard disk. We want to open the file before

we start recording the macro because Photoshop can automatically open any file we ask it to perform an Action on. So, opening the file does not have to be part of the macro, and can cause problems if it is.

2   Examine the Actions palette, shown in Figure 16-1. You'll see five buttons at the bottom. The square is the Stop button, which ceases a recording. The filled circle is the record button, which is black when no recording is taking place, and turns to red when you click it to start recording. The right-pointing triangle is the Play button, which activates the macro or step you've highlighted in the palette. (You don't have to start playing a macro from the beginning—you can begin at any step within the macro.) The icon of the page with the up-turned lower left corner is the New Action button, and the Trash can icon is used to discard a highlighted macro or step.

FIGURE 16-1
The Actions palette has five buttons along the bottom of its window: Stop, Record, Play, New Action, and Trash.

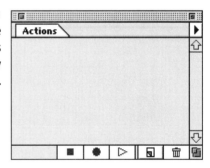

3   Click the New Action button. The New Action dialog box, shown in Figure 16-2, pops up. Fill in Save As JPEG as the title for the macro.

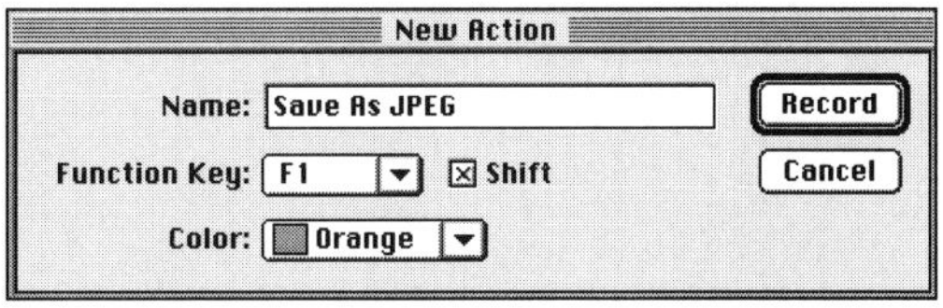

FIGURE 16-2
Type in a name for the macro in the New Action dialog box.

4   The Function Key and Color fields are optional, especially because we don't plan to reuse this macro, but now is a good time to learn how they work. You can assign any of the function keys from F1 to F15 as a shortcut that will activate this macro. Choose F1 from the drop-down list, and check the Shift box, so that Shift-F1 will become the shortcut for this new Action.

5 You may also select a color, which will be applied to a button on the
   Actions palette. That gives you three ways to activate this macro: You
   can use the shortcut key assigned previously, press the colored button,
   or choose the macro's name in the Actions palette's list. Choose
   Orange from the drop-down list. Then click Record to start capturing
   your actions. The Record button in the Actions palette will turn red.

STEP 3: RECORDING A MACRO THAT SAVES IN JPEG FORMAT

We've divided the steps that will be recorded in our macros into four separate tasks, as
follows:

⊡ Save each image file in its full size in the JPEG folder you just created,
   in the JPEG format, using enough image compression to squeeze the
   file down to a more manageable size. We'll take care of this step in the
   following macro.

⊡ Take the same file and reduce it in width so it will fit on a monitor at
   a resolution as low as 640 × 480, which is the lowest-common-
   denominator screen resolution used in both the Macintosh and PC
   environments.

⊡ Sharpen the reduced image to add a little snap.

⊡ Save the reduced image in the PCX format in the PCX folder, using
   file names that conform to the Windows eight-character/three-
   character extension format. We'll handle this step in a separate macro.

Ordinarily, it would take you at least several minutes to load a file, perform all the
preceding functions, and then move on to the next file. This next set of steps carries out
the first task in our list.

1 Select File ⇨ Preferences ⇨ Saving Files, and change the Append File
   Extension drop-down list to read Always. Photoshop will then add a
   .PCX or .JPG file extension for us automatically.

2 From the File menu, select Save As. The Macintosh's standard File
   Save dialog box appears, as shown in Figure 16-3.

3 From the drop-down Format list, select JPEG.

4 Click Save to start saving the file.

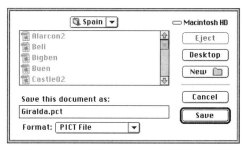

FIGURE 16-3
The standard Mac File
Save dialog appears.

5 The JPEG Options dialog, shown in Figure 16-4, appears. Change the
quality slider to a value of 2. Click on OK and the file will be saved to
the disk.

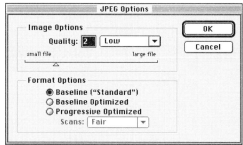

FIGURE 16-4
Set the JPEG Options
quality slider to 2.

6 Click the Stop button to stop recording this macro.

STEP 4: REDUCING THE IMAGE SIZE

Next, we'll record a second macro to reduce the size of the images and store them in the
PCX format. Scott may not know that his PC users could easily read the JPEG-format
files we just saved. However, he says they want PCX files, and in a size that will fit on
even the smallest monitors, so we are happy to oblige him. Here's how to do it:

1 Click the New Action icon, and name the macro Reduce/Save as PCX.

2 From the Image menu, select Image Size. The Image Size dialog box
appears.

3 Change the Width field to 600 pixels, switching the drop-down
measurements list from percent to pixels if necessary. Make sure the
Constrain Proportions and Resample Image checkboxes are marked, as
shown in Figure 16-5.

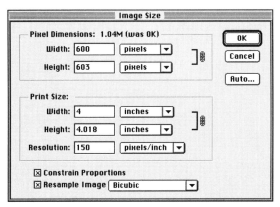

FIGURE 16-5
Use Image Size to set
the width to 600 pixels.

4 Click on OK to resize the image. Scott said that the image quality for
   these snapshots he's sending his relatives isn't critical. He's more
   concerned about having them fit the width of their screens. You decide
   to resize all the images so they are 600 pixels wide, and will thus
   display on 640 × 480, 800 × 600, or even larger screens. Some of the
   vertical shots will probably be taller than 480 pixels when resized, but
   that won't matter. You figure the relatives can always scroll down to
   view the rest of the picture if they need to. Having the images fit the
   width of the screen is the most important thing.

5 You know that Photoshop will do a decent job of interpolating
   the images down to a 600 pixel width, but that some fuzziness is
   inevitable. It's not worth using sophisticated sharpening techniques on
   these snapshots, so you just select Filter ⇨ Sharpen ⇨ Sharpen to add
   some generic sharpness to the image.

STEP 5: SAVING IN PCX FORMAT

We can continue with the same macro, because Photoshop is still recording our actions.
The last image-processing step for this macro is to save the file as a PCX-format file. Just
follow these directions carefully:

1 Select File ⇨ Save As once more, and indicate PCX as the format for
   the file.

2 Click Save A Copy to store the file on the hard disk using the new
   format and extension.

3 Click the Stop button to cease recording this macro. The Actions palette will look like Figure 16-6.

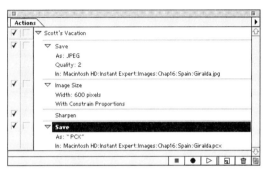

FIGURE 16-6

The finished macros appear in the Actions palette.

NOTE Note that all the steps you just carried out are displayed on separate lines, with check marks next to them. The checks indicate that the particular action is active and will be executed the next time the macro is run. You can disable a particular action by unchecking its box.

STEP 6: RUNNING A MACRO IN A BATCH

Now we're ready to run the macros on Scott's vacation pictures. We didn't include all 500 in our set: the 25 images we've included are enough to let you observe how a batch macro operates. Even with just 25 pictures, it will take several minutes to run. Just follow these directions:

1 Highlight Save As JPEG in the Actions palette. You could also highlight an individual action and start the macro from there, but we want to let the whole thing execute.

2 From the Actions palette's fly-out menu, choose Batch. The Batch dialog box, shown in Figure 16-7, appears.

3 The Source drop-down list box has two choices. If you select Import, the list changes to Photoshop's File ➪ Import menu. In that case, you could select TWAIN and Photoshop would run your scanner's capture program, then process the resulting image using the remainder of the macro. In our case, however, we want to work with files we've placed in the Spain folder. Make sure Folder is showing in the Source list.

FIGURE 16-7

The Batch dialog box lets you define whole groups of files on which to perform a single macro.

4   Click the Choose button, and the standard Mac folder navigation dialog box appears, as shown in Figure 16-8. Find the Spain folder and click the Select "Spain" button at the bottom of the dialog box.

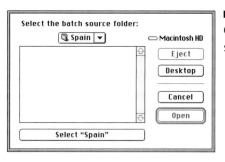

FIGURE 16-8

Choose the Spain folder as the source for the files to be processed.

5   In the Destination drop-down list, make sure that Folder is also selected.

6   Now, click the Choose button, find the JPEG folder, and select it.

7   Click on OK to start the macro. It processes each of the files in turn, and saves the new .jpg files in the JPEG folder.

8   Next, highlight Reduce/Save as PCX.

9   From the Actions palette's fly-out menu, choose Batch, as you did before.

10   Click the Choose button, and double check to make sure the Spain folder appears. (It should if you haven't done anything else between Steps 7 and 8.) Click the Select "Spain" button at the bottom of the dialog box.

11   Next, click the Choose button, find the PCX folder, and select it.

12   Click on OK to start the macro. It processes each of the files in turn, reduces and sharpens them, and saves the new .pcx files in the PCX folder. And so much more easily than doing them one at a time yourself!

MORE ABOUT ACTIONS

Here are some more things you'll want to know when using Actions:

- You can select any step in a macro by highlighting it in the Actions palette and then clicking the Play button. The macro runs from that point onward.
- You can disable any step in a macro by unchecking the box next to its name in the Actions palette. Do this to temporarily disable any step you don't want to perform.
- You can play back only a single command in a longer macro by highlighting its name in the Actions palette, and then Command-clicking the Play button.
- You can save whole sets of macros under individual names and retrieve them when you need them. You can thus avoid having the Actions palette filled with macros you aren't currently using. Load only the macros you need, when you need them. Better yet, create a macro to load them for you.
- The Button Mode command turns the Actions palette into a list of color-coded buttons (if you've specified a color for an Action), without showing the individual commands in each macro. Use this mode when you don't need to work with individual commands.
- You can drag commands within the Actions palette to change the order in which they execute. If you decide to sharpen an image before resizing it, rather than vice versa, just drag the sharpen command in the palette to move it above the resizing command.
- You can delete or copy individual commands. Just highlight the command name and choose Delete or Copy from the Actions palette's fly-out menu. You can also delete a command by dragging it to the palette's trash can, or simply by selecting it and Option-clicking the palette's trash can.

STEP 7: ADDING STOPS TO AN ACTION

Some kinds of actions can't be captured in a macro. For example, you can't paint with a brush or any other tool, nor can you make a selection with a selection tool within a macro. This chapter's final exercise shows you how to allow for individual actions such as these "undoable" ones within a macro. We'll assume you want to go through all 25 of Scott's vacation pictures and crop them individually. The following directions demonstrate how to automate the process:

1 Open the Giralda file in the Spain folder.

2 Click the New Action button, and name the macro Crop.

3 Click Record to start recording the macro.

4 Click the Actions palette's fly-out menu, and select Insert Stop. The Record Stop dialog box appears. Enter the following message: `Crop the image and then click the Play button in the Actions palette. Click on OK`.

5 Choose the rectangular marquee to select the area you want to crop.

6 Use Image ⇨ Crop to crop the image.

7 Select File ⇨ Save As to save the cropped image.

8 Click the Stop button to stop recording the macro.

9 Use the Actions palette's Batch command to select the folder containing the images you want to crop, and a destination folder.

10 When you start the macro, each image will be loaded in turn, and the dialog box will pop up asking you to crop the image. Click Stop, crop the image, and then click the Play button in the Actions palette as the dialog box told you to do. The image will be cropped, saved, and the next image will appear.

WHAT YOU'VE LEARNED

This chapter hardly scratched the surface of all the things you can do with macros within Photoshop. However, you know that:

- Photoshop's Actions are easy to use and enable you to perform most Photoshop procedures.

- Actions let you combine a series of steps into a single command that you can activate by typing a shortcut key, choosing the command from a menu, or by pressing a button.

- You can start in the middle of an action, or pause to perform another step.

- Actions can be carried out in batches, which can operate on entire folders of files.

- You may assign a function key or button color to an action, and activate it at a key press or from a set of buttons in the Actions palette.

In the next chapter, we'll explore a new way to create textured backgrounds.

Creating a Textured Background
Applying What You've Learned

Kitchen Table International is launching a new scheduling program called Big Ben, and wants to use a textured image of the original Big Ben clock tower in London as a background for the packaging. Luckily for the KTI ad budget, Scott has just come back from England, and hands you a snapshot of the famous tower to use. The problem? The photo is a little distorted, the colors are muted, and there's a large street lamp right in the middle of the picture. This is your opportunity to use several of the tools you already worked with in previous chapters in new ways to fix this image.

THE TOOLS
- ☐ Transform ⇨ Perspective
- ☐ Crop tool
- ☐ Toning tool
- ☐ Filter ⇨ Texture ⇨ Texturizer

In most of the previous chapters, we've concentrated on learning one or two tools in their most simple incarnations. In your real work, you'll find you'll need to apply quite a few different techniques, as we do in this chapter.

 tone \tone\ *n* **1:** A state of physical perfection achieved only by male and female models who sell exercise equipment in infomercials, although they didn't actually use the products involved. **2:** In acoustics, a sound that can be recognized by its regularity of vibration (*see also* tone deaf: karaoke). **3:** In linguistics, a variation of the voice while speaking. **4:** In image editing, that quality of an image that is never quite correct.

STEP 1: STRAIGHTENING BIG BEN

Our first step is to straighten out Big Ben. How did England's venerable tower get tilted to a Pisa-like angle in the first place? Those of you with professional photographic experience will look at the photograph in Figure 17-1 and realize that we've got a serious case of perspective distortion.

FIGURE 17-1
Our unaltered photo has Big Ben with a severe tilt.

Ideally, when photographing a tall building such as Big Ben, the camera back (where the film plane lies), the lens, and the building itself should all be parallel to one another. Often, though, we tilt the camera to take in the top of a tall subject. That produces a distorted, leaning back effect. Pros have special cameras and lenses that enable the lens and film to be moved up and down, swung, and tilted independently so that virtually any subject can be photographed while maintaining the necessary parallel relationships and eliminating the distorted effect.

This photographer didn't have those tools, so we've got a tilted view of Big Ben that, fortunately, we can fix with Photoshop's perspective controls. Just follow these directions:

1 Copy the bigben.tif file from the Chapter 17 folder of your CD-ROM to the hard disk, and then open it in Photoshop.

2 Use Select ⇨ Select All (or learn the shortcut for this common operation: Command-A).

3 Select the View ⇨ Show Rulers from the menu bar (or press Command-R) to turn on the rulers, if you haven't done so already.

4 From the Layer menu, select Transform ⇨ Perspective. Tiny selection handles appear at the corners of the image, and in the center along each side. The cursor changes to an arrow shape.

5 Place the cursor on the handle at the upper left corner. Move it toward the right until the tower appears straight. It should be about ⅛th inch on the ruler.

6 Press Return to accept the change. The whole image has been straightened, but we're showing you just the corner that contains Big Ben, where the effect is more dramatic, in Figure 17-2.

FIGURE 17-2
The leaning tower of Big Ben
has been straightened out.

STEP 2: CROPPING THE IMAGE

In earlier exercises, when you cropped an image, we had you simply select it with the rectangular marquee and use the Image ⇨ Crop command to trim off the excess. You'll find the crop tool is a bit more flexible. We don't need all of its capabilities for this picture, but now is a good time to get to know this tool. Here's what you do:

1 Hold down the Option key and click in the marquee tool square until the crop tool appears.

2 Drag a rectangle bounding box in the straightened Big Ben image that includes only the portions that contain part of the image. You'll have to trim tall triangles of extraneous image at the right and left sides, as you can see in Figure 17-3.

FIGURE 17-3
Extra image area has to be trimmed away.

3 Adjust the boundaries of the crop selection if necessary. Unlike the selection rectangle, the crop tool's boundaries have selection handles that you can drag to move the top, bottom, or sides in any direction. This

enables you to adjust the selection more accurately, when compared to the routines needed to add or subtract from a conventional selection. But there's more. You can also scale the image or rotate it using the same techniques you learned with Free Transform. (Place the cursor on a corner handle and move diagonally to scale, or outside a handle to rotate.) We don't need to scale or rotate this image, however.

4   Press Return to accept the cropping you've done.

 TIP   You'll find the crop tool is a great time saver because you can select the area to be cropped, rotate and resize the image, or even change the resolution of the finished image (in the Crop Tool Options palette), all with a minimum number of steps.

STEP 3: TONING UP THE IMAGE

You can use the toning tool (dodge/burn/sponge) to make some additional corrections to our image. Follow these directions to get some additional experience with all three modes:

1   The Houses of Parliament building to the right of Big Ben is a little too light. Hold down the Option key and click the toning tool until the burn tool (represented by a cupped hand icon) appears.

2   Double-click the icon to produce the Toning Tool Options palette. Move the Exposure slider to 15% (to make our adjustments small and easy to control), and then select Highlights from the drop-down list to the left of the Exposure slider.

3   Choose the 35-pixel brush from the Brushes palette. We want to darken fairly broad areas at one time to make the burned areas less obvious. The unaltered area of the image looks like Figure 17-4.

4   Use the Burn tool to darken the Houses of Parliament building to more closely match Big Ben. The effect should look like Figure 17-5.

5   The color of Big Ben and Parliament have been muted by the overcast sky. The Sponge tool can brighten them up. Option-click the toning tool until the sponge appears.

6   Double-click the sponge to bring the Toning Tool Options palette to the front again, and then choose Saturate from the drop-down list box to the left of the Pressure slider.

FIGURE 17-4
The unaltered image area looks like this.

FIGURE 17-5
The Houses of Parliament have been darkened.

7   Using the 35-pixel brush, enrich the color of the buildings by painting
    over them with the sponge tool. We can't show you a screen shot of
    the color change on a black-and-white page, but if you're working
    along you should see a much brighter looking, more cheerful image.

8 Option-click the Toning tool one more time to select the Dodge tool. Set exposure to 15%, and set the drop-down list box to the left of the Exposure slider to Shadows. We're now going to lighten the left side of the Big Ben tower so we can see more detail. Figure 17-6 shows the tower prior to enhancement.

9 Using the 35-pixel brush, lighten the left side of the tower. The effect appears in Figure 17-7.

LEARNING ABOUT CMYK

As you move beyond this book and learn more about CMYK, you'll discover that this color model is just as important to professional applications as the RGB system used to display color on your Macintosh. You'll probably use RGB to edit images, as Photoshop displays RGB color most accurately, and then frequently convert to CMYK at some point for production. You'll need to become familiar with the potential problems of working in these dual modes.

One important thing to keep in mind is that CMYK systems can't reproduce all the colors available under RGB, because their *gamuts* are different. Color gamuts are often represented by map-like images that represent a particular system's *color space*. The RGB color space is a bit larger than CMYK's, and even though they overlap, a rather large area within the RGB gamut falls entirely outside the CMYK color space. A smaller amount of color space can be represented by CMYK that extends a little outside the RGB gamut. More simply, you can see quite a few RGB colors on your screen that can't be reproduced by CMYK, and a few CMYK hues can't be duplicated in RGB. You'll find that CMYK colors are often more subdued and less bright, which is logical, because they must be viewed by reflected light (which is limited) rather than the transmitted light that can be pumped up brighter and brighter.

Any time you switch from one color model to another, the colors that can't be represented by the destination system are lost. That's why switching back and forth between RGB and CMYK isn't a good idea: you may lose some colors each way. To help minimize this problem, Photoshop includes a CMYK Preview command in the View menu, which you can activate by pressing Command-Y. In this mode, you can view an RGB image as it will be reproduced in CMYK (or as closely as Photoshop can duplicate the view) without making an actual conversion.

Photoshop also has a View ⇨ Gamut Warning command (which you can activate by pressing Shift-Command-Y) that shows you out-of-gamut colors, so you can make corrections. You'll also need to be aware of out-of-gamut conditions when you work with tools that change the brightness or saturation of colors, as we did with the sponge tool in this chapter. These tools can easily alter an image so that it can no longer be represented by CMYK. Use the Gamut Warning commands frequently to help you avoid this condition. Also, to learn more about calibrating your monitor and color theory, see Appendixes A and B at the end of this book.

FIGURE 17-6
We're going to lighten the shadows that obscure Big Ben's left face.

FIGURE 17-7
The left side of the tower has been lightened.

STEP 4: REMOVING ONE STREET LAMP

Several of the street lamps in the photo are unobtrusive, but the tallest and closest one obscures our view of the buildings. A quick revisit to the Rubber Stamp Tool can remove the lamp for us. You've already used this tool in several previous chapters, so consider this a refresher. Just follow these directions:

1 Double-click the rubber stamp tool to bring the Rubber Stamp Tool Options palette to the front. Make sure Opacity is set to 100%, blending mode is Clone (aligned), and the drop-down list box to the left of the Opacity slider is set to Normal.

2 Option-click in an area of the sky around the street lamp, and paint over the lamp to remove it from the image, as shown in Figure 17-8. Use a small, feathered brush of any size you feel comfortable using for this step.

FIGURE 17-8
This street lamp is being turned off permanently.

3 Where the lamp overlaps the building, trees, or cars, use a smaller brush to clone parts of the surroundings over the lamp. The section will look like Figure 17-9 when you're finished.

TIP Another way of performing this last step is to create a new layer and remove the street lamp on that layer. While the step is a simple one, performing the change on a layer gives you extra protection in case you goof up. You could copy back the parts of the image you damaged from the original background, or, if you erred in a major way, delete the cloning layer and start over with a fresh copy. Use Merge Down to combine the cloned layer with the original when you finish.

FIGURE 17-9
The lamp is completely removed.

STEP 5: CREATING BIG BEN TEXTURE FILES

Although we've added textures earlier in this book, you can use a texture of your own design if you like. We'll explore several ways to do this in the following sections. Just follow these directions to create a Big Ben texture file you can use to apply a texture to any image, including the one we've been working on:

1 In the Magic Wand Options palette, set the tool's Tolerance to 32. Then use the magic wand to select the sky around Big Ben.

2 Use Select ⇨ Inverse to invert the selection so that everything except the sky is selected.

3 Use the rectangular marquee tool to deselect the rest of the image except for the Big Ben tower. Hold down the Option key and drag the deselection rectangles that each remove some of the rest of the image, until only the tower itself remains selected.

4 You can switch to Quick Mask mode to see if you've successfully selected the tower, as shown in Figure 17-10.

5 Press Command-C to copy the tower, and then use File ⇨ New to create a new file to drop it into. Click on OK in the New File dialog box to create the file, and then press Command-V to paste in the tower.

FIGURE 17-10
Quick Mask shows that only
the tower is selected.

6   In the new file, select Image ⇨ Image Size, and change from pixel to
    percent measurements in the drop-down Width list box, and then type
    in 33 percent for the final size. Click on OK to reduce the image to
    one-third its former size.

7   Select Filter ⇨ Unsharp Mask, and apply a 200 percent sharpening
    factor to the new, reduced image of Big Ben. Leave Radius and
    Threshold at their default values of 1.

8   Use Image ⇨ Canvas Size, and adjust the size of the Big Ben file to
    1-inch × 1-inch.

9   Select File ⇨ Save A Copy, and store the file under the name Big Ben
    Pict, using the PICT format. Add the .PCT extension, which the
    Macintosh doesn't require, but will be beneficial if you share the file
    with a PC user, because Windows machines do use extensions to
    determine likely file formats.

10 Next, return to the Big Ben image and select only a portion of its brick
    façade, using the rectangular marquee tool.

11 Press Command-C to copy the selection, and then use File ⇨ New and
    Command-V as you did in Step 5 to create a new file containing only
    the selection.

12 Select Filter ⇨ Unsharp Mask and apply a 200 percent sharpening factor
    to the brick. Leave Radius and Threshold at their default values of 1.

13 Choose File ⇨ Save A Copy, and store a PICT version of this file under
    the name Big Ben Brick Pict.

STEP 6: APPLYING TEXTURES

We can add these textures to our Big Ben image. The following directions demonstrate how to combine them both into an interesting background:

1 Return to the Big Ben image and create a new, empty layer using Layer ⇨ New ⇨ Layer.

2 Press D to make sure your default colors are black/white, and use Edit ⇨ Fill (or press Shift-Delete) to fill the new layer with a 35 percent gray tone.

3 Choose Filter ⇨ Texture ⇨ Texturizer, and the Texturizer dialog box, shown in Figure 17-11, appears.

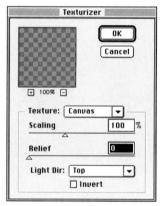

FIGURE 17-11
The Texturizer dialog box looks like this before we've loaded one of our custom textures.

4 Click the Load Texture button, and select the Big Ben Brick Pict file from the standard Macintosh file navigation dialog box that pops up.

5 Back in the Texturizer dialog box, change Scaling to 50 percent with the slider, reducing the size of the texture in proportion to the rest of the image. Then adjust the Relief slider to 50 to produce a 3D effect. Set the Light Dir (light direction) drop-down list box to top right, as shown in Figure 17-12.

6 Click on OK to apply the effect. The layer look like Figure 17-13.

FIGURE 17-12
The Texturizer dialog box
should look like this.

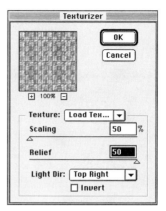

FIGURE 17-13
The Big Ben Brick Pict texture
has been applied to the layer.

7 Select Filter ⇨ Texture ⇨ Texturizer again (or press Option-Shift-F to bring up the dialog box), and change the Scale to 100.

8 Click the Texture button, and load the Big Ben Pict file as the new texture.

9 Change the Light Dir drop-down list box so the light comes from the top left.

10 Click on OK to apply the texture. The finished texture layer will look like Figure 17-14.

FIGURE 17-14
The finished texture
layer looks like this.

STEP 7: COMBINING TWO LAYERS

Finally, we need to combine the background layer and the texture in an attractive way. We'll do that by following these directions:

1 Make sure both the background and texture layers are available by clicking their eyeball icons. The image looks like Figure 17-15.

2 Too much of Big Ben has been obscured. The reason for this is that we have chosen the Normal blending mode between the two layers. In this mode, the pixels of each layer are overlapped, giving equal weight to those in both layers. Photoshop has a broad selection of modes, each of which uses a different type of calculation to determine which pixel gains preference over the other. The best way to see the effects of each mode is to try them out individually.

3 In the Layers palette, use the drop-down list to try out a few of the available modes. You might try Darken, in which Photoshop examines each pixel in both layers and uses the darker of the two as the result pixel. Lighter pixels are replaced by darker ones. You can see this effect in Figure 17-16.

FIGURE 17-15
The two layers look like this together.

FIGURE 17-16
Darken mode produces an effect like this.

4   You'll want to experiment with other modes to see how they work.
    However, after you're done testing, select Multiply, which is the mode
    we'll use to add our texture. In this mode, Photoshop examines the
    pixels and multiplies them together, and then divides the result by
    255. This has the effect of darkening the image, but takes into account
    the brightness level of the pixels in both layers, unlike Darken mode,
    which simply replaces the lighter pixel with the darker one.

5   Change the Opacity slider to 70 percent. You'll see that this has the
    effect of emphasizing the texture in the lighter areas of the image, such
    as the sky, and allowing most of the darker image areas to show
    through, as you can see in Figure 17-17.

FIGURE 17-17
With Opacity set to 70 percent, the texture and background blend
together attractively.

6   Select the texture layer, and from the Layers palette, choose Merge
    Down. This merges the current layer with the layer below it. This
    technique enables you to merge two layers without completely
    flattening the image. The other layers, if any, remain unchanged.

WHAT YOU'VE LEARNED

In this chapter, you got to combine several different techniques you've already been exposed to in new ways. Among the things you learned:

- ☐ You can use the Layer ➪ Transform ➪ Perspective command to straighten images that have perspective distortion.

- ☐ Several new common shortcuts, including Command-A to select all of an image, Command-R to show or hide rulers, and Shift-Delete to fill in a color.

- ☐ The Crop tool provides a more flexible way of trimming images, because it can also rotate and scale a selection before cropping.

- ☐ You can use the toning tool's dodge/burn/sponge modes to lighten, darken, and modify the color saturation of sections of an image using painting tools.

- ☐ PICT files that you save can be used as textures.

In the final chapter of this book, we'll learn how to combine another set of techniques to produce color images suitable for display.

Fine-Tuning Color
Preparing Images for Display

THE PROJECT

Kitchen Table International's president would like to create some overhead transparencies of the vacation images you modified in Chapter 16. Now he wants 256-color versions to put on his personal Web page. Many of the pictures have a strong magenta color cast, which, he suspects, is due to leaving his camera in the trunk of the car for a few weeks. Can you correct the color in these photographs, and reduce them from 16.7+ million colors to 256? After that, he also wants you to resize a copy of the photos so he can print a full-page preview at the proper size on his ink-jet. You think you're up to the task, so you hop right in. Besides, your job's on the line.

THE TOOLS
- ⊡ Adjustment Layers
- ⊡ Color Balance
- ⊡ Levels
- ⊡ Image Size
- ⊡ Image ⇨ Mode ⇨ Indexed Color

Color correction is one of the highest-stakes activities you are likely to encounter in Photoshop. The reasons are obvious: If the final destination for color images is the printed page, you or your employer may have thousands of dollars in time and direct costs tied up in production costs alone. Fortunately, Photoshop has all the tools you need to provide the best possible color images. Simple color and density corrections can be made with the Image ➪ Adjust ➪ Variations dialog box we last used in Chapter 5. By viewing sample images, you can often judge how much of a particular color needs to be added or subtracted from an image to produce optimum results. The Levels dialog box we used in Chapter 3 can also be applied separately to the individual color channels of an image to improve the appearance.

Because the stakes are so high, an introductory book like this one shouldn't purport to teach you everything you need to know about color correction, color separating, and the prepress process. Entire books twice the length of this one deal with professional techniques for using Photoshop with scanners, interfacing with color prepress systems, and making digital color separations. Our goal in this chapter is to provide you with a little more exposure to some of the tools you'll be using as you move on to the next level.

We're going to take one of Scott's photos, discover exactly why the color is so bad, correct it, and then prepare the image for his Web page. We're going to let Scott handle reducing them to whatever size he wants to use on the page, and instead give him some resized versions he can output on his color printer for reference. While this project is less ambitious than what you'll encounter in professional applications, the skills you learn will provide a good foundation to build on.

If you aren't already familiar with basic color theory, you'll want to read Appendix A of this book for an introduction to calibrating your system for accurate color reproduction, and also Appendix B to learn about the most common color models. For some of the illustrations for this chapter, we'll refer you to the color insert in the center of this book, because color information doesn't seem to reproduce very well in grayscale figures.

histogram \hiss' to gram\ *n* **1:** A nasty missive transmitted to an evil person. **2:** Unit of measurement for cold remedies. **3:** A sort of EKG administered to an image by Photoshop to see if there is any possibility of bringing it to life.

STEP 1: CREATING ADJUSTMENT LAYERS

Color correction is the perfect use for Photoshop's Adjustment Layers, because they allow you to preview the effects of a color change without permanently applying it to an image. You can make as many modifications as you like, save the file with the Adjustment Layers intact, and make a duplicate copy of the image to produce a "final" image. You'll still be able to re-open the original file at any time, make additional adjustments, and produce a new final copy. In this next section, we'll open one of Scott's images and create the Adjustment Layers we need. Just follow these directions:

1 Copy the file tower.tif from the Chapter 18 folder of your CD-ROM to your hard disk, and open it in Photoshop. It has a distinct magenta cast, as you can see from the image Color 8-1 in the color insert. The basic image is also shown in grayscale here in Figure 18-1.

FIGURE 18-1
The image of the tower needs color correction.

2 Select Layer ⇨ New ⇨ Adjustment Layer to display the New Adjustment Layer dialog box, as shown in Figure 18-2.

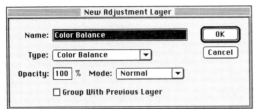

FIGURE 18-2
You can create nine different types of Adjustment Layers from this dialog box.

3 The Type field should have Color Balance selected from the drop-down list box. If not, choose it now. Color Balance is automatically filled in the Name field as a name for this layer. Opacity should be 100%, and blend mode Normal. Click on OK to create the new Adjustment Layer.

4 The Color Balance dialog box appears. We don't need to work with it yet, so click on OK.

5 Repeat Step 2 to access the New Adjustment Layer dialog box once more. This time select Levels from the drop-down Type list box, and click on OK.

6 The Levels dialog box appears. Click on OK to close it, and then examine the Layers palette, as shown in Figure 18-3.

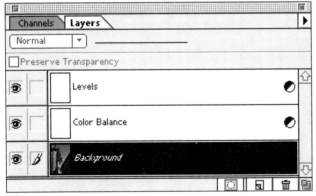

FIGURE 18-3
After you've added two Adjustment Layers, the Layers palette looks like this.

NOTE Adjustment Layers are similar to Layer Masks, and, in fact, are represented by mask icons in the Layers palette, as you can see in Figure 18-3. Each kind of layer changes a different kind of image attribute in all of the visible image layers that are stacked beneath in the Layers palette. You can choose from Levels, Curves, Brightness/Contrast, Color Balance, Hue/Saturation, and four additional lesser-used attributes, such as Invert and Posterize.

NOTE Because Adjustment Layers are a type of mask, you can paint on them to limit the adjustments they provide to only the unpainted area. For example, if you filled the top half of a Color Balance Adjustment Layer with black, only the bottom half of the layers below it would be affected. If you want to apply some changes to some image layers, and other changes to different layers, you can use the stacking order and painted areas to determine which image layers and parts of layers are modified by individual Adjustment Layers. If you were combining two images that had different color balance problems, you could create two Color Balance Adjustment Layers, and tweak each image separately.

STEP 2: REMOVING THE MAGENTA CAST

We'll start by adjusting the color balance of our image. The overall magenta cast applies to the entire image, so we don't need to mask off part of the picture to protect it from the Color Balance Adjustment Layer's effects. We could, if we needed to, select the sky area in the background image, and then switch to the Color Balance Adjustment Layer, fill the selection with black, and proceed to balance only the rest of the image. However, in this case, we'll proceed as follows:

1 Double-click the Color Balance Adjustment Layer. The Color Balance Layer dialog box appears, as shown in Figure 18-4.

FIGURE 18-4

You can adjust the color balance of an image in this dialog box.

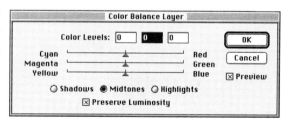

2 Good color can be somewhat subjective, although drastic defects such as the cast in our sample picture are very obvious. Ideally you should have a target image to use as a reference, but you may not always have one available. You can use Color 8-2 from the color insert, or load the Figure 18-2 file from the Chapter 18 folder of the CD-ROM. Look at either one now to get an idea of what color balance we're trying to achieve.

3   Click the Midtones button in the dialog box. Because the color cast seems to be evenly distributed in the highlights, midtones, and shadows, we can simply work with the midtones. The changes we make will be applied to all three.

4   Make sure the Preview checkbox is marked. This enables us to see the changes we make immediately in the original image.

5   Images can appear to have too much of any one or two of the three primary additive colors. That is, they can have too much red, green, or blue, or too much of both blue and green (the color cast will seem cyan), too much blue and red (excess magenta), or too much red and green (producing a yellow cast.) Extra amounts of red, green, and blue cancel each other out, so color casts are always produced by too much of one or two of the primary colors. To prove this, move all three of the sliders in the Color Balance Layer dialog box to the right an equal amount, and see what happens. The image has the same color balance, but is darker.

6   Move the sliders back to the zero point. The image appears to have too much magenta, which means we can reduce that color cast in one of two ways: by removing equal amounts of red and blue (which, added together, produce magenta), or by adding magenta's complement, green. We can accomplish the first by moving the Cyan-Red slider toward the cyan end of the scale (subtracting red effectively adds its complement, cyan), then adjusting the Yellow-Blue slider an equal amount, removing blue/adding yellow.

7   However, we can do the same thing by moving only the Magenta-Green slider toward the green. That, logically, subtracts some of the magenta that we see by adding green. Adjust the Magenta-Green slider to the right until the image looks more neutral. That should be at about the +25 point on the scale. Click on OK to apply the change to the Color Balance Adjustment Layer.

STEP 3: FINE-TUNING THE COLOR

If you look at the image now, you'll see that the objectionable magenta cast is gone, but now the picture seems to have too much cyan in it. That's likely to be typical of images that you work with, and a good example of why it may be easier for you, at first, to make corrections as we did in the last step by adding a complement to the unwanted hue, rather than trying to subtract the two component colors. Follow these directions to get rid of the cyan:

1   Double-click the Color Balance Adjustment Layer again to open the dialog box.

2   We can now get rid of the cyan cast by simply adding a little green. Move the Cyan-Red slider toward the right until the image takes on the rich, brownish colors of the original.

3   Uncheck the Preview box. The view of the image will return to the last adjustment you made (that is, with the magenta removed), so you can compare the most recent version with your current changes by checking and unchecking the box.

4   A change of about +35 should provide the fix we're looking for. When you're satisfied, click on OK to apply the modification to the Adjustment Layer.

5   Note that we've only made this change in the Adjustment Layer. The original image is unchanged. You can confirm this by making the Color Balance Adjustment Layer invisible. Click its eyeball icon to see the original image underneath, still with too much magenta and cyan.

 NOTE   Wait a minute! If our image had too much magenta and cyan, then wouldn't it be correct to say that it was too blue—because cyan and magenta "make" blue? While that would be true if equal amounts of excess were in both colors, in this case we had to remove varying amounts of each. It's difficult to judge from looking at the image alone. This picture, after all, looked as if it had far too much magenta—which is why learning to deal with individual colors as we're doing in this chapter is a good idea.

STEP 4: ADJUSTING TONAL RANGE

We haven't enhanced the image as much as we can. While the color is closer to what we want, the tonal range is far from perfect. If this were a grayscale image, we'd think it was a bit too dark, with not enough detail in the shadows. We can use the Levels Adjustment Layer to improve the tonal range. Here's how:

1   Double-click the Levels Adjustment Layer to produce the Levels dialog box, as shown in Figure 18-5. The histogram display shows the levels for the combined red, green, and blue layers.

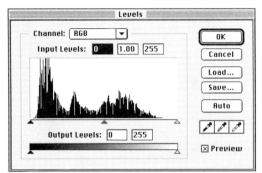

FIGURE 18-5
The Levels dialog box shows the combined histograms for the red, green, and blue layers.

2   Choose Red in the Channels drop-down list. The Red channel's histogram, shown in Figure 18-6, appears.

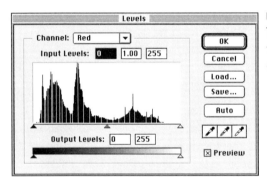

FIGURE 18-6
The Red channel's histogram shows the distribution of tones in the red channel of the image.

3   Adjust the black and white point triangles so they correspond to the first black tones and last white tones in the histogram, as you learned to do in Chapter 3. Slide the black triangle over to the right to the point where the histogram shows the black tones begin, and then slide the white triangle toward the left to where the white tones end.

4   Next, choose Green from the Channels drop-down list. The Green channel's histogram appears, as shown in Figure 18-7.

5   Adjust the black and white sliders to match this histogram's black and white points.

6   Next, choose Blue from the drop-down Channels list box. The Blue histogram looks like Figure 18-8.

7   Click on OK to apply the changes to the Levels Adjustment Layer.

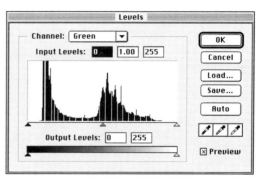

FIGURE 18-7
The Green channel's histogram looks like this before modifications are made.

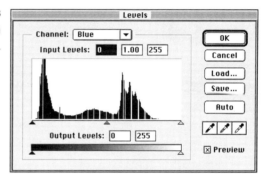

FIGURE 18-8
The Blue channel's histogram also needs tweaking.

8 Save a copy of this file in Photoshop format with all the Adjustment Layers intact. You can return to it at any time to make additional changes to these layers.

9 Use Layer ⇨ Flatten Image to combine all the changes we've made in the Adjustment Layers with the original image, and save this file in TIFF format as tower2.tif.

STEP 5: CHANGING PRINT SIZE

Photoshop enables you to create an image in any size you like, and then specify a different size to use when printing out the file. You can select a print size to best fit the image on the paper you'll be using. Because this image will be printed out on 8½ × 11-inch paper, we need to make sure it fills the sheet. Follow these directions to adjust the print size:

1 Select File ⇨ Page Setup ⇨ Options, and make sure the default paper size of 8½ × 11 is selected.

2   Place the mouse pointer in the document status box at the bottom of its window, and hold down the mouse pointer. A preview image like the one shown in Figure 18-9 pops up. This box shows the relative size of the image compared to the page size you have selected in File ⇨ Page Setup ⇨ Options.

FIGURE 18-9
The relative size of the image appears in this preview box.

3   Examine the image. You can see from the preview that the image is too small to fill the page. Moreover, it appears to be taller in proportion to the paper than it is wide. That is, if the image nearly fills the long dimension of the page, there will be extra space at either side.

4   Choose Image ⇨ Image Size. The Image Size dialog box, shown in Figure 18-10, appears.

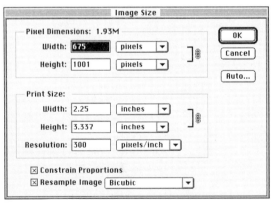

FIGURE 18-10
The Image Size dialog box shows the dimensions of the image, and the size it will print.

5   Because the proportion, or aspect ratio, of the image is extra tall, we need to specify the height of the image as it prints, and allow Photoshop to select a proportionate width. We also don't want the image to print too close to the edge of the paper, as most printers have a limited printable area that must be taken into account. Make sure that inches are the unit of measurement for the Height field, and then type in a value of 8.00 inches. This setting allows 1½ inches at both

the top and bottom of the paper as a safety margin, because the area that printers can actually print varies. Photoshop automatically adjusts the width to 5.395 inches.

6   Click on OK to apply the new print size to the image. Photoshop calculates a new image size and performs the interpolation necessary to resize the image.

7   Save the file as tower.tif. This is your full-color, RGB version of the image, which you'll use in Step 6 in a moment.

8   Next, go to the Image ➩ Mode menu item and select CMYK color. The image will be converted to the CMYK mode that Scott will use to print out his full-page, full-color versions of the images.

9   Save the CMYK version of the image as tower-4.tif or some other name that will help you remember that this is a CMYK version.

TIP One of the most common complaints of both novice and professional users is that the colors on the printed page don't look like what they saw on their monitors. Because so many low-cost continuous-tone color printers proliferate the market, even beginning users will encounter this problem. The simplest fix is to save files as CMYK when you're ready to print them. As a result, your output will look more like the CMYK preview or final version you saw. Edit in RGB, but print in CMYK.

STEP 6: REDUCING TO 256 COLORS

Next, we're going to change the image's color palette to 256 colors. We're doing this as the final step because Photoshop is unable to perform many of its functions on indexed color images of this type. You lose all the soft-edged brushes, for example, and will definitely not like the results of using hard-edged brushes for functions such as cloning. Follow these directions to reduce from 16.7+ million colors to 256 hues:

1   Reopen the RGB version of our image, tower.tif, that you saved in the previous exercise before you created the CMYK version.

2   Use the magic wand tool, with its tolerance set to 32, and select by clicking and Shift-clicking as many sky pixels as possible in the image.

3   Choose Select ➩ Inverse to invert the selection so that the tower and surrounding buildings are selected. The selection is not critical. We're selecting as much of the building and as little of the sky as possible because Photoshop will use a selection you make to determine which

256 hues out of 16.7+ million possible colors it should use to build a palette for this image. Because the buildings have been selected, the colors will be weighted toward them, although the blues of the sky will not be ignored. This gives us smoother color transitions in the buildings in the final picture, because more colors will be able to represent them. The sky may suffer a little, but we don't care.

4 Select Image ➪ Mode ➪ Indexed Color, and the Indexed Color dialog box, as shown in Figure 18-11, appears.

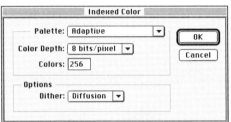

FIGURE 18-11
Use the Indexed Color dialog box to choose a palette for 256 (or fewer) color images.

5 Select Adaptive from the Palette drop-down list box. With this palette, Photoshop samples all the colors in an image (or in the selection we just made) and tries to find the 256 most frequently used colors for our palette.

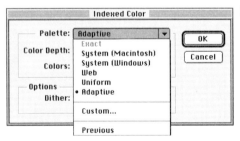

FIGURE 18-12
Five main palettes are available for indexing color.

6 For Color Depth, make sure 8 bits/pixel is chosen (so we'll get a full 256 hues), and that the Diffusion dither option is selected. We need this latter setting because our Adaptive palette may not contain all the colors Photoshop needs to represent an image. By allowing diffusion dithering, Photoshop can add pixels of colors that are close to the one needed to simulate that hue. A random pattern is used that keeps the dithering as unobtrusive as possible.

7 Click on OK to apply the mode change. Because a broad range of colors isn't needed to reproduce this image, the final picture looks very much like the modified image in Color 8-2 in the color insert. If an image has many colors, especially multicolored gradients and transitions, you'll probably get some banding where Photoshop must use a small number of colors to represent the smooth progression of hues in the original.

8 Save this image as tower.gif—using the GIF format, which can present only 256 or fewer colors.

NOTE Five palette types are available, depending on what sort of image you are working with. You can see the drop-down list box in Figure 18-12. The Exact palette is available only if the image already has 256 or fewer colors: Photoshop can construct a palette that includes every color already in the image. The System palette is the Macintosh's default eight-bit palette (you can also choose the Windows default, even if you're using a Mac), a uniform sampling of colors. (Because our image is heavy in the browns and blues, this palette is unlikely to match ours very closely, so we wouldn't have enough of the colors we need to represent the image.) The Web palette uses the colors built into Web browsers. The Uniform palette is another evenly distributed palette, created for a specific color depth. (You can choose 8 bits/pixel (256 colors), 7 bits/pixel (128 colors), and so forth in the Color Depth drop-down list.) You may also design your own Custom palette by selecting individual colors, or use the Previous palette, which is useful if you want a succession of images to all use the same palette of colors (say, to display on the same Web page).

USING 256 OR FEWER COLORS

You'll want to use 256 or fewer colors on many occasions. Web pages benefit especially from indexed color images. If you have a graphic that can be represented by 256, 128, 64, or even 16 colors, you'll always end up with a smaller file that's faster to download and display if you reduce the colors to the smallest possible palette.

Web browsing software packages have default color sets, and if you can confine your images to those exact colors you'll have a better chance of previewing how an image will display over the Web. For example, if you place multiple images on a page that use different palettes, visitors to your Web site who are using 256-color monitors may see bizarre color shifts as their browsers attempt to display each image using the skimpy available hues. You can use Photoshop's Web palette when you're indexing images to minimize these effects.

WHAT YOU'VE LEARNED

In this last chapter of the book, we've tried to give you a taste of what lies ahead of you now that you've gained a solid understanding of Photoshop's most important features. You learned some of the basics of color correcting, which you can use to progress into more sophisticated aspects of fixing bad color and creating color separations. Among the things you learned are the following:

- Adjustment Layers are perfect for color correction, because they allow you to preview effects without permanently changing an image.

- Adjustment Layers are similar to Layer Masks.

- You can choose from Levels, Curves, Brightness/Contrast, Color Balance, Hue/Saturation, and four additional lesser-used attributes, such as Invert and Posterize for Adjustment Layer modifications.

- Adjustment Layers affect only the layers stacked below them.

- You can create several Adjustment Layers of the same type to apply changes to particular layers or parts of layers.

- Images can appear to have too much of any one or two of the three primary additive colors. That is, they can have too much red, green, or blue, or too much of both blue and green (the color cast will seem cyan); too much blue and red (excess magenta), or too much red and green (producing a yellow cast).

- You can use the Levels dialog box to modify the tonal range of each color channel separately.

- Photoshop enables you to create an image in any size you like, and then specify a different size to use when printing out the file. You can select a print size to best fit the image on the paper you'll be using.

- Photoshop offers five different indexed color palettes. The Exact palette is available only if the image already has 256 or fewer colors: Photoshop can construct a palette that includes every color already in the image. The System palette is the Macintosh's default eight-bit palette (you can also choose the Windows default, even if you're using a Mac), a uniform sampling of colors. The Web palette uses the colors built into Web browsers. The Uniform Palette is another evenly distributed palette, created for a specific color depth. The Adaptive palette is an optimized palette of as many as possible of an image's current colors.

We hope you've enjoyed learning Photoshop through these exercises, even if Kitchen Table International is not likely to hit your résumé as a reference.

Calibrating Your Monitor

This appendix introduces the topic of calibrating your system, with emphasis on calibrating your monitor. We'll explain a little about why calibration is important, give an overview of how it's done, and help you calibrate your monitor so your view of a particular file looks a lot like what other users should see with the same file on their systems.

In an introductory book like this one, it's not possible to lead beginners through all the complex steps needed to fine-tune systems for prepress operations. It would be absurd to jump from teaching you how to make a selection into the complexities of color separating, dot gain, or the mysteries of current hot subjects such as stochastic screening. However, we hope that after finishing this book you'll be ready to move on to a more advanced book that does cover these essential parts of professional imaging.

Indeed, one of the first things new Photoshop users notice is that images that look great on their display screens may look completely different when they transport those images to a colleague's computer, or print the image out using a desktop color printer. You may have spent hours adjusting the color and density of an image only to find it looking darker and flatter, or perhaps lighter and more contrasty when viewed on someone else's monitor, or even more divergent from what you thought you were getting when you print it out.

The same picture captured by the scanner on your desktop can appear drastically different when grabbed by a different scanner. By the time your work reaches the printing press, it may bear no resemblance to what you saw on your screen. Fortunately, there's a solution.

WHAT'S THE PROBLEM HERE?

Once you read Appendix B, you'll know that these disparities occur because different technologies are used to capture and reproduce colors. Scanners use red, green, and blue light sources (or a white light source and red, green, and blue filters) and (often) use charge-coupled device (CCD) sensors to snatch images. The light sources, filters, and solid-state sensors all have characteristics of their own that can affect the color balance and density of scanned images.

Then the images are displayed on computer monitors using red, blue, and green phosphors that glow when struck by light. These phosphors, too, vary from manufacturer to manufacturer, so you might find one display that shows bright, vivid colors and another that has more muted hues—with both of them adding a subtle color cast.

Any RGB image, of course, is only an approximation of the way colors look when printed using cyan, magenta, yellow, and black pigments, inks, dyes, toner, or some other printing method. Not only do scanners, monitors, and printers vary in the way they reproduce color, they have different subsets of all the available hues that they can produce. More specifically, your scanner may capture colors that are impossible to display on your monitor, which, in turn may show hues that are outside the capabilities of a CMYK printing system to reproduce.

So, how can you possibly hope to reproduce color that's even acceptably accurate? The answer, of course, is to calibrate your entire system so that each component "knows" the limitations, capabilities, and biases of the other components. The following simplified example shows you how this is done.

A QUICK CALIBRATION EXAMPLE

A particular scanner may be supplied with an image file that has been carefully tested by the scanner manufacturer, which also provides a profile of the characteristics of the file. If you print this image using your desktop color printer, and then place it on the scanner, and capture an image of the printout, the scanner can compare the colors and densities of the scan with the stored profile information that specifies the characteristics of the original file.

The scanner can then produce a fudge-factor file of its own: To reproduce this kind of green on your printer, the scanner needs to add so much of this other color. To get a good red, it must subtract a particular amount of density and/or another hue. In other words, the scanner can alter the way it reproduces color to more accurately reflect what's going to be printed from your printer.

Note that once you've calibrated your scanner and printer with each other, even though these two components may walk in lock-step, that doesn't mean the colors will look accurate on your display screen. It wouldn't matter much if you planned to just scan and print, and ignore the screen display. But if you plan to make adjustments to color or density, you'll want the image on the monitor to resemble what will be printed by the printer.

It's also important to realize that calibration is not something you do once and forget about. You need to prepare separate calibration profiles for every scanner you work with, every display screen, and every output device. So, if you use a color ink-jet printer to get a rough look at what a color image looks like, you'll still need to calibrate for whatever proofing system and printing inks you'll be using. You may be required to recalibrate for any of these components as they age or change characteristics. If your scanner vendor doesn't provide a file to use for calibration, you can use the Olé No Moiré file in the Calibration folder on the Photoshop CD-ROM.

CALIBRATING YOUR MONITOR'S DISPLAY

Calibrating your own monitor is an important step you should carry out soon after you begin using Photoshop. Your monitor is adjusted using a Control Panel, not Photoshop itself, so the following steps will be the only ones in this book that don't require having Photoshop loaded. Make sure that your monitor has been switched on for 30–60 minutes so it will be warmed up and the colors stabilized, and adjust the room lighting to the average level it will be at when you're working with your computer. Then follow these directions:

1   Find the Gamma control panel and open it. The easiest way to find it is to pull down the Apple menu and click the cascading Control Panels choice, and then scroll down to the Gamma control panel. If the Gamma control panel hasn't been installed on your computer, you'll find it in the Goodies ⇨ Calibration folder on the Photoshop CD-ROM. Drag it to the System Folder and it will be placed in the correct subfolder automatically. The Gamma control panel's dialog box looks like Figure A-1.

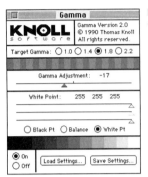

FIGURE A-1

The Gamma control panel looks like this.

2 In the Target Gamma section, click the 1.8 button. That's the setting that's best suited to producing a screen display that matches CMYK images and the typical gamma used by other applications. You may find you need a higher value if you output to video devices. However, 1.8 is a good all-around setting.

3 Move the Gamma slider until the two sets of alternating gray boxes appear exactly the same, or as close as you can make them.

4 Place a piece of white paper near the monitor screen. Click the button labeled White Pt (for White Point) and then move the red, green, and blue sliders until the monitor screen appears to be a neutral white that matches the paper as closely as possible. Many monitors have a slight color cast, and this step lets you compensate for that tendency.

5 Click the Balance radio button, and move the red, green, and blue sliders until the alternating boxes in the gray step-scale below the sliders have no color cast.

6 You can click the Black Pt radio button, and adjust the sliders to remove any remaining color tint that you might detect in the black areas on your screen.

7 Click the Save button and store the settings under a name of your choice.

8 Close the Gamma Control panel to make the changes permanent. You shouldn't have to adjust the gamma again unless you switch monitors or change your room lighting.

9 If you use your Mac with dual monitors, as some professionals do (for example, a large screen monitor for documents mated with a smaller monitor for file management and other functions) you can drag the Gamma Control panel to the second monitor and calibrate that one as well.

CALIBRATING PHOTOSHOP FOR YOUR MONITOR

You'll also need to tell Photoshop what kind of monitor you have, so the application will have the information it needs to display CMYK previews. To do that, follow these directions:

1 Select File ⇨ Color Settings ⇨ Monitor Setup. A dialog box like the one shown in Figure A-2 will appear.

FIGURE A-2

The Monitor Setup dialog box enables you to calibrate your display for Photoshop.

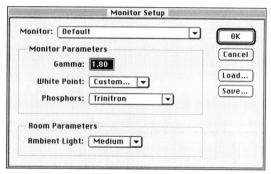

2 Look through the Monitor drop-down list box. If you find your own monitor listed, use that. Otherwise, let the Default setting remain.

3 In the Monitor Parameters area, type in the gamma value you set in the previous exercise (probably 1.8) if it's not already filled in for you as the default.

4 In the White Point field, select 6,500 degrees K in the drop-down list. The settings here represent color temperature for the light source used to view your image, with 6,500K being the most typical. If you have a monitor calibration device that can actually measure the color temperature of your monitor, use that value instead. If the exact color temperature doesn't appear in the drop-down list box, select Custom and type in the value you require. Incidentally, color temperature is an actual temperature, being the amount of heat, in degrees Kelvin, generated by something called a black-body radiator. At 6,500K, the light generated approximates noon daylight.

5 You can leave the Phosphors setting at the default Trinitron setting, unless your particular monitor appears in the skimpy drop-down list box, or you happen to have RGB chromacity coordinates provided by your monitor vendor. (If you own a 20-inch or larger professional quality monitor, that's possible.)

6 In the Ambient Light field, you can leave the setting at Medium, unless you work in a room that has either very bright or very dim illumination, in which case you can make an adjustment from the drop-down list box.

7 Click the Save button to save the settings under a name of your choice. Then click on OK to make the settings you've selected permanent.

As you work with Photoshop more and need to prepare images that are ready for prepress, you'll want to learn how to calibrate for printing inks, dot gain, and the color proofing system you use. As we said, these are all beyond the scope of this book.

An Introduction to Color Theory

This appendix provides a general introduction to the color theories you'll need to be familiar with as you use Photoshop 4.0. We'll cover the most frequently used color models and explain the differences between the way color is displayed on your monitor and the way it is output by an offset press or printer.

Human perception of color is a strange and wonderful thing. Most of us remember a little of how the eye sees from our high school science class: The retina of the eye contains tiny rods and cones that somehow react to light and provide information to the brain that we interpret as sight.

Color vision is a miracle of sorts, and trying to duplicate our ability to see color using mechanical devices such as computers and printing presses is a source of much vexation for software and hardware designers. Color vision derives from three different types of cone cells, which respond to different wavelengths of light. Our eyes are able to detect only a relatively narrow band of frequencies, ranging from 400 nanometers at the short (violet) end of the visible spectrum to 700 nanometers at the long (red) end.

Artificial color systems, including computer scanners, monitors, printers, and other peripherals, attempt to reproduce (or *model*) the colors that we see, using various sets of components of color. If the model is a good one, all the colors we are able to detect with our eyes are defined by the parameters of the model. The colors within the definition of each model are termed its *color space*. Colors that don't fit within the space of a particular model are referred to as *out of gamut*. Photoshop has the ability to flag out-of-gamut colors for you, as you may have noticed when an exclamation point pops up in the Color palette.

The international standard for specifying color was defined in 1931 by the Commission Internationale L'Eclairage (CIE); it is a scientific color model that can be used to define all the colors that humans can see. However, Photoshop users most often work with one of three or four other color models, including RGB or CMYK, that are more practical because they are based on the actual systems used to reproduce the colors, rather than some scientific definitions.

Although none of these real-world systems can generate all the colors in the full range of human perception, they are the models we must use. Some efforts are underway to define new models, but so far nothing that will completely take over the industry in the near future has appeared on the horizon. Because most image-editing and scanning programs support the most-used color models, your best bet is to learn about the most common models.

Of the three most common models, the ones based on the hue-lightness-saturation (HLS) and hue-saturation-value (HSV) color models are the most natural for us to visualize, because they deal with a continuous range of colors that may vary in brightness or richness. Unfortunately, Photoshop users most often actually work with two other models—RGB (or additive color) and CMYK (or subtractive color)—both of which are somewhat easier for computers to handle, because the individual components are nothing more than basic colors.

Additive color is commonly used in computer display monitors, while subtractive color is used for output devices such as printers. Because you need to understand how color works with these peripherals, we'll explore the additive and subtractive models first.

RGB: ADDITIVE COLOR

Color monitors produce color by aiming three electronic guns at sets of red, green, and blue phosphors coated on the screen of your Cathode Ray Tube (CRT). The guns excite the phosphors in proportion to the amount of red, green, or blue light in a given pixel of the image. The phosphors glow, and our eyes add their illumination together, perceiving a color image. If none of the phosphors glows, we see a black pixel. If all three glow in equal proportions, we see a neutral color—gray or white, depending on the intensity.

Such a color system uses the additive color model—so called because the colors are added together. Systems can produce a huge selection of colors by varying the combinations of light. In addition to pure red, green, and blue, we can also produce cyan (green and blue together), magenta (red and blue), yellow (red and green), and all the colors in between. As with grayscale data, the number of bits used to store color—usually eight bits per hue—determines the number of different tones that can be reproduced. Eight bits (256 different shades) multiplied by three colors equals 24 bits in all, or $256 \times 256 \times 256$ colors—a total of 16.8 million.

No CRT device available today produces pure red, green, or blue light. Only lasers generate absolutely pure colors, and they aren't practical for display devices. We see images through the glow of phosphors, as mentioned, and the ability of phosphors to generate absolutely pure colors is limited. Color representations on a monitor differ from brand to brand and even from one monitor to another within the same brand.

Moreover, the characteristics of a given monitor change as the monitor ages and the phosphors wear out. Some phosphors, particularly blue ones, change in intensity at a different rate than others. In other words, identical signals rarely produce identical images on CRTs, regardless of how closely the monitors are matched in type, age, and other factors. Appendix A provides more information on this topic in the discussion of calibration.

ADDITIVE COLOR AND YOUR MONITOR

In practice, most monitors display far fewer colors than the total of which they are theoretically capable of displaying. The number of colors that can be displayed is largely a function of the amount of memory available to store and manipulate color. A Mac with 1MB of VRAM, for example, may be able to display thousands of colors at 640×480 to 832×624 pixel resolution, and only 256 colors at 1024×768. Increasing the amount of VRAM to 2MB or more can give you millions of colors at the higher resolutions. If you're using Photoshop, you should upgrade your video memory so you can display millions of colors; 16-bit color just can't represent all the colors you'll be working with in an image.

CMYK: SUBTRACTIVE COLOR

A second way of producing color that is familiar to computer users is *subtractive color.* It, too, has a color model that represents its color gamut. When we represent colors in hard copy form, the image is viewed by light that strikes the paper or other substrate, is *filtered* by the image on the paper, and then is reflected back to our eyes.

This light starts out with equal quantities of red, green, and blue light and looks white to our eyes. The pigments the light passes through before bouncing off the substrate absorb part of this light, subtracting it from the spectrum. The light that remains reaches our eyes and is interpreted as color. That's why this color model is known as the subtractive system: Various components of light are subtracted from white to produce the hues you see.

The three primary subtractive colors are cyan, magenta, and yellow, and the model is usually known as the CMY model. When black is added (for reasons explained shortly), it becomes the CMYK model (black is represented by its terminal character, k, rather than b to avoid confusion with the additive primary blue).

In subtractive output devices, cyan, magenta, yellow, and usually black pigments are used to represent the full gamut of colors. It's obvious why additive colors won't work for hard copies: It is possible to produce red, green, and blue pigments, and you could print red, green, and blue colors that way (that's exactly what is done for spot color), but you can't mix additive primary pigments to generate other colors. For example, red pigment reflects only red light; green pigment reflects only green. When they overlap, the red pigment absorbs the green, and the green absorbs the red, so no light is reflected at all and we see black.

The cyan pigment, on the other hand, absorbs *only* red light. It reflects both blue and green, producing the blue-green shade we see as cyan. Yellow pigment absorbs only blue light, reflecting red and green, while the magenta pigment absorbs only green, reflecting red and blue. When we overlap two of the subtractive primaries, some of at least one color still reflects. Magenta (red-blue) and yellow (red-green) together produce red, because the magenta pigment absorbs green and the yellow pigment absorbs blue. Their common color, red, is the only one remaining.

Of course, each of the subtractive primaries can be present in various intensities or percentages, just as with the additive colors. Computers can keep track of how much cyan, magenta, and yellow is present using eight bits of information and 256 different shades of each, just as with additive, RGB images. However, an extra eight bits are required to track how much black is in an image; because four colors are used, CMYK files actually represent 32-bit (not 24-bit) color.

Why is black added? Theoretically, you can represent virtually any color within the CMY color space using the correct percentages of cyan, magenta, yellow. However, you'll recall that RGB monitors aren't perfect because the color of the phosphors can vary. So, too, is it impossible to design pigments that reflect absolutely pure colors.

Equal amounts of cyan, magenta, and yellow pigment *should* produce black. More often, what you'll get is a muddy brown. With many output systems, that's what you'd have to settle for. It's a complicated enough procedure to lay down sets of cyan, magenta, and yellow pigment in perfect register.

However, better results can be obtained by adding black as a fourth color. Black can fill in areas that are supposed to be black and add detail to other areas of an image. While the fourth color does complicate the process a bit, the actual cost in processes such as offset printing is minimal. Black ink is used to print text anyway, so no additional press run is needed for black. Moreover, black ink is cheaper than critical process color inks, so it's possible to save money by using black instead of laying on three subtractive primaries extra thick.

The output systems you use to print hard copies of color images use the subtractive color system in one way or another. Most of them are unable to print varying percentages of each of the primary colors. Offset presses, ink-jet printers, color laser printers, and thermal wax transfer printers are examples of these. All of these systems must simulate other colors by dithering, which is similar to the halftoning system discussed earlier. A few printers can vary the amount of pigment laid down over a broader range. Thermal dye sublimation printers are an example of this type. These printers can print a full range of tones, up to the 16.7 million colors possible with 24-bit systems.

COMPLICATIONS

Now that you understand the two most commonly used color models, you can probably grasp the problems Photoshop users have to wrestle with. Our monitors can display only RGB colors with reasonable accuracy. Our output devices, on the other hand, use a completely different color model to create hard copies. That wouldn't be as much of a problem if the two color spaces were exactly the same. In practice, many colors can be displayed by the RGB color model that can't be reproduced by CMYK—and vice versa.

Many complex reasons make this the case. Phosphors can generate colors that pigments can't reproduce, and the reverse is true. You can always create a lighter, brighter color by pumping more light into an additive system, whereas subtractive colors are limited by the brightness of the paper substrate onto which the colors are laid. The best we can hope for is to approximate colors between these two color systems.

In Photoshop, the problems become most evident when you try to display subtractive colors on an RGB monitor. If you open a file saved in CMYK format, Photoshop must convert it to RGB to display the image on the screen. If you change modes from RGB to CMYK and back again, some colors will be lost during each conversion. That's why Photoshop lets you preview color renditions between one mode and another without actually making a conversion.

OTHER COLOR MODELS

Other color models that have been developed include hue-saturation-brightness and hue-lightness-saturation, known as HSB and HLS respectively. Both models are supported by many software packages, including Photoshop. However, exotic color models such as these are beyond the scope of this book.

Another color "system" is the Pantone Matching System, or PMS. This system is Pantone, Inc.'s check-standard trademark for color reproduction and color reproduction materials. At least, that's the legal terminology that Pantone is quite zealous about insisting on from helpless writers like us. In simpler language, PMS is just another way of referring to colors. Instead of using a set of descriptive parameters to define every possible color, PMS takes a different approach. Pantone has identified hundreds of colors and defined the formulas needed to produce pigments of those colors. Each color is given a number. You use a printed matching guide—actually an ink swatch book, which is available at most graphic arts supply stores—to select the color. The samples are printed on both coated and uncoated paper. You can select a color and specify it by number. Your printer can then use the PMS formula to mix the proper ink. This is extremely useful when you want a specific spot color for, say, corporate trade dress or product packaging.

As useful as Pantone colors are for spot color, they can't be used to print full color images; to reproduce 256 different colors, you would need 256 different inks and press runs. If you don't need an exact shade, it may be less expensive to let your printer use the three process colors to produce the spot color you want. That's because using a specially mixed color requires cleaning the press and other additional make-ready steps.

You can also use the Pantone Matching System just as a way to specify colors. You can choose a Pantone color and then tell your printer to approximate it as closely as possible using the four-color process.

If the RGB, CYMK, and HSB color models produce continuous color models, the Pantone model might be thought of as discrete points of particular color within the larger color space that humans can perceive. While the Pantone color selection is huge, it can't represent all possible colors, as the other models can.

As you can see, color is a complicated topic. But the more you know about color theory, the more you can anticipate—and prevent—color and calibration problems with your computer and with Photoshop especially.

Sample Filter Effects

On the following pages you'll find single images that have been processed by each of Photoshop's filters using the default values of each filter. They have been grouped by the same subdivisions you'll find in the Filter menu, as follows:

- Artistic
- Blur
- Brush Strokes
- Distort
- Noise
- Pixelate
- Render
- Sharpen
- Sketch
- Stylize
- Texture
- Other

Samples for the two Video filters—De-Interlace and NTSC Colors—are not provided, because their effects aren't visible in the grayscale images in this appendix.

ARTISTIC FILTERS

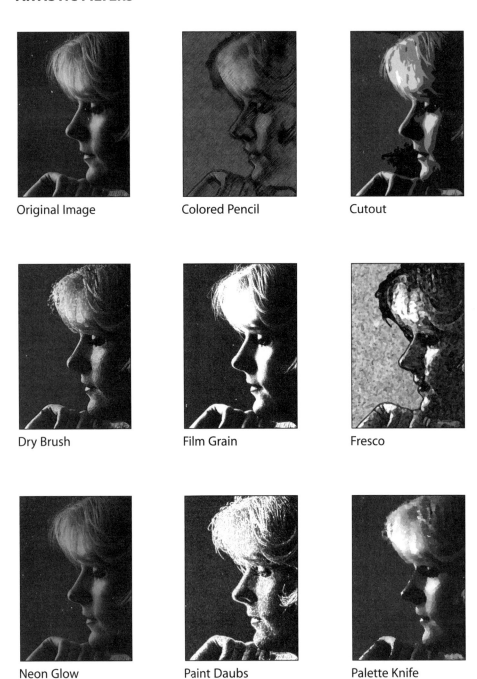

Original Image

Colored Pencil

Cutout

Dry Brush

Film Grain

Fresco

Neon Glow

Paint Daubs

Palette Knife

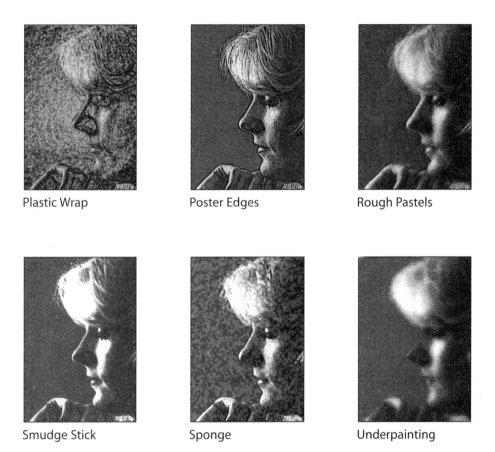

Plastic Wrap

Poster Edges

Rough Pastels

Smudge Stick

Sponge

Underpainting

Watercolor

BLUR FILTERS

Blur

Blur More

Gaussian Blur

Motion Blur

Radial Blur

Smart Blur

BRUSH STROKES FILTERS

Accented Edges

Angled Strokes

Crosshatch

Dark Strokes

Ink Outlines

Spatter

Sprayed Strokes

Sumi-e

DISTORT FILTERS

Diffuse Glow

Displace

Glass

Ocean Ripple

Pinch

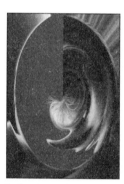

Polar Coordinates

Ripple

Shear

Spherize

Twirl

Wave

ZigZag

NOISE FILTERS

Add Noise

Despeckle

Dust & Scratches

Median

PIXILATE FILTERS

Color Halftone

Crystallize

Facet

Fragment

Mezzotint

Mosaic

Pointillize

RENDER FILTERS

Clouds

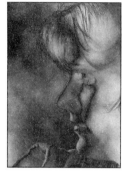

Difference Clouds

Lens Flare

Lighting Effects

Texture Fill

SHARPEN FILTERS

Sharpen

Sharpen Edges

Sharpen More

Unsharp Mask

SKETCH FILTERS

Bas Relief

Chalk & Charcoal

Charcoal

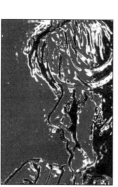

Chrome

Conte Crayon

Graphic Pen

Halftone Pattern

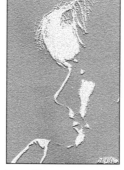

Note Paper

Photocopy

Plaster

Reticulation

Stamp

Torn Edges

Water Paper

STYLIZE FILTERS

Diffuse

Emboss

Extrude

Find Edges

Glowing Edges

Solarize

Tiles

Trace Contour

Wind

TEXTURE FILTERS

Craquelure

Grain

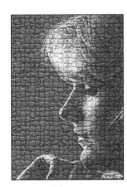

Mosaic Tiles

Patchwork

Stained Glass

Texturizer

OTHER FILTERS

Custom

High Pass

Maximum

Minimum

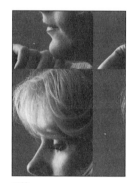

Offset

Toolbox Reference Guide

This appendix includes a chart that shows the function of each of the tools (with shortcut keys) in Photoshop's toolbox. You can use this section as a quick reference to the functions of each of the tools.

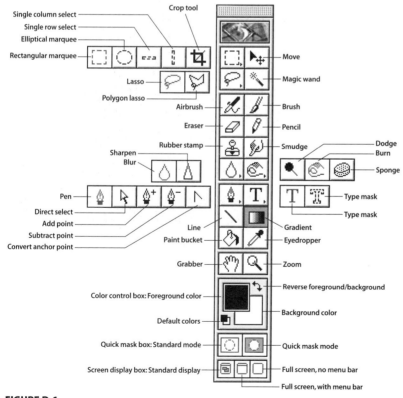

FIGURE D-1

Photoshop's toolbox shows many—but not all—of the tools available at any one time.

RECTANGULAR MARQUEE (M)   Selects rectangular portions of images; Shift-drag to select a square.

ELLIPTICAL MARQUEE   Selects oval shapes; Shift-drag to select a perfect circle; Option-Shift to create a circle from a center point.

SINGLE ROW MARQUEE   Selects a single row of pixels.

SINGLE COLUMN MARQUEE   Selects a single column of pixels.

CROP TOOL (C)   Allows rotating or resizing of images before trimming.

LASSO (L)   Makes freehand selections.

POLYGON LASSO   Makes freehand selections between points you click.

AIRBRUSH (A)   Paints soft-edged strokes.

ERASER (E)   Erases pixels and restores from a stored image.

RUBBER STAMP (S)   Copies portions of images.

BLUR (R)   Unsharpens images.

SHARPEN   Sharpens images.

PEN (P)   Draws paths.

DIRECT SELECT   Selects portions of paths.

ADD POINT   Adds points to a path.

DELETE POINT   Removes points from a path.

CONVERT POINT   Changes straight line segments to curved, and vice versa.

LINE TOOL (N)   Draws straight lines.

PAINT BUCKET (K)   Fills selected areas with color.

HAND (H)   Moves entire image.

FOREGROUND COLOR   Click to change the foreground color from the Color Picker.

USE DEFAULT COLORS (D)   Changes the foreground color to black, and the background color to white.

STANDARD MODE (Q)   Turns off Quick Mask.

STANDARD SCREEN (F)   Shows the normal screen with menu bars and palettes.

FULL SCREEN WITH MENU BAR   Shows the full screen view with palettes hidden.

FULL SCREEN MODE   Shows the full screen view with palettes and menu bars hidden.

QUICK MASK MODE   Represents selected or masked areas by a red overlay.

BACKGROUND COLOR   Click to change the background color from the Color Picker.

SWAP FOREGROUND/BACKGROUND COLORS (X)   Exchanges the values of the two colors.

ZOOM (Z)   Magnifies or reduces the document image.

EYEDROPPER (I)   Changes foreground or background color from a sample you select.

GRADIENT (G)   Fills the selection with a gradual transition from one color to another.

TYPE TOOL (T)   Creates filled type.

TYPE MASK   Creates a selection from the type.

DODGE TOOL (O)   Lightens the area.

BURN TOOL   Darkens the area.

SPONGE TOOL   Adds or reduces color saturation.

SMUDGE (U)   Blends pixels.

PENCIL (Y)   Draws hard-edged lines.

PAINTBRUSH (B)   Draws brush strokes on an image, using hard-edged or soft-edged brushes, or user-defined brushes.

MAGIC WAND (W)   Selects pixels based on brightness/color similarity.

MOVE TOOL (V)   Moves a selected area.

About the CD-ROM

The accompanying CD-ROM contains folders where you'll find all the graphics used in this book. A folder exists for each chapter, for three of the appendixes, and for the color insert. Each chapter folder has two subfolders:

- Figures
- Working Files

The Figures folder contains the figures used throughout the book. The Working Files folder contains the figures in the various stages of each project.

EXTRAS

On the CD-ROM, you'll also find a Clip Art folder that contains photos and art files from the authors for you to experiment with, as well as the following:

BACKGROUNDS FROM TEXTURE FARM   Superb photographic-quality background images in Kodak Photo CD format. You can access these backgrounds from Adobe Photoshop or any other Photo CD-savvy graphics application.

KAI'S POWER TOOLS TRYOUT FROM METATOOLS   Award-winning special effects filters for Adobe Photoshop. This package provides save-disabled versions of Kai's Power Tools for Macintosh and Windows. To install Kai's Power Tools Tryout click on the Install 1 icon and follow the instructions.

CONVOLVER TRYOUT FROM METATOOLS   Award-winning special effects and texture generator for Adobe Photoshop. To install, click on the Demo Version icon and follow the instructions.

PHOTOSHOP SPECIAL EFFECTS FILTERS DEMO FROM XAOS TOOLS   Includes TypeCaster 1.1, Paint Alchemy 2, and Terrazzo. To install, double-click on installer icons.

DEBABELIZER LITE LE   This version of the award-winning Macintosh graphics translator will read and write BMP, GIF, PICT, and TIFF (Mac and IBM) files. To run, click on the Demo Version icon.

DEBABELIZER TOOLBOX DEMO   This is a full demo of the premiere Macintosh graphics translator, which reads and writes 64 graphics formats. To install, double-click on the installer icon.

Glossary

Part of being a Photoshop Instant Expert means encountering terms you may not understand from time to time. We tried to define most words we thought you might not understand the first time they appeared in this book. However, it wasn't practical to explain every term, synonym, or jargonism you might encounter without bogging down the text with continual digressions. You can check this comprehensive glossary whenever you encounter a new or obscure word, whether you're working with this book, talking turkey with a service bureau, or just trying to sound smart among your other Photoshop-using colleagues. While I haven't defined every single Photoshop palette and tool, I've tried to describe in some detail features new to Photoshop 4.0.

achromatic color A color with no saturation, such as a light gray.

additive colors The primary colors of light—red, green, and blue—that, when combined, produce white light. Your monitor (or home television, if you're a couch potato) is probably the most common source for RGB images you see on a regular basis, and most Photoshop images are manipulated in this mode.

adjustment layer A layer that affects the brightness and hues of all layers below it without affecting the actual pixels in those respective layers.

airbrush An atomizer used for spraying paint. Photoshop's airbrush-like tool can apply a fine spray of a given tone to a specified area, and features fully controllable airbrushes that enable you to adjust the size of the airbrush spray, its density or concentration, and the speed at which the spray flows.

alpha channel   An optional grayscale "layer" of an image that can be created to store selections and other modifications and may be saved with the image if it is stored in TIFF or Photoshop's proprietary PSD format. *See also* channel.

ambient lighting   The overall nondirectional lighting that fills an area. When using Photoshop's lighting effects filters, you can place specific lights around your subject, and use ambient lighting to fill in the dark areas not illuminated by one of the main lights.

anamorphic   An image that has been enlarged or reduced more in one direction than another. The image looks "squashed" or "stretched" in a given dimension.

anti-aliasing   A process that can be used to remove the appearance of jaggies or stair-stepping in an image. Anti-aliasing smoothes out diagonal lines by placing dots of an in-between tone in appropriate places.

applications program interface (API)   A common interface that enables software engineers to write programs that will operate with a broad range of computer configurations. Photoshop's ability to accept plug-in filters or acquisition add-ons such as TWAIN modules is an example of an API that can be used by third-party software developers.

archive   To store files that are no longer active. Programs such as STUFFIT combine and compress files into an archive file for more compact, easier storage.

ascender   The portion of an uppercase letter that extends above the *x-height* (*see also*). The letter *d* is an example of a character with an ascender.

ASCII   No definition is needed for ASCII. Even Bob Dole knows what ASCII is.

aspect ratio   The relative proportion of the length and width of an image. For example, if you scan an original image that measures 4×6 inches, it will have an aspect ratio of 4:6 or 2:3. To maintain the same proportions, you must place it in your desktop publishing document with dimensions that conform to the same ratio. That is, it could be sized at 2×3 inches, 1.5×2.25 inches, and so on. CRT screens and printers also have aspect ratios.

attribute   Characteristics of a page, character, or object, such as line width, fill, underlining, boldface, or font.

autotrace   A feature found in many object-oriented image editing programs or stand-alone programs that enables you to trace a bitmapped image and convert it to an outline or vector format.

background   The ability to run a program unattended while another program is executing, such as background printing. In Photoshop, the background is the bottom layer of an image.

backlighting   A lighting effect produced when the main light source is located behind the subject. If no front, fill, or ambient lighting is used in conjunction with backlighting, the effect is a silhouette. You can simulate backlighting with filters.

back up   To make a copy of computer data as a safeguard against accidental loss. The copy that is made is called the backup.

baseline   An imaginary line on which all the characters in a line rest.

Bézier curve   A cubic polynomial in mathematical terms (ouch!) or, simply, a way of representing a curve that enables great flexibility in manipulating the curve. Bézier curves are adjusted using endpoints and anchor points, as you might do with Photoshop's paths tool.

bilevel   In scanning, a binary scan that stores only the information that tells whether a given pixel should be represented as black or white. Photoshop works with such scans while in Bitmap mode.

bit   A binary digit—either a 1 or a 0. The only time Photoshop users need to be concerned about bits and bytes is when dealing with color depth. Image files typically use multiple bits to represent information about each pixel of an image. A 1-bit scan can store only black or white information about a pixel. A 2-bit scan can include four different gray levels or values—00, 01, 10, or 11; A 4-bit scan can include 16 gray levels/colors; a 5-bit scan 32; a 6-bit scan 64; a 7-bit scan 128; an 8-bit scan 256; a 15-bit scan 32,767 colors; a 16-bit scan 65,535 (or "thousands of colors"); and a 24-bit scan 16,777,216 colors (or "millions of colors").

bitmap   A representation of an image in row and column format in which each individual pixel is represented by a number. A single bit or up to as many as 32 can be used with each increment representing a larger amount of gray or color information about the pixel. You'll often hear service bureaus and others talking about a bitmap as a bilevel, black/white image.

black   The color formed by the absence of reflected or transmitted light.

black printer   The plate used for the black ink in the four-color printing process. It provides emphasis for neutral tones, detail in shadow areas of the image, and a deeper black than can be provided by combining cyan, magenta, and yellow alone. Black printers can take two forms. A skeleton black adds black ink only to the darker areas of an image. A full-range black printer adds some black ink to every part of the image.

bleed   An image that continues off the edge of the page. This effect is often accomplished by having the image extend past the edge and then trimming the page to the finished size. Depending on the printer, an image should extend from ¼ to 1 inch beyond the trim.

blend   To create a more realistic transition between image areas, as with Photoshop's smudge tool. Image editing software often enables you to merge overlapping sections of images to blend the boundary between them.

blur   To soften part of an image, making it less distinct.

brightness   The balance of light and dark shades in an image. *See also* luminance.

buffer   An area of computer memory set aside to store information meant for some sort of Input/Output (I/O) process, such as printing or writing to disk. This enables the device supplying the information to feed it into memory faster than the device meant to accept it can handle it. A printer buffer, for example, enables an application to quickly dump a document for printing and then go on to something else. The buffer can then feed the information to the printer at a slower rate. In scanning, buffers are often used to store images awaiting processing.

bug   An error in a program that results in some unintended action. *Some* software publishers think of these distractions as features.

burn   In photography, to expose part of a print for a longer period, making it darker than it would be with a straight exposure. Photoshop's equivalent is the Burn mode of the toning tool. In lithography, to expose a printing plate.

bus   A hardware interface used to connect a computer to peripherals or other computers. You'll often see references to the SCSI bus or PCI, which are both used by Macintosh computers.

byte   One byte consists of eight bits, which can represent any number from 0000000 to 11111111 binary (0 to 255 decimal).

cache A fast memory buffer used to store information read from disk or from slower RAM to enable the operating system to access it more quickly. Cache programs use various schemes to make sure that the most frequently accessed sectors, as well as the most recently accessed sectors, remain in the buffer as long as possible. A *disk cache* stores data that would otherwise be retrieved from a floppy disk, hard disk, optical disk, or CD-ROM, while a *processor cache* stores instructions and data that the microprocessor needs to work with. PowerPC chips have a cache built into them, but an additional L2 (level 2) secondary cache can be provided in the form of an add-on board plugged into the Mac.

calibration A process used to correct for the variation in output of a device such as a printer or monitor when compared to the original image data you get from the scanner.

camera ready Art work that is printed in hard copy form and can be photographed to produce negatives or plates for printing.

cast A tinge of color in an image, particularly an undesired color.

CCD Charge-Coupled Device. A type of solid-state sensor used in scanners and video capture devices. Compared to older imaging devices, including video tubes, CCDs are more sensitive and less prone to memory problems that can cause image blurring.

channel One of the layers that make up an image. An RGB image has three channels—one each for the red, green, and blue information. A CMYK image has four channels—cyan, magenta, yellow, and black. A grayscale image contains just one channel. Additional masking channels, or *alpha channels (see also)*, can be added to any of these.

chooser The Macintosh desk accessory used to select from devices such as printers, and direct their communications through either the printer or modem port.

chroma Color or hue.

Chromalin The DuPont trademark for a type of color proof made from color separations, used for representing how color halftones will appear on the printed page.

chromatic color A color with at least one hue available, with a visible level of color saturation.

chrome Photographer-speak for a color transparency, from film names such as Kodachrome or Ektachrome.

clip art   Artwork that is purchased or otherwise available for scanning or other uses in desktop publishing with few restrictions.

Clipboard   A memory buffer that can hold images or text so it can be freely interchanged within and between applications. Photoshop uses its own internal Clipboard, but can export and import to and from your operating system's own Clipboard.

clipping   Compressing a range of values into a single value, as when a group of highlight tones are compressed to white or a set of shadow tones are represented as black. *See also* threshold.

clone   In image editing, to copy pixels from one part of an image to another, as with Photoshop's rubber stamp tool.

CMYK   *See* process colors.

color   *See* hue.

color correction   Changing the color balance of an image to produce a desired effect, usually a more accurate representation of the colors in an image. Color correction is used to compensate for the deficiencies of process color inks, inaccuracies in a color separation, or an undesired color balance in the original image. Color correction is done using one of several available color models, including RGB (red-green-blue), CMYK (cyan-magenta-yellow-black), and LHS (luminance-hue-saturation).

color key   A set of four acetate overlays, each with a halftone representing one of the colors of a color separation and tinted in that color. When combined, color keys can be used for proofing color separations.

color separation   The process of reducing an image to its four separate color components—cyan, magenta, yellow, and black. These separations are combined using an individual plate for each color on a press. Percentages of each primary color, plus black, are combined to create any other hue.

color wheel   A circle representing the spectrum of visible colors.

comp   A layout that combines type, graphics, and photographic material, also called a *composite* or *comprehensive*.

complementary color Generally, the opposite hue of a color on a color wheel, which is called the *direct complement*. For example, green is the direct complement of magenta. In addition, two other types of complements are the *split complement* (a color 30° away from the direct complementary color) and the *triadic complement* (a color 120° in either direction from the selected color).

compression Packing of a file or image in a more efficient form to improve storage efficiency. Compression and decompression take some time, so it takes longer to save and open compressed files. Some types of compression can degrade images.

constrain To limit in some way, as to limit the movement of a selection by holding down the Shift key as you begin to move it with the mouse.

contiguous In reference to hard disks, contiguous sectors are those that are arranged consecutively on the disk. Your system software tries to allocate sectors to a file contiguously so that the disk drive can read as many sectors of a file as it can with a minimum of read/write head movement. However, as a hard disk fills, the unallocated sectors gradually become spread out and fragmented, forcing the operating system to choose more and more noncontiguous sectors. Fragmented files can be much slower to access.

continuous-tone image Images that contain tones from black to white with an infinite range of variations in between.

contrast The range between the lightest and darkest tones in an image. A high-contrast image is one in which the shades fall at the extremes of the range between white and black. In a low-contrast image, the tones are closer together.

control character A nonprinting character used to send information to a device, such as the control characters used to communicate special formatting commands to a printer.

convolve To twist, roll, or twine together. As applied to imaging, the term is used to describe the way filters use the values of surrounding pixels to calculate new values when generating a special effect, as with MetaTools' KPT Convolver.

copy dot Photographic reproduction of a halftone image, in which the halftone dots of a previously screened image are carefully copied as if they were line art. The same technique can be used in scanning to capture a halftoned image. If the original dot sizes are maintained, the quality of the finished image can be good.

creator code   A four-letter code used by your system software to keep track of which application was used to generate a given document. This code enables the Mac to launch the right application when you double-click on a file. Because many applications can create several different types of files, a second code, called a *type code*, is used to differentiate them. *See also* type code.

crop   To trim an image or page by adjusting the side or boundaries.

crop mark   A mark placed on a page that is larger than the finished page to show where the page should be trimmed to final size.

cursor   A symbol that indicates the point at which the next action the user takes—text entry, line drawing, deletion, and so on—will begin.

CYMK color model   A model that defines all possible colors in percentages of cyan, magenta, yellow, and black.

darken   A feature that enables gray values in selected areas to be changed, one value at a time, from the current value to a darker one. This is equivalent to the burning procedure used in conventional darkrooms. *See also* burn.

data compression   A method of reducing the size of files, such as image files, by representing the sets of binary numbers in the file with a shorter string that conveys the same information. Many image editing programs offer some sort of image compression as an optional mode when saving a file to disk.

default   A preset option or value that is used unless you specify otherwise.

defloat   To merge a floating selection with the underlying image. The defloated portion of the image is still selected, but if you move or cut it, the area it previously covered will be filled with the background color.

defringe   To remove the outer edge pixels of a selection, usually to merge the selection with the underlying image more smoothly.

densitometer   A device that measures the density of an image.

desaturate   To reduce the purity or vividness of a color. Desaturated colors appear washed out and diluted.

descender   The portion of a lowercase letter that extends below the *baseline (see also)*. The letter *p* is an example of a character with a descender.

diffusion The random distribution of gray tones in an area of an image, often used to produce a mezzotint effect.

digitize To convert information, usually analog information, such as that found in continuous-tone images (or music), to a numeric format that can be accepted by a computer.

displacement map A file used to control the shifting of pixels in an image horizontally or vertically to produce a particular special effect.

dithering A method of simulating gray tones by grouping the dots shown on your CRT display or produced by your printer into large clusters of varying size. The mind merges these clusters and the surrounding white background into different tones of gray.

dodge In photography, to block part of an image as it is exposed, lightening its tones.

dot A unit used to represent a portion of an image. A dot can correspond to one of the pixels used to capture or show an image on the screen, or groups of pixels can be collected to produce larger printer dots of varying sizes to represent gray.

dot etching A technique in photographic halftoning in which the size of the halftone dots is changed to alter tone values.

dot gain The tendency of a printing dot to grow from the original size when halftoned to its final printed size on paper. This effect is most pronounced on offset presses using poor quality papers, which enable ink to absorb and spread.

dots per inch The resolution of an image, expressed in the number of pixels or printer dots in an inch. Abbreviated *dpi*. Scanner resolution is also commonly expressed in dpi, but, technically, scanners use an optical technique that makes *samples per inch* a more accurate term.

download To receive a file from another device. For example, soft fonts are downloaded from your computer to your printer.

driver A software interface used to enable an application to communicate with a piece of hardware, such as a scanner.

drop cap The first letter of a paragraph, set in a larger point size than the rest of the text. It may rise above the first line or extend below, in which case the drop cap is inset into the text block.

dummy   A rough approximation of a publication, used to gauge layout. IDG Books has an excellent fictitious publication on how to create these, called *Dummies for Dummies*.

duotone   A printed image, usually a monochrome halftone, that uses two different colors of ink to produce a longer range of tones than would be possible with a single ink density and set of printer cells alone.

dye sublimation   A printing technique in which solid inks are heated directly into a gas, which then diffuses into a polyester substrate to form an image. Because dye sublimation printers can reproduce 256 different hues for each color, they can print as many as 16.7 million different colors.

dynamic RAM   Type of memory that must be electrically refreshed many times each second to avoid loss of the contents. All computers use dynamic RAM to store programs, data, video information, and the operating system.

emboss   To change an image or selection so it appears to be raised above the surface, in a 3D effect.

emulsion   The light-sensitive coating on a piece of film, paper, or printing plate.

emulsion side   The side of a piece of film that contains the image, usually with a matte, nonglossy finish. This side is placed in contact with the emulsion side of another piece of film (when making a duplicate) or the printing plate. That way, the image is sharper than it would be if it were diffused by the base material of the film. Image processing workers need to understand this concept when producing images oriented properly (either right-reading or wrong-reading) for production.

Encapsulated PostScript (EPS)   An outline-oriented image format that represents graphics and text in terms of mathematical descriptions of how to draw them. Software such as Photoshop can import these files, while vector-oriented draw programs can often modify them.

export   To transfer text or images from a document to another format. Some applications provide a Save As option to save the entire file in the optional format, while others let you save a selected portion of the image or file in another file format. Photoshop offers both Save As and Export options in the File menu.

extrude   To create a 3D effect by adding edges to an outline shape as if it were clay pushed through a Play-Dough Fun Factory.

eyedropper An image editing tool used to "pick up" color from one part of an image, so it can be used to paint or draw in that color elsewhere.

feather To fade the edges of a selection to produce a less-noticeable transition.

file A collection of information, usually data or a program, that has been given a name and allocated sectors by the operating system.

file format A way in which a particular application stores information on a disk. This standardization makes it possible for different applications to load each others' files, because they know what to expect from a predictable file format. PICT and TIFF are file formats found on the Mac.

file name The name given to a file, which can be quite long in the Macintosh/Windows 95 environment, but is, in contrast, limited under older versions of MS-DOS to just eight characters and an optional three-character extension.

fill To cover a selected area with a tone or pattern. Fills can be solid, transparent, or have a gradient transition from one color or tone to another.

filter In scanning, image filters are used to process an image to blur, sharpen, or otherwise change it. Programs such as Photoshop have advanced filters that will spherize, change perspective, and add patterns to selected portions of the image.

Finder The part of the Macintosh system software that takes care of opening, closing, renaming, moving, and erasing files and folders from your desktop. The Finder also formats (initializes) and ejects disks.

flat A low-contrast image. Also, the assembled and registered negatives or positives used to expose a printing plate.

font A group of letters, numbers, and symbols in one size and typeface. Garamond and Helvetica are typefaces; 11-point Helvetica bold is a font.

format To initialize or prepare a disk for use by writing certain information in magnetic form. Formatting divides the disk into tracks and sectors and sets up a directory structure, which appears in the Macintosh world as folders and icons.

four-color printing Another term for process color, in which cyan, magenta, yellow, and black inks are used to reproduce all the hues of the spectrum.

FPO For Position Only. Artwork deemed not good enough for reproduction, used to help gauge how a page layout looks. *See also* position stat.

fractal A kind of image in which each component is made up of ever smaller versions of the component. Sets of fractal images can be calculated using formulas developed by mathematicians such as Benoit B. Mandelbrot, and used as textures in images with tools such as KPT Fractal Explorer. More recently, fractal calculations have been used to highly compress image files; when the image is decompressed, fractal components are used to simulate portions that were discarded during the archiving process.

frame grabber A device that captures a single field of a video scanner or camera.

frequency The number of lines per inch in a halftone screen.

frisket Another name for a mask, used to shield portions of an image from the effects of various tools that are applied to other areas of the image.

galley A typeset copy of a publication used for proofreading and estimating length.

gamma A numerical way of representing the contrast of an image, appearing as the slope of a line showing tones from white to black.

gamma correction A method for changing the brightness, contrast, or color balance of an image by assigning new values to the gray or color tones of an image. Gamma correction can be either linear or nonlinear. Linear correction applies the same amount of change to all the tones. Nonlinear correction varies the changes tone-by-tone, or in highlight, midtone, and shadow areas separately to produce a more accurate or improved appearance.

gamut A range of color values; those present in an image that cannot be represented by a particular process, such as offset printing or CRT display, are said to be out of gamut.

gang scan The process of scanning more than one picture at a time, used when images are of the same density and color balance range.

Gaussian blur A method of diffusing an image by using a bell-shaped curve to calculate which pixels will be blurred, rather than blurring all pixels in the selected area uniformly.

gigabyte A billion bytes of information; a thousand megabytes. Only ten 8.5 × 11-inch full color images scanned at 600 dpi use about one gigabyte of disk space.

graduated fill A pattern in which one shade or hue smoothly blends into another; also called a gradient fill.

graphics tablet A pad on which you draw with a pen-like device called a *stylus*, used as an alternative to a mouse.

gray balance The proportion of ink in each of the three process colors (cyan, magenta, and yellow) that will combine to produce a neutral gray color.

gray component removal A process in which portions of an image that have all three process colors have an equivalent amount of their color replaced by black to produce purer, more vivid colors. *See also* undercolor removal.

gray map A graph that shows the relationship between the original brightness values of an image and the output values after image processing.

grayscale The spectrum of different gray values an image can have.

guides New to Photoshop 4.0, a set of user-definable grid lines used to help position objects in an image.

gutter The inner margin of a page that must be included to allow for binding.

halftoning A method for representing the gray tones of an image by varying the size of the dots used to show the image.

handles Small squares that appear in the corners (and often at the sides) of a square used to define an area to be scanned or an object in an image editing program. The user can grab the handles with the mouse cursor and resize the area or object.

hardware The physical components of a computer system, including the CRT, keyboard, microprocessor, memory, and peripherals.

highlight The brightest values in a continuous-tone image.

histogram A bar-like graph that shows the distribution of gray tones in an image.

HPGL Hewlett-Packard Graphics Language. Used to define images to be printed with plotters.

HSB color model   A model that defines all possible colors by specifying a particular hue and then adding or subtracting percentages of black or white. HSB stands for hue/saturation/brightness.

hue   A pure color. A continuous range of hues exists in nature.

icon   A small graphic that represents an object or function on the computer screen.

image acquisition   Capturing a digitized version of a hard copy or real-world image, as with a scanner or video camera.

image editor   A program such as Adobe Photoshop, used to edit bitmapped images.

imagesetter   A high-resolution PostScript printer that creates camera-ready pages on paper or film.

ink-jet   A printing technology in which dots of ink are sprayed on paper.

input   Incoming information. Input may be supplied to the computer by the user or to a program by either the user or a data file.

instruction cache   A type of high-speed memory used to store the commands that the microprocessor used most recently. A cache "hit" can eliminate the need to access slower RAM or the hard disk, thus increasing the effective speed of the system.

intelligent disk drive   Having sufficient programming built in to carry out certain tasks independently. An intelligent disk drive can accept requests from the operating system, locate the data, and deliver it without detailed instructions on how to do the physical I/O (*see also*).

interlacing   A way of displaying a video image in two fields—odd-numbered lines first, then even-numbered lines, thereby updating or refreshing half the image on the screen at a time. With interlaced video, half the image on the screen (called a field) is updated or refreshed, and then the other half is updated. Most computer displays are noninterlaced, which means the entire screen is painted line-by-line, pixel-by-pixel in one continuous series.

interactive   Enabling user input during run-time.

interpolation A technique used, when resizing or changing the resolution of an image, to calculate the value of pixels that must be created to produce the new size or resolution. Interpolation uses the tone and color of the pixels surrounding each new pixel to estimate the correct parameters.

invert To change an image into its negative; black becomes white, white becomes black, dark gray becomes light gray, and so forth. Colors are also changed to the complementary color: green becomes magenta, blue turns to yellow, and red is changed to cyan.

I/O Input/Output. Used to describe the process whereby information flows to and from the microprocessor or computer through peripherals such as scanners, disk drives, modems, CRT screens, and printers.

jaggies Staircasing of lines that are not perfectly horizontal or vertical. Jaggies are produced when the pixels used to portray a slanted line aren't small enough to be invisible, because of the high contrast of the line and its surrounding pixels, such as at the edges of letters.

JPEG compression Reducing the size of an image through algorithms specified by the Joint Photographic Experts Group. The image is divided into blocks, and all the pixels within the block are compared. Depending on the quality level chosen by the user, some of the pixel information is discarded as the file is compressed. For example, if all the pixels in a block are very close in value, they may be represented by a single number rather than the individual values.

justified Text that is aligned at both the right and left margins.

K Kilobyte. In computer terminology, 1 kilobyte amounts to 1,024 bytes, so that 16K represents 16,384, 64K equals 65,536, 512K corresponds to 524,288, and so on.

kern To adjust the amount of space between two adjacent letters.

knockout Area on a spot color overlay in which an overlapping color is deleted, so the background color shows through.

landscape The orientation of a page in which the longest dimension is horizontal, also called *wide orientation. See also* portrait.

lasso A tool used to select irregularly-shaped areas in a bitmapped image.

launch To start a Macintosh or Windows application.

layers   Separation of a drawing or image into separate "transparent" overlays, that can be edited or manipulated separately, yet combined to provide a single drawing or image.

layer mask   A kind of grayscale mask applied only to one layer of a Photoshop image.

leading   The amount of vertical spacing between lines of text from baseline to baseline (*see also*).

lens flare   In photography, an effect produced by the reflection of light internally among elements of an optical lens. Bright light sources within or just outside the field of view cause lens flare. It can be reduced by the use of coatings on the lens elements or with the use of lens hoods, but photographers (and now digital image workers) have learned to use it as a creative element.

LHS color correction   A system of color correction based on based on the luminance, hue, and saturation of an image.

ligature   A combination of two characters squeezed together to form a composite character. Ligatures can confuse OCR programs (*see also*)that use pattern matching until the software has been trained to recognize each ligature combination.

lighten   An image-editing function that is the equivalent to the photographic darkroom technique of dodging. Gray tones in a specific area of an image are gradually changed to lighter values. *See also* dodge.

line art   Usually, images that consist only of black and white pixels.

line screen   The resolution or frequency of a halftone screen, expressed in lines per inch. Typical line screens are 53 to 150 lines per inch.

lines per inch   Abbreviated *lpi*, lines per inch is the yardstick used to measure halftone resolution.

linking   The ability to join several Photoshop layers together.

lithography   Another name for offset printing, a reproduction process in which sheets or continuous webs of material are printed by impressing them with images from ink applied to a rubber blanket on a rotating cylinder from a metal or plastic plate attached to a another cylinder.

lossless   A compression scheme that reduces file size by representing some number values by shorter codes while preserving all of the original image information, so no degradation in quality occurs.

lossy   A compression scheme that discards some of the image information to reduce the file size. Used by file formats such as JPEG, lossy schemes choose what information to discard by dividing an image into blocks. All the pixels within the block are compared. Depending on the quality level selected, some of the pixel information is averaged together, so that if the pixels in the block are very close in value, they may be represented by a single number rather than the individual values.

luminance   The brightness or intensity of an image. Determined by the amount of gray in a hue, luminance indicates the lightness or darkness of a color. *See also* saturation.

LZW compression   A method of compacting TIFF files using the Lempel-Zev-Welch compression algorithm. It produces an average compression ratio of 2:1, but larger savings are produced with line art and continuous-tone images with large areas of similar tonal values.

magic wand   A tool that selects contiguous pixels that have the same brightness value, or that of a range you select.

mapping   Assigning colors or grays in an image.

marquee   The selection tool used to mark rectangular and elliptical areas.

mask   To cover part of an image so it won't be affected by other operations.

mass storage   Permanent storage of computer information, usually on magnetic disk but also on magnetic tape, optical disk, bubble memory, and other nonvolatile storage media.

mechanical   Camera-ready copy with text and art already in position for photographing.

memory buffer   An area of RAM (*see also*) used to store a file or an image between certain operations, such as printing, storing to disk, or display in an image-editing program.

mezzotint   An engraving that is produced by scraping a roughened surface to produce the effect of gray tones. Image editing and processing software can produce this effect with a procedure called error diffusion.

microprocessor   The computer-on-a-chip that is the brains of a personal computer.

midtones   Parts of an image with tones of an intermediate value, usually in the 25–75% range.

millisecond   One-thousandth of a second.

moiré   In scanning, an objectionable pattern caused by the interference of halftone screens—often produced when you rescan a halftone and a second screen is applied on top of the first. *See also* stochastic screen.

monochrome   Having a single color.

monospaced   Text in which each character takes up exactly the same amount of horizontal space. Some OCR programs require specifying that text to be scanned is monospaced. *See also* proportional spacing *and* OCR program.

mount   To activate a floppy or hard disk or other external media for use. Disks must be mounted before you can open them.

multibit   Any scan that uses more than 1 bit to store information about a pixel.

multisession CD   A CD-ROM that can have images placed on it several times, as opposed to *single-session CDs*, which are written to once only.

multitasking   The ability of a computer system to handle several different chores simultaneously. Because microcomputers have only one main processor, this is usually done by slicing processor time into individual segments and enabling the programs to share the slices in rotation. Some recent computers are equipped with multiple microprocessors, and can share tasks between them.

negative   A representation of an image in which the tones are reversed. That is, blacks are shown as white, and vice versa.

neutral color   In RGB mode, a color in which red, green, and blue are present in equal amounts, producing a gray. *See also* RGB color model.

noise   Random pixels added to an image to increase apparent graininess.

NTSC   National Television Standard Code, the standard for video in the United States.

object graphics   Vector-oriented graphics, in which mathematical descriptions, rather than bitmaps, are used to describe images.

OCR program Optical Character Recognition. A scanning program that uses optical means to convert printed (hard copy) text to electronic text. *See also* scanner.

offset printing *See* lithography.

opacity The opposite of transparency—the degree to which a layer obscures the view of the layer beneath. High opacity means low transparency.

origin The starting horizontal and vertical reference point for a scan.

overlay A sheet laid on top of another to specify spot colors for printing.

point A unit of typographic measurement, approximately 72 to the inch.

page description language A programming language that can be used to tell a printer how to handle a given page. PostScript is the most widely used page description language for printing and publishing.

palette A set of tones or colors available to produce an image, or a row of icons representing tools that can be used.

Pantone Matching System A registered trade name for a system of color matching. If you specify to your printer the PMS number of the color you want, that color can be reproduced exactly by mixing printing inks to a preset formula.

Parallel processing To move data several bits at a time, rather than one at a time. Usually, parallel operation involves sending all 8 bits of a byte along eight separate data paths at one time. This is faster than serial movement. Most scanners use parallel connections to move image information. *See also* serial processing.

parameter A qualifier that defines more precisely what a program is to do.

peripheral Any hardware part of a computer system other than the microprocessor itself and its directly accessible memory. We usually think of peripherals as printers, modems, scanners, and so on.

Photo CD A special type of CD-ROM developed by Eastman Kodak Company that can store high quality photographic images in a special space-saving format, along with music and other data. Photo CDs can be accessed by CD-ROM XA-compatible drives, using Kodak-supplied software or compatible programs such as Photoshop.

phototypesetting   A process used to expose text and images onto materials that will later be used to produce printing plates. Phototypesetters generally have much higher resolutions than laser printers.

PICT   A graphic image and file format used by the Macintosh and its Clipboard. PICT2 is an enhanced version that can be used in both 8-bit and 24-bit formats.

pixel   A picture element of a screen image; one dot of the collection that makes up an image.

plate   A thin, light-sensitive sheet, usually of metal or plastic, that is exposed and then processed to develop an image of the page. The plate mounted on the printing press to transfer ink or dye to a surface, generally paper.

plugging   A defect on the final printed page in which areas between dots become filled due to dot gain, producing an area of solid color. *See also* dot gain.

plug-in   A module that can be accessed from within a program such as Photoshop to provide special functions. Many plug-ins are image-processing filters that offer special effects.

point   Approximately $1/72$ of an inch outside the Macintosh world, exactly $1/72$ of an inch within it. Points are used by printers to measure things such as type and other vertically oriented objects.

Port   A channel of the computer used for input or output with a peripheral. The serial and parallel ports of the PC are the most widely used.

Portable Network Graphics   A new RGB file format supported by Photoshop 4.0. It offers progressive, interleaved display, such as GIF and progressive JPEG, for the gradual display of images on Web pages, but is *lossless* (unlike JPEG, which can discard some image information). *See also* lossless.

portrait   The orientation of a page in which the longest dimension is vertical, also called tall *orientation*. *See also* landscape.

position stat   A copy of a halftone that can be placed on a mechanical to illustrate positioning and cropping of the image. *See also* FPO.

posterization   A photographic effect produced by reducing the number of gray tones in an image to a level at which the tones are shown as bands, as on a poster.

PostScript   Developed by Adobe Systems, PostScript is the most widely used page description language for PCs. It provides a way of telling the printer, typesetter, or imagesetter how to generate a given page.

prepress   The stages of the reproduction process that precede printing, when halftones, color separations, and the printing plates themselves are generated.

preview scan   A preliminary scan that can be used to define the exact area for the final scan. A low-resolution image of the full page or scanning area is shown, and a frame of some type is used to specify the area to be included in the final scan.

primary colors   The basic colors used to produce all other colors in a color system: red, green, and blue for the additive color system, and cyan, magenta, and yellow in the subtractive color system. *See also* additive color, subtractive color, *and* secondary color.

process camera   A graphic arts camera used to make color separations, photograph original artwork to produce halftones and page negatives, and to perform other photographic enlarging/reducing/duplicating tasks.

process colors   Cyan, magenta, yellow, and black. The basic ink colors used to produce all the other colors in four-color printing.

proof   A test copy of a printed sheet, which is used as a final check before a long duplication run begins.

proportional spacing   Text in which each character takes up a varying amount of horizontal space. *See also* monospaced.

quadtone   An image printed using black ink and three other colored inks.

quantization   Another name for *posterization (see also)*.

RAM   Random Access Memory. The volatile memory used as temporary storage for program instructions and working files while the computer is turned on.

raster image   An image defined as a set of pixels or dots in row and column format.

raster image processor   Abbreviated RIP, this is the hardware/software used to process text, graphics, and other page elements into a raster image for output on a printer.

rasterize   The process of turning an outline-oriented image, such as a PostScript file or an Adobe Illustrator drawing into a bitmapped image.

ray tracing   A method for producing realistic highlights, shadows, and reflections on a three-dimensional rendering by projecting the path of an imaginary beam of light from a particular location back to the viewpoint of the observer.

ResEdit   The Apple resource editor, which enables you to modify applications, data files, and system files (if you're brave enough to experiment).

reflection copy   Original artwork that is viewed and scanned by light reflected from its surface, rather than transmitted through it.

register   To align images, usually different versions of the same page or sheet. Color separation negatives must be precisely registered to one another to ensure that colors overlap in the proper places.

register marks   Small marks, also known as *registration marks*, placed on a page to make it possible to align different versions of the page precisely.

registers   The basic memory locations of a microprocessor, through which all information that is processed passes.

rendering   To produce a realistic 3D image from a drawing or other data.

resampling   The process of changing the resolution of an image, adding pixels through interpolation, or removing pixels to reduce resolution.

resolution   The number of pixels or dots per inch in an image, whether displayed on the screen or printed.

retouch   To edit an image, usually to remove flaws or to create a new effect.

RGB color correction   A color correction system based on adjusting the levels of red, green, and blue in an image.

RGB color model   A way of defining all possible colors as percentages of the three additive primary colors, red, green, and blue.

right-reading image   An image, such as on film used to produce a printing plate, that reads correctly, left to right, when viewed as it will be placed down for exposure. *See also* wrong-reading image.

RIP   Raster Image Processor. A device found in printers that converts page images to a format that can be printed.

RISC Reduced Instruction Set Computer. A computer system, like the Power Macintosh that includes an optimized instruction set designed to complete each instruction in one clock cycle (although advanced chips such as the PowerPC 604e can actually execute four instructions per clock cycle).

ROM Read-Only Memory. Memory that can be read by the system but not changed. Read-only memory often contains system programs that help the computer carry out services.

rubber stamp A tool that copies or clones part of an image to another area.

saturation Purity of color—an attribute of a color that describes the degree to which a pure color is diluted with white or gray. A color with low color saturation appears washed out. A highly saturated color is pure and vivid.

scale To change the size of a piece of artwork.

scanner A device that captures an image of a piece of artwork and converts it to a bitmapped image that the computer can handle. *See also* OCR program.

screen The halftone dots used to convert a continuous-tone image to a black-and-white pattern that printers and printing presses can handle. Even expanses of tone can be reproduced by using tint screens that consist of dots that are all the same size (measured in percentages—a 100% screen is completely black).

screen angle The alignment of rows of halftone dots, measured from the horizontal (which would be a 0° screen angle).

SCSI Small Computer Systems Interface. An intelligent interface, used for most scanners in the Macintosh world and for other devices, including hard disk drives. Pronounced as "scuzzy."

SCSI ID The number from 0 to 7 assigned to each device on the SCSI bus. You make this assignment by adjusting a jumper or DIP switch on your equipment, or sometimes, through software. No two devices can have the same ID number. The Mac itself always has SCSI ID 7, and the boot disk is typically ID 0.

secondary color A color produced by mixing two primary colors. For example, mixing red and green primary colors of light produces the secondary color magenta. Mixing the yellow and cyan primary colors of pigment produces blue as a secondary color. *See also* primary color.

selection   The act of marking various portions of an image or document so you can work on them apart from the rest of the image or document. A selection is the area that has been marked, usually surrounded by a marquee or an outline that is sometimes colorfully called "marching ants."

separation   *See* color separation.

separations   Film transparencies, each representing one of the subtractive primary colors (cyan, magenta, and yellow) plus black, used to produce individual printing plates.

serial   Passing information one bit at a time in sequential order. *See also* parallel processing.

serif   Short strokes at the ends of letters. Thought to help lead the eye and make text easier to read. Sans serif type lacks these strokes. Serifs can sometimes touch in tightly spaced text, causing problems for OCR program (*see also*).

shade   A color with black added.

shadows   The darkest part of an image, generally with values ranging from 75 to 100 percent.

sharpening   Increasing the apparent sharpness of an image by boosting the contrast between adjacent tones or colors.

smoothing   To blur the boundaries between tones of an image, often to reduce a rough or jagged appearance.

smudge   A tool that smears part of an image, mixing surrounding tones together.

snap   A feature that causes lines or objects to be attracted to a visible or invisible grid or special guidelines in an image or drawing.

solarization   In photography, an effect produced by exposing film to light partially through the developing process. Some of the tones are reversed, generating an interesting effect. In digital photography, the same effect is produced by combining some positive areas of the image with some negative areas.

spot   The dots that produce images on an imagesetter or other device.

spot color   Individual colors used on a page. Usually limited to one or two extra colors besides black to accent some part of a publication.

spot color overlay   A sheet that shows one of the colors to be used in a publication for a given page. A separate overlay is prepared for each color and all are combined to create the finished page.

stochastic screen   A halftoning method that uses small random dots instead of larger, regularly placed patterns of halftone dots, producing a higher resolution grayscale or color image that does not usually result in any moiré patterns. *See also* moiré.

strip   To assemble a finished page by taping or otherwise fastening pieces of film containing halftones, line art, and text together in a complete page negative or positive. The most common format is as a negative, because dirt and other artifacts show up as pinholes that can be easily spotted or opaqued out before the printing plates are made.

substrate   A base substance that is coated with another. In printing, the substrate is generally paper or acetate, and the second substance is usually ink or dye.

subtractive colors   The primary colors of pigments. When two subtractive colors are added, the result is a darker color that further subtracts from the light reflected by the substrate surface.

surface properties   The transparency, texture, and reflective qualities of a 3D surface.

template   A publication that is used as a framework to provide the basic structure and layout for a publication.

text file   Usually an ASCII file, often created by selecting Save Text Only from within an application.

thermal wax transfer   A printing technology in which dots of wax from a ribbon are applied to paper when heated by thousands of tiny elements in a printhead.

threshold   A predefined level used by a scanner to determine whether a pixel will be represented as black or white.

thumbnail   A miniature copy of a page or image that gives you some idea of what the original looks like without having to open the original file or view the full-size image.

TIFF   Tagged Image File Format. A standard graphics file format that can be used to store grayscale and color images.

tint   A color with white added to it. In graphic arts, tint often refers to the percentage of one color added to another.

tolerance level A brightness range used to determine how close in value to a selected pixel surrounding pixels must be to be included in the selection when using a tool such as the magic wand, or filled with paint when using a tool such as the paint bucket.

toner A pigmented substance used in page printers (and office copiers) to produce an image on a page.

trapping The ability of an ink to transfer as well to another layer of ink as to the bare paper itself. In halftoning, poor trapping results in tonal changes in the final image. In desktop publishing, trapping has an additional meaning—printing some images of one color slightly larger so they overlap another color, avoiding unsightly white space if the two colors are printed slightly out of register. Printers call this technique *spreading* and *choking*.

triad Three colors located approximately equidistant from one another on the color wheel. Red, green, and blue make up a triad; cyan, magenta, and yellow make up another. However, any three colors arranged similarly around the wheel can make up a triad.

trim size The final size of a printed publication.

tritone An image printed usually with black ink (or another color) plus two other colored inks.

true color A system in which any pixel in the image can be any of the 16.8 million colors available in 24-bit color mode. This is in contrast to systems that also access the full 16.8 million color gamut but limit a given image to a smaller palette of colors chosen from the larger range. For example, you may be able to use only 256 colors even though any of the millions available can be selected for that palette.

type code A four-letter code that tells the Macintosh what kind of document a file is. It is used with the *creator code*, which represents the particular application that created the file. Some applications can create several different types of documents. *See also* creator code.

undercolor removal A technique that reduces the amount of cyan, magenta, and yellow in black and neutral shadows by replacing them with an equivalent amount of black. It can compensate for trapping problems in dark areas. *See also* gray component removal.

unfragmented A hard disk that has most of its files stored in consecutive sectors, rather than spread out over the disk. Such an arrangement promotes a more efficient reading of data, requiring less time to move the read/write head to gather the information.

unsharp masking   The process for increasing the contrast between adjacent pixels in an image, raising the apparent sharpness.

utility   A program that performs some useful system or maintenance function, as opposed to a main application.

vector image   An image defined as a series of straight-line vectors. Instructions specifying the beginning and ending points of each line are stored and later adjusted as the image is sized.

vignette   In prepress terminology, an image with a continuous gradation of tones.

virtual disk   An electronic, or RAM, disk created in memory to mimic a real disk drive—only much faster.

virtual memory   Hard disk space used when not enough RAM is available to carry out an operation. Photoshop and your Mac each have their own virtual memory systems—if you use Photoshop a great deal, you'll want to turn off the Mac's version and let Photoshop work exclusively with its optimized version.

VRAM   Video Random Access Memory. A special, fast kind of memory used for video cards that can be read from and written to simultaneously, enabling very fast transfers of large amounts of screen information. *See also* RAM.

wire frame   A rendering technique that presents only the edges of a 3D object, as if it were modeled from pieces of wire. This is much faster than modeling the entire object, including all surfaces.

WORM   Write Once Read Many (or Mostly). An optical disk technology that enables writing to the disk by the user, although a given section cannot be erased and reused.

wrong-reading image   An image that is backward relative to the original subject—that is, a mirror image. *See also* right-reading image.

x-height   The height of a lowercase letter, excluding ascenders and descenders.

zoom   To enlarge part of an image so that it fills the screen, making it easier to work with that portion.

Index

Credits

Senior Vice President and Group Publisher
Brenda McLaughlin

Director of Publishing
Walt Bruce

Acquisitions Editor
Michael Roney

Marketing Manager
Melisa M. Duffy

Managing Editor
Terry Somerson

Development Editor
Michael Koch

Copy Editor
Michael D. Welch

Editorial Assistant
Sharon Eames

Production Director
Andrew Walker

Supervisor of Page Layout
Craig A. Harrison

Production Associate
Christopher Pimentel

Media Archive Coordination
Leslie Popplewell

Project Coordinator
Phyllis Beaty

Graphics & Production Specialists
Vincent F. Burns
Craig A. Harrison
Jude Levinson
Dale Smith

Quality Control Specialist
Mick Arellano

Proofreader
Christine Langin-Faris

Indexer
Ty Koontz

Book Design
Vincent F. Burns
Margery Cantor
Kurt Krames

Cover Design
three 8 Creative Group

About the Authors

David D. Busch

Since 1980, David D. Busch has demystified computer technology for busy professionals through more than four dozen books and thousands of magazine articles in publications like *Macworld* and *HomePC*. The first two-time winner of best-book honors from the Computer Press Association, Busch earned his first award in 1986 for an exposé of Kitchen Table International, the world's leading fictitious supplier of hardware, software, firmware, and limpware.

Dave graduated *minima sine laude* from the University of California at Kent (Ohio) in 1970 with a degree in Slide Rule Design, and immediately built a multi-thousand dollar empire marketing one of the world's first symmetric multiprocessor computers. This product, the KTI Oblivion, was discontinued when it was discovered that, at best, only one of the two chips actually functioned at any given time, and, at worst, they spent a lot of time fighting over whose turn it was. Today, he is an active beta tester of products such as Adobe Photoshop 4. When vendors want to see if a product is truly idiot-proof, they call on him.

David Field

David Field has been the director of the Boston Computer Society's Desktop Publishing group, which had over 3,000 members. He also writes a monthly column and numerous articles in *Technique* magazine, for which he is a contributing editor. For three years he also contributed monthly to the *Desktop Publishers Journal*.

Field currently teaches various computer subjects for two sections of the University of New Hampshire. He has also taught at MIT, Northeastern University, and the University of Massachusetts, and is a consultant and trainer in the Boston area. He has taught different courses for the Boston Computer Society since 1989, and also answered around 1,000 phone queries a year with BCS Dial Help.

IDG Books Worldwide
License Agreement

must include the most recent update and all prior versions. Each shareware program has its own use permissions and limitations. These limitations are contained in the individual license agreements that are on the software discs. The restrictions include a requirement that after using the program for a period of time specified in its text, the user must pay a registration fee or discontinue use. By opening the package which contains the software disc, you will be agreeing to abide by the licenses and restrictions for these programs. Do not open the software package unless you agree to be bound by the license agreements.

4. Limited Warranty. IDG warrants that the Software and disc are free from defects in materials and workmanship for a period of sixty (60) days from the date of purchase of this Book. If IDG receives notification within the warranty period of defects in material or workmanship, IDG will replace the defective disc. IDG's entire liability and your exclusive remedy shall be limited to replacement of the Software, which is returned to IDG with a copy of your receipt. This Limited Warranty is void if failure of the Software has resulted from accident, abuse, or misapplication. Any replacement Software will be warranted for the remainder of the original warranty period or thirty (30) days, whichever is longer.

5. No Other Warranties. To the maximum extent permitted by applicable law, IDG and the author disclaim all other warranties, express or implied, including but not limited to implied warranties of merchantability and fitness for a particular purpose, with respect to the Software, the programs, the source code contained therein and/or the techniques described in this Book. This limited warranty gives you specific legal rights. You may have others which vary from state/jurisdiction to state/jurisdiction.

6. No Liability For Consequential Damages. To the extent permitted by applicable law, in no event shall IDG or the author be liable for any damages whatsoever (including without limitation, damages for loss of business profits, business interruption, loss of business information, or any other pecuniary loss) arising out of the use of or inability to use the Book or the Software, even if IDG has been advised of the possibility of such damages. Because some states/jurisdictions do not allow the exclusion or limitation of liability for consequential or incidental damages, the above limitation may not apply to you.

7. U.S. Government Restricted Rights. Use, duplication, or disclosure of the Software by the U.S. Government is subject to restrictions stated in paragraph (c) (1) (ii) of the Rights in Technical Data and Computer Software clause of DFARS 252.227-7013, and in subparagraphs (a) through (d) of the Commercial Computer—Restricted Rights clause at FAR 52.227-19, and in similar clauses in the NASA FAR supplement, when applicable.

Replacement Disc. If a replacement disc is needed, please write to the following address: IDG Books Disc Fulfillment Center, Attn: *Macworld Photoshop 4 Instant Expert*, IDG Books Worldwide, 7260 Shadeland Station, Indianapolis, IN 46256, or call 800-762-2974.

Fuel your imaging with MetaTools bundle prices!

✔ **1.** Choose from:

☐ **Kai's Power Tools 3**   Mac or Windows 95/NT
☐ **Convolver**   Mac or Windows 3.1/95/NT
☐ **Vector Effects**   Mac

☐ **Power Photos I**
    Natural & Urban Backgrounds, Textures, Sports and Food
☐ **Power Photos II**
    Bugs, Nostalgia, Winter & Fall Holidays and Kids Toys
☐ **Power Photos III**
    Retro Toys, Tropical Paradise, Junk & Spring & Summer Holidays
☐ **Power Photos IV**
    Africa, Business Elements, Flowers, Papers, & Fall Foliage

✔ **2.** Select your bundle:

☐ **Buy any 1 product**   ... **$99**
☐ **Buy any 2 products**   ... **$189**
☐ **Buy any 3 products**   ... **$279**
☐ **Buy any 4 products**   ... **$369**
☐ **Buy any 5 products**   ... **$459**
☐ **Buy any 6 products**   ... **$549**

✔ **3.** Additional Specials*:

☐ **Bryce 2** Mac   ... **$129**
☐ **Final Effects AP** Mac or Win 95/NT ... **$149**
☐ **Kai's Power GOO** Mac or Win 95/NT ... **$49**.95

Take advantage of these mix and match specials today and save.

800.472.9025

Limited time. Limited offer.
Discount code: ABPN

*Not included in bundle offer.

IDG BOOKS WORLDWIDE REGISTRATION CARD

Title of this book: Macworld® Photoshop® 4 Instant Expert

My overall rating of this book: ❏ Very good [1] ❏ Good [2] ❏ Satisfactory [3] ❏ Fair [4] ❏ Poor [5]

How I first heard about this book:

❏ Found in bookstore; name: [6] _____   ❏ Book review: [7] _____

❏ Advertisement: [8] _____   ❏ Catalog: [9] _____

❏ Word of mouth; heard about book from friend, co-worker, etc.: [10] _____   ❏ Other: [11] _____

What I liked most about this book:

_____

_____

What I would change, add, delete, etc., in future editions of this book:

_____

_____

Other comments: _____

_____

Number of computer books I purchase in a year: ❏ 1 [12]   ❏ 2-5 [13]   ❏ 6-10 [14]   ❏ More than 10 [15]

I would characterize my computer skills as: ❏ Beginner [16] ❏ Intermediate [17] ❏ Advanced [18] ❏ Professional [19]

I use ❏ DOS [20] ❏ Windows [21] ❏ OS/2 [22] ❏ Unix [23] ❏ Macintosh [24] ❏ Other: [25]_____
(please specify)

I would be interested in new books on the following subjects:
(please check all that apply, and use the spaces provided to identify specific software)

❏ Word processing: [26] _____   ❏ Spreadsheets: [27] _____

❏ Data bases: [28] _____   ❏ Desktop publishing: [29] _____

❏ File Utilities: [30] _____   ❏ Money management: [31] _____

❏ Networking: [32] _____   ❏ Programming languages: [33] _____

❏ Other: [34] _____

I use a PC at (please check all that apply): ❏ home [35] ❏ work [36] ❏ school [37] ❏ other: [38] _____

The disks I prefer to use are ❏ 5.25 [39] ❏ 3.5 [40] ❏ other: [41]_____

I have a CD ROM: ❏ yes [42]   ❏ no [43]

I plan to buy or upgrade computer hardware this year: ❏ yes [44]   ❏ no [45]

I plan to buy or upgrade computer software this year: ❏ yes [46]   ❏ no [47]

Name: _____   Business title: [48] _____   Type of Business: [49] _____

Address (❏ home [50] ❏ work [51]/Company name: _____   )

Street/Suite# _____

City [52]/State [53]/Zipcode [54]: _____   Country [55] _____

❏ **I liked this book!** You may quote me by name in future
IDG Books Worldwide promotional materials.

My daytime phone number is _____

IDG BOOKS

THE WORLD OF
COMPUTER
KNOWLEDGE

❑ YES!

Please keep me informed about IDG's World of Computer Knowledge.
Send me the latest IDG Books catalog.